The Golden Age of the English Theatre

Other books by the author:

Directors' Theatre
Women in Shakespeare
Shakespeare's Players
Backstage
At the Sign of the Swan – An Introduction to Shakespeare's Contemporaries
Who Killed Hilda Murrell?
Daphne – A Portrait of Daphne du Maurier
The Slicing Edge of Death

THE GOLDEN AGE OF THE ENGLISH THEATRE

JUDITH COOK

SIMON & SCHUSTER

LONDON · SYDNEY · NEW YORK · TOKYO · SINGAPORE · TORONTO

First published in Great Britain by Simon & Schuster Ltd, 1995
A Paramount Communications Company

Simon & Schuster Ltd
West Garden Place
Kendal Street
London W2 2AQ

Simon & Schuster of Australia Pty Ltd
Sydney

A CIP catalogue record for this book is available from the
British Library.

ISBN 0-671-71229-2

Typeset in 11/13pt Baskerville
Typeset in London by Harrington & Co.
Printed and bound by Butler & Tanner Ltd, Frome and London

In memory of Peter Hewitt, who inspired so many of us with his passion for Shakespeare and his contemporaries.

'What things we have seen,
Done at the Mermaid! Heard words that have been
So nimble, and so full of subtle flame,
As if that every one from whence they came,
Had meant to put his whole wit in a jest . . .'

Francis Beaumont

Contents

PROLOGUE

It is a fine day in April, not too cold for the time of year. A visitor to London, sauntering down towards the Thames on the Middlesex side, soon finds himself caught up in a great crowd all moving steadily in the same direction. Bands of young apprentices, flushed with drink, push and jostle each other as they shout out crude witticisms. Solid tradesmen proudly shepherd their wives who are dressed in their best. Every now and then a whole group of pedestrians have to flatten themselves against a convenient wall to allow the passage of a packed carriage also making its way to the river bank.

The visitor eventually finds himself on the approach to London Bridge and looks across to the Bankside. High above the houses he can see the roofs of the playhouses, each crowned with a small covered platform, 'the hut', attached to which is a large flagpole. Flags are flying today at both the Globe and Swan theatres so the playgoers flooding south will have a choice of plays. As he arrives at the entrance to London Bridge he hears the sound of competing trumpets from both theatres, a call which announces that today's performance will begin in an hour's time.

At the river bank many of those who are better off will take a boat across to the Bankside. Theatre afternoons provide rich pickings for the watermen who jostle fiercely for custom; the more refined parents cover their children's ears to avoid their hearing the language indulged in by the competing boatmen who have a reputation for being foulmouthed. But if our visitor wants to hoard his small amount of money, he will cross by London Bridge, marvelling at the splendid array of goods displayed outside the small shop fronts.

By the time he reaches Southwark the trumpets have sounded for the second time. Should he stop now and have a plate of food at on of the many cheap cafés known as 'ordinaries', or should he buy some bread and cheese or a pie and a bottle of ale and make his way into the playhouse to ensure a good view? He decides on the latter and buys a pie. Bottle ale and oranges will be on sale inside the theatre.

Bills advertising the afternoon's entertainments have been flyposted on any available flat surface and fortunately he can read. Shall he see Mr Richard Burbage and the Lord Chamberlain's Men in Mr William Shakespeare's *Twelfth Night* at the Globe, or wallow in blood and revenge at the Hope, where the Lord Admiral's Men are presenting an old, but still popular, play, *The Spanish Tragedy* by the late Thomas Kyd? He tosses a coin and makes his choice. He will see *Twelfth Night*, which will also enable him to tell his friends of the wonders of the new Globe Theatre, the largest and most magnificent playhouse in London. As he makes his way towards the entrance, the trumpet sounds again.

Getting into the building at all is difficult due to the press of people, not all of whom are actually planning to see a play. He has never seen so many whores all in one place at the same time, some old and eaten with disease, some garishly painted and sporting gaudy finery, some, newer to the game, who still have the rosy flush of the countryside. They brazenly accost any man whose eye they can catch, offering their services then and there, during the play (if the customer will pay their entrance charge) or, failing either, afterwards.

It is a slow and tedious business even though the Gatherer, who collects the entrance money, has an assistant this particular afternoon. Some playgoers do not have the right money and there are always arguments over change. It costs a penny to stand in the open area in front of the stage, more to have a seat in one of the galleries running round three sides of the building. The visitor decides to pay sixpence, sufficient not only to purchase a seat in a gallery but to rent a cushion as well.

Before he can even make for his place he is beset by vendors wanting to sell him fruit, ale or posies and pomanders to help stifle any unpleasant smells. The open sky above the pit disperses the worst of these but many hundreds of bodies in close proximity still give off a highly unpleasant odour and this will get worse as the latrine buckets, helpfully placed in suitable spots, fill up during the show. There are no intervals.

Clutching his bottle of ale, an orange and his pie, the visitor finds a place on a bench; not before time as every tier of galleries is rapidly filling by the time the final trumpet sounds. Friends call to each other across the auditorium, while the members of the crowd down below push and elbow each other out of the way to get a better view. The floor of the Globe is raked to enable those at the back to see something of what is going on but those who are both short in height and arrive late will spend most of the afternoon viewing a solid wall of backs.

The visitor passes the time watching the crowd and also having a good look at the inside of the theatre, admiring the painting of moons, suns and stars on 'the heavens', the solid canopy which covers the back of the vast, thrust stage and the simulated marble effect of much of the inside woodwork. The noise from the playgoers is almost deafening.

Behind the stage, unseen by the audience, the actors put the finishing touches to their make-up and their elaborate costumes. The young boys, the apprentices who play the women's roles, are helped into their farthingales and gowns, their wigs adjusted and their faces plastered with a *maquillage* of flour and paint, while the Bookman or Bookkeeper, who is in charge of the scripts, runs through a speech for the last time with a new actor. From time to time an actor peers through a tiny gap in the heavy curtains which cover the 'discovery space', the small intimate area at the back of the stage.

At the last moment a noisy party of affluent young men arrive, hire themselves stools, and clamber on to the stage with them. The actors sigh. This now commonplace practice is not popular with the actors as all too often these playgoers come to be seen as much as to see the play and their fidgeting, comments and occasional interruptions are extremely distracting to the actors.

The musicians take their place in the gallery above the discovery space and very gradually the theatre begins to quieten down. There is an expectant hush. The musicians strike up a popular air, the curtain of the discovery space is pushed aside and Richard Burbage enters as Orsino, Duke of Illyria, attended by his courtiers. He is magnificently dressed in a bronze velvet doublet trimmed with copper lace. There is a scatter of applause which he acknowledges. Then he walks firmly to the front of the stage:

> If music be the food of love, play on,
> Give me excess of it, that, surfeiting,
> The appetite may sicken, and so die.

The play begins.

Part One

1

The Beginning

Within the ten year period 1554 to 1564 a number of boys were born who were, under normal circumstances, unlikely ever to have known each other. Their homes were in different parts of the country and on the face of it they had little in common, except that most of them were the sons of honest artisans and belonged to the first generation of such lads to obtain places in the new grammar schools.

John Lyly, the oldest, was born in 1554, a year of great political upheaval, which saw the execution of Lady Jane Grey, the 'nine day's Queen', and the imprisonment of the then Princess Elizabeth in the Tower of London on a charge of suspected treason. From birth to death Elizabeth's life was to be one of theatricality and drama in an age redolent of it and her arrival by barge in pouring rain at the Traitors' Gate of the Tower of London was worthy of a scene in a historical epic. Stepping out onto the steps, over her shoes in water and with her long, red hair dripping down her back, she had announced: 'Here lands as true a subject as ever landed at these stairs. Before thee, O God, do I speak it having no other friend than thou alone.' At which point some of the yeoman warders drawn up to receive her had fallen on their knees and shouted 'God Preserve Your Grace!' Deeply embarrassed, the Lieutenant of the Tower tried to hustle her in, only to be reminded in salutary fashion by the Earl of Sussex, who was one of the party, 'Let us take heed, my Lords, that we go not beyond our commission. For she was our King's daughter and the

Prince next in blood!'

Lyly, born in that time of high drama, was the first of what would become a new breed of professional writers, the poet–playwrights, but virtually nothing is known of his background except that he possibly went to the King's School, Canterbury, and from there to Magdalen College Oxford.

In 1558 the dying Mary I finally named Elizabeth as successor. A posse of lords and courtiers galloped out of London to Hatfield House in Hertfordshire, where Elizabeth was living quietly and biding her time, to find her sitting, exquisitely dressed, under a large oak tree reading an improving book. When William Cecil handed her her sister's ring as a token, she fell on her knees and thanked God, for what he had done was 'miraculous' in her eyes. It was another scene in Elizabeth's life worthy of the stage. Her accession dowsed the fires of Smithfield and ushered in a new era.

George Peele and Thomas Kyd were both born that year. Peele's family had come to London from Devonshire and his father was a city salter and Clerk to Christ's Hospital, a post which brought with it a rather fine property in which the family lived. He was obviously considered to be of great value in his position as Clerk as he both taught bookkeeping and wrote about it and is credited with introducing the Italian system of bookkeeping into the country.

Thomas Kyd was also born in London and was christened at the church of St Mary Woolnoth on 6 November, eleven days before Queen Elizabeth's accession. He was the son of Francis Kyd who was, like Milton's father, a scrivener – a professional copyist and writer of letters, documents, etc. This was a useful craft in an age when the majority of ordinary people were illiterate. Also like Milton's father, Francis Kyd was the 'writer of the Court Letter of London' and a Freeman of the Company of Scriveners. His wife, Anna, Thomas's mother, was the legatee of a publisher.

A year later George Chapman was born in Hitchin in Hertfordshire, one of the five surviving children of Thomas and Joan Chapman, the grandson of a George

Nodes, sergeant to the buckhounds of Henry VIII. At about the same time, or possibly a year later, Robert Greene was born in Norwich. As with Lyly, almost nothing is known of his family background except that he said of his parents that they were 'respected for their gravity and honest life', which is more than would later be said of him.

* * *

In 1564 the young wives of two artisans gave birth to healthy sons. The families, although many miles apart, had much in common. In both cases the father had been apprenticed in leatherwork and at the time each boy was born the parents were in comfortable circumstances, although both fathers were later to run into debt due, in part, to their predilection for litigation.

Katherine Marlowe's child was born at the beginning of February. As it was not until the nineteenth century that births had to be officially registered, the only record we have of a birth is when the child was christened and recorded in the Parish Register, known popularly as 'the Church Book'. As baptism was considered essential for eternal life and infant mortality was extremely high, the ceremony usually took place without loss of time, generally about three days after birth. Indeed, the Book of Common Prayer bade parents not to postpone christening their child beyond the first Sunday or Holy Day after birth.

The Marlowes were established Canterbury leatherworkers and Katherine's husband, John, was the third generation to go into the family business. His father, Christopher, was comfortably off with both a substantial town house in Canterbury and a further property in the Kent countryside, with a meadow and twenty grazing acres. John, who specialised in shoemaking, had married Katherine Urry, a Dover girl, on 22 May 1560 at the church of St George the Martyr.[1] Their home was a handsome house in the main street, renowned in its day for carved panelling of such beauty that it attracted a great deal of envy, so much so that years later a local squire removed it to decorate his own country manor. John Marlowe's house stood at the corner of St George's Street and Little St George's Lane close to the church.[2] All that remains now of house and church is the latter's tower, the rest having fallen victim to wartime bombing.

The first child of the marriage, a daughter, Mary, was born in 1562 but died almost immediately. The second, a son named Christopher after his grandfather, was baptised at St George's on 6 February 1564. He was to be followed by another daughter, Margaret, and two more boys, one of whom died at birth, unnamed, while the second, Thomas, lived only twelve days. A fourth son, also called Thomas, came next followed by a further three daughters, Joan, Anne and Daretye (Dorothy).

Two months after the birth of Christopher Marlowe, Mary, the wife of the second artisan, John Shakespeare, gave birth to her first son in the small market town of Stratford-upon-Avon in Warwickshire. John Shakespeare had been born in the country, in the village of Snitterfield. His father was a tenant farmer on the estate of the Arden family of Wilmcote and young John, the first of his family to be apprenticed in leatherwork, had been sent to Stratford to serve his time.

Once eligible to call himself a master craftsman, he set up in his own right as a glover and tanner and, later, trader in wool. He acquired his first house, in Henley Street, some time before 1552 at a ground rent of sixpence a year for he is recorded as living in the property that year and being fined a shilling for making a dunghill in the street outside his door, instead of at the end of it under the trees like everyone else. John's business prospered so that a few years later he was able to take on the lease of the larger house next door and knock the two together to make them one. The second property had the benefit of a garden at a ground rent of thirteen pence a year.[3]

John married Mary in 1557. His bride, Mary Arden of Asbys, was a very good match for a craftsman, being the daughter of his father's landlord and a young woman very definitely above his own station. She was the eighth, and favourite, child of a family who were said to have been great lords in Warwickshire before the Conquest, and as well as bringing her young husband a hefty dowry, when her father died he left her not only money but the entire Asbys estate and the home farm.[4]

By the time John married Mary he was already a Burgess of Stratford and the Town Aletaster, a man prominent in its affairs and soon to be Chamberlain to the Borough, a position which allowed him to process grandly to church of a Sunday in a fine robe alongside the rest of the local worthies. A year after their marriage Mary had a daughter, Joan, but she, like the little Mary Marlowe, did not survive. Neither did the Shakespeare's second daughter, Margaret.

William Shakespeare was born on or about 23 April in the Henley Street house and his birth was duly recorded in the Register of Holy Trinity, the parish church on the bank of the River Avon. St George's Day, 23 April, is traditionally celebrated as the birth of England's greatest poet as it fits neatly with the fact that he also died on that date.

The new baby survived, in spite of the fact that 1564 was one of the great plague years of the sixteenth century, the disease having been brought back from Le Havre by the Earl of Warwick. It spread rapidly throughout the country but was particularly virulent in Warwickshire as many of his soldiers had been levied in the county. *'Hic incipit Pestis'* wrote the Rev. John Bretchgirdle, vicar of Stratford, 'here the Plague rages', noting that entire households had been wiped out. Councillor John Shakespeare had to meet his colleagues in the Guild Hall garden under the apple trees instead of in the council chamber, in an effort to avoid infection.[5]

William was followed by a second son, Gilbert, another daughter christened Joan, Anne (who lived only until she was eight), Richard and, finally, the baby of the family, Edmund, born in 1580, only three years before William's own eldest child. Mary Shakespeare's childbearing was spread over eighteen years. Possibly there were miscarriages in the gaps between the births, something that was then extremely commonplace. The large proportion of infant deaths in the Marlowe and Shakespeare families was typical of the time and such appaling infant mortality ensured that Tudor children grew up fully aware of the uncertainty and fragility of life.

However, both Christopher Marlowe and William Shakespeare thrived and were healthy. Had they not been, the history of English literature, not to mention that of the theatre, would have been very different. For these two were to take the English language and shape it in such a way that it would never be the same again.

2

The New Professionals

Both boys were extraordinarily fortunate in that they were born and grew up in the age they did, a time of tremendous creativity in both the arts and the new science and with a Court presided over by a Queen with a passion for literature, poetry and theatre. For a would-be playwright, there would never be a better time.

Elizabeth had come to the throne full of hope, with a driving desire to heal wounds and pull her country together and in the early years to a large extent she succeeded. She was endlessly exhorted to marry, but steadfastly refused to do so, keeping a host of suitors continually dangling after her both at home and abroad. Politically it suited her to appear to be willing to consider marriage to a foreign prince, while at home she could play one favourite off against another for as long as it amused her to do so.

It is likely that there were also psychological problems. A woman who had seen first her mother, then her cousin, beheaded by her own father, had watched her sister become a fanatic under the influence of a foreign husband and who had been in mortal danger herself through the over-ambition of a much older man, must have viewed any marriage with deep misgivings sufficient to remain single by choice.

It was, however, a hazardous one particularly as time went by. She had said that she sought no windows into men's souls and to begin with those who remained true to the Catholic faith were left alone so long as they remained discreet about it and loyal to the crown. Any Catholic who kept out of trouble and paid their weekly fine had no need to fear the stake. It has sometimes been suggested that John Shakespeare was a recusant because he was fined several times for not attending the parish church regularly, but there is a far more prosaic explanation which is given in the excellent booklet *Shakespeare in the Public Record Office,* published by the Stationery Office. At the time John was being fined for the offence he was also heavily in debt and dared not step out of his house for fear the bailiffs would catch up with him. Since theoretically everyone had to attend church, it was not uncommon for process servers to hang about churchyards waiting for debtors. In John Shakespeare's case he would have been impossible to miss since, as an Alderman, he would have walked in the slow procession of town worthies every Sunday.

But as time went on attitudes towards Catholics hardened and the years of the birth and growth of professional theatre and that glittering age of drama need to be set against a darkening landscape as Elizabeth was threatened not only from abroad by Catholic Spain, but also by her cousin Mary, Queen of Scots.

Mary Stuart would have made a highly suitable subject for the later Jacobean playwrights had she not been the mother of their King. The child bride of the French king, later married to the weak and vicious Darnley, she had been made to watch, while heavily pregnant, her favourite musician stabbed to death in front of her eyes by the jealous Darnley's servants. Scandal followed her every move. Darnley was mysteriously blown up and killed shortly after the birth of their son, an action in which she may have been implicated, and the notorious Earl of Bothwell, at whom the finger of suspicion pointed, was said to be her lover. Whether he was then is not clear but he certainly became so later after he had abducted her. Brought back to Edinburgh pregnant by the Earl, she miscarried twins before escaping to England dressed as a boy to plead with her cousin to give her sanctuary.

Mary was both beautiful and sexually charismatic and

drew men to her like moths to a candle but she had neither Elizabeth's intellect nor her political talents. However, her mere presence in the country ensured that she would provide the focus for every dissenter with dreams of overthrowing the Queen. In showing compassion to Mary after her flight from Scotland, Elizabeth set in train a series of events which would throw long shadows over the rest of her reign.

Her action was also to have a bearing on the history of the early Elizabethan theatre for when, in 1573, the Queen appointed Sir Francis Walsingham Secretary of State to the Privy Council, she agreed to his proposal that he should set up an efficient and professional network of spies and informers for the defence of the realm, a sixteenth-century MI5. Ten years later Walsingham expanded his secret service further, looking to Cambridge University for bright new recruits and he also charged his most efficient agent, a man called Robert Poley, with the task of infiltrating the ranks of Mary Stuart's increasingly active supporters, actions which were later to have a catastrophic effect on the lives of two of the most popular early dramatists.

* * *

It was in the early 1580s that theatre made the leap from the amateur or semi-amateur to the truly professional, from the religious play cycles performed by guilds of craftsmen and the plays offered on public holidays by local amateur worthies, to the beginnings of properly set up theatre companies. Hitherto there had been the tumblers and the clowns and the small groups of strolling players who were forever moving on, setting up their carts at fairs and in inn yards. By the end of the decade professional actors were playing in custom-built buildings patronised by the aristocracy or even, by royal command, in one of the royal palaces before the Queen herself.

Since medieval times, players had been considered little better than rogues and vagabonds but as early as the late 1560s it was becoming fashionable for noblemen to set up their own private companies of players. In 1569, when John Shakespeare was a bailiff in Stratford-upon-Avon and young William was only five years old, a troupe calling themselves the Queen's Men played in the town and were paid nine shillings. They were followed a few weeks later by the Earl of Worcester's Men who received only one, although this did not take into account the amount collected at their performances.[1]

But players were still treated with considerable suspicion by the authorities, national and local, until the introduction of the Act which changed everything. The 1572 Vagabonds Act forced all serious acting companies on to a professional basis for the first time for it required each one to be authorised by one nobleman and two judicial dignitaries of the realm, although this latter restriction was dropped in a later Act in 1598. The Statute says:

> . . . all Fencers, Bearewards, Common Players in Enterludes and Minstrels, not belonging to any Baron of this Realme, or towards any other honourable Personage of greater Degree; all Jugglers, Pedlars, Tinkers and Petty Chapman; which said Fencers, Bearewards, Common Players, Minstrels, Jugglers, Pedlars, Tinkers and Petty Chapman, shall wander abroad and have not Licence of two Justices of the Peace at the least, whereof one to be of the Quorum when and in what Shire they shall happen to wander . . . shall be taken and adjudged to be deemed Rogues, Vagabonds and Sturdy Beggars.

It is obvious from the wording of the Act that even though players had been given a certain amount of respectability so long as they had patronage, those who had drafted it still saw them as all of a piece with the other itinerants listed and rated theatrical performances little higher than those of acrobats or dancing bears. However, following the new legislation, various prominent and well-heeled members of the nobility began to vie with each to become patrons of theatre companies; with the accession of James even royalty would do so.

Not surprisingly, the Queen's flamboyant favourite, Robert Dudley, Earl of Leicester, was one of the first to put his name to a company almost immediately after the introduction of the 1572 Act, hiring James Burbage and his players who then became known as the Earl of Leicester's Men. One of Leicester's homes was Kenilworth Castle, only a few miles from Stratford, and in 1573 when Shakespeare was nine, his actors visited Stratford, returning again in 1576 and also in 1587. The new company of another local grandee, the Earl of Warwick, played Stratford for the first time in 1575, while the Earl of Worcester's Men returned no less than six times between 1569 and 1587. In fact Stratford audiences did very well for there are records of visits by the companies of Lord Berkeley, Lord Strange, Lord Derby, the Countess of Essex, the Earl of Essex and the Lord Chandos while in 1587, a year crucially significant in Shakespeare's life, no fewer than five companies visited the town, including that of Burbage.[2]

Just what they brought with them is virtually unknown. There were early Tudor comedies such as those written by John Heywood, and adaptations from Roman writers like Terence and Plautus. Plautus' bawdy comedies provided rich pickings for the Elizabethans (and not only for the Elizabethans: some of their plots, thinly disguised, appeared well into the twentieth century in the Frankie Howerd television series *Up Pompeii!*).

Broad comedy humour was certainly popular. The anonymous *Jack Jugeler* is a straightforward piece about rogues trying to get the best of each other (including a scene where Jack comes face to face with his double), while Nicholas Udall's *Ralph Roister Doister* foreshadows a host of similar storylines, including *The Merry Wives of Windsor*, where a swaggering braggart who fancies himself a devil with the ladies finds the woman he is after is more than a match for him. Another play which might well have toured is the anonymous *Gammer Gurton's Needle*, a highly sophisticated piece which anticipates classic farce.

Marlowe and Shakespeare were not the only theatrical rivals born within a short time of each other. They were followed by the two great actors who were to head the rival companies with which each playwright was associated.

Edward Alleyn was born on 1 September 1566 to a Bishopsgate publican, who died when he was four. His mother then married within a short time a haberdasher called John Brown. The young Alleyn presumably fancied neither innkeeping nor haberdashery, for by the time he was sixteen he was touring in Leicester with the Earl of Worcester's company. We know this because he was hauled up with the rest of the players before the local Justices, as the company appears to have mislaid its Justices' Licence, although they still had one from the Earl. In spite of this and in defiance of the Mayor of Leicester, they had proceeded to put on a performance anyway. Afterwards they apologised to the Mayor, pleading with him not to tell their patron.

Alleyn's rival, Richard Burbage, was born less than a year later into the first truly theatrical family for his father James was already well established as an actor and what we would today call a company manager. Richard went straight into his father's company as a boy player and by the time he was thirteen his brother Cuthbert was describing him as 'brilliant', presumably in the women's roles which were then allotted to young lads.

Also born around this time were three famous comic actors, Richard Tarleton, Will Kempe and Robert Armin. Tarleton is said to have started out in life apprenticed to a watercarrier before becoming a publican in Colchester. He later moved to London, kept the Saba Tavern in Gracechurch Street and also ran an ordinary in Paternoster Row. He might well have graduated into theatre proper after giving comic turns to customers in his own inns. He has been described as a 'Charlie Chaplin figure' and perhaps this is not too far off the mark; the drawings of him which have come down to us show a little man with bushy hair, squinty eyes and a squashed nose, dressed in large baggy trousers and wearing oversize shoes. He is usually featured blowing a penny whistle and banging a small drum or tabor.[3] We know little or nothing of Tarleton's early years and even less of those of Kempe and Armin, both of whom were to interpret Shakespeare's great comic roles.

The clowns are followed by more prospective dramatists. It is not surprising that there is so little hard information on the origins of early theatre people for even at the height of their powers neither dramatists nor actors were considered people of any real importance.

Thomas Dekker was born about 1570, probably in London, Thomas Heywood in either Rothwell or Ashby-cum-Fenby in Lincolnshire, possibly to Robert Heywood who was the rector of these parishes. John Marston, whose family came from Shropshire, was born in Coventry in 1575 and baptised in Wardlington, Oxfordshire. His mother is said to have been the daughter of an Italian surgeon, his father, after the family moved to London, a lecturer at the Middle Temple. Of Cyril Tourneur, possibly born the same year, we know almost nothing except that he was probably a son of the Sir Richard Tourneur who spent his life in the service of the Cecil family.

Now enters the dramatist about whom we know most, thanks to his own self-publicity: Ben Jonson, that Falstaffian figure who was to span almost the entire era of Elizabethan and Jacobean theatre, living on until just before the Civil War. He was born in the summer of 1572, probably in London. Later he was to tell William Drummond of Hawthornden, during a notorious visit to him which was duly recorded by his increasingly reluctant host[4] that he thought his grandfather had come to Carlisle from Annandale. He went on to embroider this. His grandfather had been a gentleman in the service of King Henry VIII, but his son lost 'his whole estate' under Mary Tudor and, having been 'cast into prison and forfeited all', went into the church on his release. So, says Drummond confidently, Ben was a 'Minister's Son'. There is no way of knowing how much truth there is in this account. All we can be sure of is that his father died during his mother's pregnancy and he was born a month after his death.

Ben Jonson changed the legend of his background over the years but we do know for certain that shortly after his father's death, his mother took up with a bricklayer from

Westminster and finally married him. Ben grew up there and was sent to Westminster School which, even then, was one of the best in London.

He proved an apt pupil and a formidable scholar, remaining proud of his knowledge of classical languages all his life, and so feeling able to patronise Shakespeare for having 'small Latin and less Greek'. However, like Shakespeare, there was no question of his going on to university and when he left school he was apprenticed to his bricklayer stepfather. He remained sensitive about this until the end of his days and a sure way to make him explode was to remind him that he was once a 'bricklayer'.

For some time after the main companies had acquired patrons, the pattern of their professional activities changed little. They continued touring, setting up where they could and when in London performing either in the yards of the big inns, like the Tabard in Southwark or the Bel Savage in Ludgate[5] or, when specially invited, in the private houses of their patrons, but as productions became more elaborate it was obvious that what was needed was some kind of purpose-built permanent venue.

In 1574 James Burbage finally decided that the only sensible solution was to build a playhouse and so set about applying for a licence to build it. This took some time to achieve as the City fathers looked on the idea with deep suspicion and distrust. However, on 3 March 1576 he finally signed a twenty-one-year lease for a piece of land just outside Finsbury Fields in north London, a well-known recreation spot for people in the City. The playhouse had to be built outside its boundaries because although they had been reluctantly persuaded to grant a licence, the City authorities remained hostile to the idea and insisted it should not sully the City itself.

Burbage called his new playhouse quite simply 'the Theatre', and it stood on a piece of land between Finsbury Fields and the public road from Bishopsgate to Shoreditch Church. His lease still exists and shows that it contained a clause stating that if he spent £200 or more on the building, a very large sum in those days, he could take it down if he wanted to when the lease expired. He was also supposed to be offered an automatic extension when the time came for the lease to be renewed and new terms negotiated.[6]

The Theatre opened its doors to the public for the first time towards the end of 1576 at about the same time a history book was published which was to be a source of inspiration for many of the dramatists whose work would be peformed there. It was called Holinshed's *Chronicles.*

One year later a second theatre, the Curtain, opened nearby. The name, though apt, was not chosen for any theatrical connections, but was that of the piece of ground on which it was built. It is not certain whose idea it was to build the Curtain but it was soon being run by Philip Henslowe, the greatest theatrical entrepreneur of his day, so it is most likely to have been his. Between them the Burbage family and Henslowes were to dominate the way theatre was run for the next twenty years.

3

Growing Up

The early years of Christopher Marlowe and William Shakespeare would have followed a similar pattern. The 'petty schools' provided the earliest schooling, catering for children (mostly boys), teaching them to read and write and learn their Catechism, grace before and after meals and the psalms. Small children learned the alphabet, numbers and simple words from horn books which could be hung from their belts. The first row on the book, which began with a cross, was known as the 'Christ-cross row'.

At around seven, already able to read, write and number, a young boy whose family was prepared to support him was ready to move up into the grammar school. The word 'boy' is used advisedly for such an education was strictly for the boys. Girls did not go to secondary school although the well-born might choose to educate them to a high standard at home. However, by the time substantial numbers of artisans' sons were going to grammar schools, it is clear that at least a proportion of their daughters were literate. We know this as so many plays, including *The Merry Wives of Windsor* and *Twelfth Night* hinge on the ability of such women to read and write and, in the latter case, for a maid to successfully forge her mistress's handwriting.

The generation of boys destined for the theatre were the beneficiaries of the new grammar schools founded by the Tudors, beginning with Edward VI. There might not have been a National Curriculum in the sixteenth century, but the same pattern of the day and the same subjects were taught throughout the land. A grammar school boy rose early, for school began at 6am in summer and 7am in winter. Having stumbled out of bed, he was expected to say his prayers, wash, dress, comb his hair and say 'good morrow' to his parents, before leaving with his satchel of books. Whether or not he crept 'like a snail unwillingly to school' he was expected to be there before the bell stopped ringing or he would be punished.

School opened and closed with Bible readings, psalm-singing and prayers. The entire syllabus was based on Latin, the pupils working from Latin grammars and phrase books before going on to read *Aesop's Fables* and Cato. Traces of these can be seen in the plays of all those working in the theatre. The first three years were spent in the Lower School and it was most likely here that the boys first came into contact with the Roman plays of Terence and Plautus which were to prove so influential.

In the Upper School they were introduced to Ovid and both Marlowe and Jonson later produced translations of his erotic verse. Alongside Latin, and some Greek, were logic and rhetoric. 'Again and again,' writes Rowse,[1] 'we find Shakespeare's expertise in dialectical argument according to the text-books turned to use, especially in the earlier plays – the sentence by sentence question and answer, the line by line statement and rejoinder, passages of wearisome antiphony to our ears, hair-splitting about words which seems obsessive to us. It was drilled into him at school, it remained with him all his days; the Elizabethans liked that sort of thing.' Although Holinshed's *Chronicles* were published while Marlowe and Shakespeare were still at school, it is unlikely they came into general use until after they had left. History was taught by use of the Latin historians and, in some cases, through the earlier Hall's *Chronicle*.

Memory training was considered vitally important and the boys were expected to learn an enormous amount by rote. Religion was ever-present, from the services which began and ended the school day, throughout the lessons taught during it, and from the powerful and influential role the church played in the lives of all children. It was this pervasive influence which later caused some playwrights, notably Marlowe, to react against religion.

* * *

John Fletcher, John Webster and Thomas Middleton were all born at the end of the 1570s. Fletcher is usually spoken of in the same breath as Francis Beaumont, with whom he had a close working relationship for a number of years. Beaumont and Fletcher are paired like Gilbert and Sullivan or Morecambe and Wise. Whether their close relationship was carried further is open to debate. The arch-gossip John Aubrey said of them:

> There was a wonderful consimility of fancy between him [Beaumont] and John Fletcher which caused the dearness of friendship between them. They lived together on the Bankside, not far from the Playhouses, both bachelors; lay together; and had one Wench in the house between them, which they did so admire; the same clothes and cloak between them.[2]

Fletcher's family was well off in his early years, his father being first a Senior Fellow of Corpus Christi College, Cambridge, then vicar of Rye where John was born. Eventually he became the Queen's own Chaplain after becoming Bishop of London. He died in 1596 leaving behind him John, a further eight surviving children and a mountain of debt.

Webster's family too were wealthy, though artisan. His father was a coach builder who lived at the corner of Cow Lane and Hosier Lane, Smithfield, in the parish of St Sepulchre-without-Newgate. His father had married a much younger woman, Sarah Peniall, when she was sixteen, and John was born at his grandparents' house when his mother was only seventeen years old. We know his father was well off because in 1597 he had to pay £12 in taxes, a large sum for those days.

Webster, known for his dark and death-laden plays, might well have been influenced by his early life for his house was close to Newgate Prison itself, and every night before the execution of prisoners, either locally or at Tyburn, the Great Bell of St Sepulchre's would toll out for those due to die next day. Moreover, horrible stories still circulated about the death at the stake of the vicar of that same church. The Reverend John Rogers was the first martyr to be condemned under Bloody Mary and was burned in Smithfield market place in front of his wife and eleven children on 4 February 1555.[3]

Thomas Middleton, one of the most brilliant dramatists of his generation, was born in 1580 and his father, like Jonson's stepfather, was a bricklayer. However, unlike his theatrical colleague, Middleton does not seem to have been paranoid about bricks and bricklaying and by the time he was five his father was dead, leaving behind a young and comparatively wealthy widow.

It might well be that Middleton was able to write believable female characters (unlike Marlowe and Jonson), because he was brought up by a strong mother and a lively older sister. Seven months after her husband's death, Anne Middleton had married a grocer called Thomas Harvey, who had lost all his money backing a disastrous venture to the New World. Perhaps she was lonely or felt the need of a father for her two small children but either way she soon discovered she had fallen prey to an impoverished man who had been on the lookout for an attractive wife with means of her own. Middleton's early comedies are much concerned with this kind of situation. However, the marriage soon proved to be a disaster and within a matter of months Anne forced Harvey to leave.

He devoted much of his time during the next few years to trying to get his hands on the money left to his wife and stepchildren and Middleton grew up in a constant atmosphere of litigation, as his mother resolutely stood her ground and would not give in. That, too, was to leave its mark.

* * *

When they reached the age of thirteen the lives of Marlowe and Shakespeare diverged markedly. Shakespeare left grammar school, as was usual for boys of his background, and joined his father in the family business, while Marlowe remained where he was, at the King's School, Canterbury, for another two years. Thereafter the two boys followed very different paths until the theatre brought them together in London seven or eight years later.

Marlowe went on to win the Archbishop Matthew Parker scholarship to Corpus Christi College, Cambridge, an award which brought brought with it sufficient funds to enable its recipient to study for his degree, on the understanding that he would then take Holy Orders. Marlowe went up to the university three weeks before Christmas 1580 and settled into the special room set aside in college for the Matthew Parker scholar.

According to the Indenture made between Archbishop Parker and the College, he was to receive his 'barber and launder freely without anything paying therefore', and his barber was to see his head was kept suitably 'polled, notted or rounded'. He was not permitted to have 'long lockes of Hayre upon his hede'. He was allowed a shilling a week while in residence, to be forfeited if he were absent. Students remained at the university all year round without vacations; absences, unless caused by dire sickness, being limited to a month at most. The ruling on the time that actually had to be spent in college in order to be awarded a degree was to play a highly significant part in Marlowe's Cambridge life.[4]

In his college room he was entitled to a corded bedstead (a bed with a wooden frame criss-crossed with cords on which the mattress rested), a feather mattress and two feather pillows, coverlets, a chair, a trestle-table, and two forms – comfortable accommodation by Elizabethan standards. Marlowe's expenditure on food and drink, noted in the college Buttery Books, shows that in one week alone he spent the prodigal sum of fifteen pence and one halfpenny.[5]

Elizabethan university students studied Latin, Greek,

Hebrew, Logic, Mathematics, Philosophy, Divinity and Dialetics, but there was also, of course, a busy social life and early in his time at Cambridge Marlowe made a friend of an interesting fellow undergraduate, Thomas Walsingham, the young cousin of the Secretary to the Privy Council, Elizabeth's spymaster Sir Francis Walsingham.

Shakespeare, meanwhile, continued learning the trade of a leatherworker and glovemaker in Stratford. John Shakespeare's shop, like that of John Marlowe in Canterbury, would have been stacked with the hides of deer, sheep and goats. John Shakespeare treated many hides himself, buying in only those of cattle and pigs.

William would know, writes Mark Eccles in *Shakespeare in Warwickshire* that neat's leather was used for shoes, sheep's leather for a bridle, horsehair for bowstrings and calves' guts for fiddles. Cheveril or kid-skin was used for gloves because of its softness and flexibility. Gloves often figure in Shakespeare's imagery and Eccles points to his reference to a tool he must often have seen used by his father when Mistress Quickly asks: 'Does he not wear a great round beard like a glover's paring knife?'

We simply do not know when young Will first became drawn towards the theatre but given the popularity of Stratford with the touring companies, he would have had ample opportunity to acquire the taste for it. The usual place for the companies to set up was the courtyard of the Bear Inn and he might well have seen there the popular *The Famous Victories of King Henry the Fifth.*

A few weeks after Marlowe went up to Cambridge for the first time an event occurred in Stratford which obviously haunted Shakespeare for years. Shortly before Christmas 1579 the body of a young girl was found in the River Avon, caught under the bare branches of the willows at Tiddington. It was thought that she had entered the water on 17 December but the Inquest was not held until 11 February 1580. The jury consisted of three gentlemen or freeholders of Alveston (on the outskirts of Stratford), John Pearse, John Lord and Thomas Townsend, and nine others good men and true. After due deliberation, they returned a verdict of death by drowning, an accident *'per infortunium'*. It was decided that 'she, going with a milk pail to draw water at the river Avon, and standing on the bank of the same, suddenly and by accident, slipped and fell into the river and was drowned; and met her death in no other wise or fashion *(et non aliter nec alio modo mortem suam devenit)*.'[6]

Because of the length of the delay, presumably due in part to the Christmas holiday, it is likely that she had already been buried, and her coffin then taken up for the Inquest eight weeks later. But the time lag might also suggest there was suspicion or argument over the sequence of events leading to her death. Was it truly an accident or could it have been suicide? Had she been jilted by a lover, was she expecting a child?

If the jury had returned a suicide verdict the result would have been a hasty interment at some nearby crossroads after the Coroner had announced 'that the deceased, regardless of salvation of her soul and led astray by the instigation of the Devil, threw herself into the water and wilfully drowned herself.' Wilfully and wittingly, she would have murdered herself *(murderavit se ipsam)* and been guilty of disobeying the sixth Commandment and, by doing so, would have forfeited her right to burial in hallowed ground. Did lingering doubts remain? Were there family friends on the jury to enable it to bring in a kinder verdict? Whatever the reason, the young woman was given the benefit of the doubt and duly buried in consecrated ground. Her name was Katherine Hamlet.

If Shakespeare was indeed seriously contemplating becoming an actor (and it is not difficult to imagine the effect such a notion would have had on his parents), then his dreams were about to be dashed. Sometime during the summer of 1582 he became heavily involved with the daughter of Richard Hathaway of Shottery. What is now called 'Anne Hathaway's Cottage' was a substantial property known then as Hewlands Farm. Anne or Agnes Hathaway (for she was known by both names) was born in 1556, eight years before Shakespeare and at the age of twenty-six would have been considered an ageing spinster by Elizabethan standards; her family were probably despairing of her finding a husband. At her age she must have been a great deal more experienced than Will.

It is highly unlikely that he had marriage in mind as he happily took what was offered to him in the long grass of the fields around Stratford but the outcome could hardly have been unexpected. Mystery surrounds his marriage, in that there are two conflicting entries. On 27 November 1582 an entry in the episcopal register at Worcester sets down the issue of a marriage licence for William Shaxpere and Anne Whateley of Temple Grafton. On the next day, two yeomen of Stratford, Fulke Sandells and John Richardson, agreed to pay £40, a very large sum of money, should any legal problem arise to prevent the marriage of 'William Shagspere and Anne Hathwey of Stratford in the Dioces of Worcester, maiden'. This asked for a marriage after one reading of the banns instead of three, and the object of the bond was to indemnify bishop or clergy from any action or suit arising from the grant of such a special licence.[7]

The argument as to whether the two ladies are, in fact, one is still unresolved, or whether Shakespeare wanted to marry a Miss Whateley but was forced into marriage with Miss Hathaway. Dr A.L. Rowse and Mark Eccles incline to the former view, Ivor Brown to the latter.[8] He points out that while it would have been possible to miswrite the surnames, it is harder to understand how the clerk was able to confuse Temple Grafton with Stratford. But Shakespeare was not an uncommon name and were there, by coincidence, two Shakespeare's marrying two Anne's? It seems unlikely. One view is that Anne Hathaway's family and friends were so powerful that, having heard William was about to marry Anne Whateley, they stepped in and forced him to make an honest woman of their pregnant relative.

Whatever the explanation, the fact remains that Shakespeare married Anne Hathaway by special licence that November, the special licence being needed because it was the beginning of Advent, during which time marriages were not solemnised. There is no record of where that hasty wedding took place, although tradition has it in a small chapel, which has now disappeared, in the village of Luddington, just outside Stratford.

In the May following the shotgun wedding Anne gave birth to the couple's first daughter, Susannah, who was swiftly followed by twins, Judith and Hamnet. As the family of five continued to live at the house in Henley Street, along with Will's parents and his brothers and sisters, it is unlikely that he had much time to moon about dreaming of the theatre and even less to set pen to paper. For the time being he had more than enough to do in surroundings which must have been disruptive and noisy.

* * *

Christopher Marlowe had different sexual tastes and it seems most likely that he and Thomas Walsingham were lovers while at Cambridge. Walsingham, as well as studying for his degree, was also being employed by his uncle Sir Francis to recruit agents, for Sir Francis was anxious to bring a more professional element into his secret service, young men with bright, trained minds, and he set Thomas to do just this. So it was that Christopher Marlowe became one of the first of the homosexual Cambridge spies, antedating Guy Burgess and Anthony Blunt by some four hundred years.

Twice during his time at Cambridge Marlowe was absent for about half a term. He became a Bachelor of Arts in 1584 but when it came to his Master's degree, the university refused to award it on the grounds that he had not fulfilled the residency criterion. It was then that Sir Francis Walsingham intervened personally and it is his letter of 29 June 1587, on behalf of the Privy Council, that confirms the tradition that Marlowe worked for the secret service: It states:

> Whereas it was reported that Christopher Marlowe was determined to have gone beyond the seas to Rheims, and there to remain, their Lordships thought it good to certify that he had no such intent; but that in all his

> actions he had behaved himself orderly and discreetly, whereby he had done her Majesty good service and deserved to be rewarded for his faithful dealing.

Their lordships requested,

> ...that rumour therefore should be allayed by all possible means, and that he should be furthered in the degree he was to take this next Commencement. Because it is not her Majesty's pleasure that anyone employed, as he had been, in matters touching the benefit of this country should be defamed by those that are ignorant in the affairs he went about.

It was signed on behalf of the Lord Archbishop, the Lord Chancellor, the Lord Treasurer, the Lord Chamberlain and Mr Comptroller.

There is no absolute proof as to how Marlowe had been employed but the consensus is that he was probably sent over to the English Seminary in Rheims. The college, originally founded in Douai by a Dr Allen, had become a centre for disaffected English students drawn to the old Faith. Allen and his colleagues did not only support Philip II of Spain in his proposed invasion of England, but also actively assisted in the various plots designed to put Mary Stuart on the English throne. The Seminary was therefore a hotbed of intrigue, so what better way to discover who was there and what was being planned than to send a bright young undergraduate along posing as a recusant? From what we know of Marlowe he must have enjoyed the intellectual game of chess involved in espionage and have revelled in the excitement of it. Thus, with his arrogance and feeling of natural superiority, he walked happily into Walsingham's net, a net from which he was never afterwards able to disentangle himself.

4

The First Playhouses

Throughout the 1580s, and indeed beyond, the City Fathers remained distinctly unenthusiastic when it came to granting licences for the building of theatres and even while James Burbage was still wrestling with them for permission, the authorities were issuing statements pointing out the unpleasant consequences of allowing plays in inn-yards which, they said, caused great congestion in the streets due both to the 'coaches of the great' and to the large number of young apprentices attending the shows. One such warning reads:

> The inordinate haunting of great multitudes of people, especially youth, to plays, interludes and shows [leads to] affrays, quarrels, and evil practices of incontinency in great Inns, having chambers and secret places adjoining to their open stages and galleries, inveigling and alluring maids, especially orphans and good Citizens children [who are] under age, to privy and unmeet shows, the publishing of unchaste, uncomeley and unshamefast speeches and doings and the withdrawing of Her Majesty's subjects from divine service and holy days. At the times such plays are chiefly shown [there] follows unthrifty waste of money by poor and fond persons, sundry robberies by picking and cutting of purses, the uttering of popular, busy and seditious matters and many other corruptions of youth and other enormities; besides that also sundry

> slaughters and mayhems of the Queen's subjects have happened by the ruining of scaffolds, frames and stages and by the engines, weapons land powders used in the plays.[1]

Until recently Burbage's Theatre was assumed to have been the very first playhouse but recent excavations show that there appears to have been an earlier one in Whitechapel, called the Red Lion, which was built about 1567 and which the Theatre replaced, but it is not thought to have been built specifically with plays in mind; its more common use would have been animal baiting as it is similar in design to the baiting rings which had been in use on the South Bank for many years. It has a direct link with the Theatre because it was built by John Brayne, Burbage's partner in the Theatre venture.

There are no drawings to tell us what either the Theatre or the Curtain looked like but it is assumed that they were of a cruder design than their successors, the Rose, Swan and Globe. Andrew Gurr[2] considers that it was likely that the Theatre was closely based on the old inn-yards, especially that of the Bel Savage, while the Curtain was more like the 'wooden O' which is familiar from later prints which show the playhouses on the Bankside, but we have no way of knowing, unless its foundations are eventually discovered. Simple in construction they may have been but both the Theatre and the Curtain were lavishly decorated inside.

Whatever their shape, they would have had several tiers of galleries on three sides of the building and a large thrust stage which pushed out well into the auditorium. The area in front of the stage was for those who stood for the performance; hence the term 'groundlings'. Although both theatres were primarily built for the presentation of plays, they were also used for a wide variety of other events such as exhibitions of sword-fighting, wrestling, bear-baiting, tumbling, vaulting and rope-dancing.

All the early playhouses were open to the sky. Those who could afford to sit in the galleries were sheltered from the weather and, as stages became more sophisticated, some provision was made upstage for the actors, but there was no protection whatsoever for the groundlings. Gurr points out how often in the text of Elizabethan plays actors are said to be wearing hats or there is stage business using hats. 'The unbonneted Hamlet familiar to modern audiences is a creation of the indoor theatre and fourth-wall staging,' he writes, 'where everyone goes hatless accordingly. Hamlet in 1600 walked under the sky in an open amphitheatre, on a platform that felt out-of-doors in comparison with modern theatres but indifferently represented indoors or out to the Elizabethans.'[3] Hats, he continued, were useful to guard the wearer's head against the sun or to keep his head warm and this went for actors and audience alike.

Over the next twenty years a distinction was drawn between public and private theatres. The latter did not mean that the theatre was privately owned or some kind of club for which you had to have membership. It merely meant that it was enclosed and had a roof. The earliest was the Blackfriars Theatre, converted from the ruins of the old monastery on the bank of the Thames, and first used for a children's company, the Earl of Oxford's Children. By the end of the century both kinds were being built.

Once the two theatres were up and running their critics became even more rancorous. John Northbrooke in his *Treatise Against Dicing, Dancing, Plays, Interludes and Other Idle Pastimes* describes the doorway into the theatre as the gate to 'hell-mouth'. The pamphlet is set out in question-and-answer form, Youth (unsurprisingly) asking the questions and Age replying:

> *Youth:* Do you speak against those places also, which are made up and builded for such plays and entertainments as the Theatre and Curtain is, and other such like places besides?
>
> *Age:* Yea, truly; for I am persuaded that Satan hath not a more speedy way and fitter school to work and teach his desire, to bring men and women into the snare of concupiscence and filthy lusts

> of wicked whoredom, than those places and plays and theatres are; and therefore necessary that those places and players should be forbidden and dissolved, and put down by authorities as brothel houses and stews area.[4]

It is hardly surprising that, following this kind of hot publicity, audiences flocked to the new entertainment in ever greater numbers. They were speeded on their way on 24 August 1578 by parson John Stockwood who attacked the theatre in a sermon preached at Paul's Cross, the Speakers' Corner of its day. Having pointed out the vast cost of these sinks of iniquity, built outside the 'liberty' of the City Walls with no expense spared, he castigated the players who, he said, ignored all criticism, their attitude being:

> . . . let them say what they will, we will play. I know now how I might, with the godly-learned most especially, more discommend the gorgeous playing place erected in the fields, than term it, as they have pleased to have called it, the Theatre . . . Will not a filthy player with the blast of a trumpet sooner call thither a thousand than an hour's tolling of a bell bring to a sermon a hundred? If you resort to the Theatre, the Curtain and other places of players in the City, you shall, on the Lord's Day find them so full as possibly they can throng.[5]

Which proves that there was Sunday opening for theatres in Elizabeth's day.

Women and young persons were considered to be particularly at risk. An anonymous pamphlet *A Third Blast of Retreat from Plays and the Theatre* says:

> Some citizens wives, upon whom the Lord for example to others hath laid his hands, have even on their death beds, with tears confessed that they have received at those spectacles such filthy infections, as have turned their minds from chaste cogitations, and made them, honest women, [into] light housewives. Whosoever shall visit the Chapel of Satan, I mean the Theatre,

> shall find there no want of young ruffians, nor lack of harlots utterly past all shame, who press to the front of the scaffolds, to the end to show their impudency, and to be as an object to all men's eyes.[6]

Young lads might never even get there:

> Sometimes he comes not to the play,
> But falls into a whorehouse by the way . . .

Theatre audiences were 'a monster of many heads, the common people which resort to theatres being but an assembly of tailors, tinkers, cordwainers, sailors, old men, young men, women, boys, girls and such like . . .'

Human nature has changed little and the more and louder the ranting, the bigger the audiences which 'thronged' to see these 'filthy' shows and entertainments; much as television audiences switch on to the dramas heavily criticised beforehand by the National Viewers and Listeners Association for being disgusting, blasphemous and overloaded with sex.

It was true that the theatres did provide a draw for all kinds of low life. The groundlings standing packed before the stage, listening and watching intently, provided easy pickings for thieves, while a whore might well make more money in an afternoon at the theatre than she would during the rest of the week. Deals were struck during or in the breaks in performance and a girl might well take away a string of clients at the end of the show and service them, one after the other, up against the outside wall of the theatre itself.

The programmes presented by the early theatres were not, of course, as their critics had it, filthy and obscene. There is little detail of what actually was put on but audiences would almost certainly have been offered morality plays and comedies such as *Ralph Roister Doister*, although most of these have not survived. The staple fare seems to have been romantic tales of knight errantry, such as *Common Conditions, The Conflict of Conscience* and *Clyomon and Clamydes*. They were described by contemporary critics as 'gallimaufreys', regarded much in the way Mills & Boon novels are today by literary reviewers, and were presented with a welter of unsophisticated special effects, which those same critics dismissed as being nothing more than coloured smoke and cardboard monsters. Audiences, however, loved them.

Elizabethan audiences whether gentry or groundlings were far from prudish and sex was a legitimate subject for jokes, especially seduction and adultery. Most comedies would have contained an element of bawdy humour but this was mainly reserved for the 'jigs' which came after the main performance. This was not, as the name suggests, a jolly dance but a turn given by the company clown. It would be a hundred years before women were allowed to become actresses in England (although they were playing in Italy and even Catholic Spain by the end of the sixteenth century), but women were among the most enthusiastic members of the audience and were not easily shocked.

The clown, Richard Tarleton, made his early theatrical reputation with his jigs and continued to perform them long after he had achieved success as a comic actor, indeed his fame was such that in a time when communications were poor and most people never travelled more than a few miles from the place of their birth, his name was known throughout the country, his jokes retold by those unlikely ever to see him. After his death it was said of him that such was his skill that he only had to walk on to a stage for his audience to collapse with laughter, and keen playgoer Henry Peachman wrote:

> Tarleton, when his head was only seen,
> The Tire-house door and tapestry between,
> Set all the multitude in such a laughter,
> They could not hold for scarce an hour after.

All those who have found a particular comedian so intrinsically funny will know exactly what he meant. Tarleton's humour was universal, appealing to city and country, rich and poor alike.

There are numerous anecdotes about him. He would,

like stand-up comedians today, single out members of the audience for special attention and it was a bold lad indeed who would set out to draw his fire in an attempt to get the better of him. Tarleton would destroy him. There is a report of one such who refused to give in until Tarleton came back with such a put-down that 'the poor fellow, plucking his hat over his eyes, went his ways'. Tarleton also considered the authorities and the City Fathers fair game and his *Jigge of a Horseload of Fools* provoked a furious response from them when he performed it at the Curtain.[7]

As primarily a comedian and a noted ad-libber, he might well have found it difficult to confine himself to a script. There are accounts of his appearing in scenes in the old play about Henry V, *The Famous Victories of Henry V*, either disrupting what was going on or, on one famous occasion, taking both his own part and that of the Judge who was supposedly sentencing him for misbehaviour. He also wrote plays himself; his *The Seven Deadly Sins*, the text of which has not survived, was a box-office winner.

Three more playwrights now enter our stage. Francis Beaumont, he who was the other half of Fletcher was, like his partner, comparatively well born, being the son of a judge, Sir Francis Beaumont, Justice of the Common Pleas. Later he was entered at Pembroke College Oxford, but only stayed up a year before being entered as a member of the Inner Temple. There is no evidence that he ever followed his father into the law.

John Ford was born in Ilsington, Devon, in 1586 into a family of Devon gentry and was related to Lord Chief Justice Popham. He too spent a short time at Oxford, at Exeter College, before going into the Middle Temple where his early years must have been disrupted and stormy for he was rusticated for two years for failing to pay his Buttery bills. The third playwright, Philip Massinger, born in Salisbury in the same year as Ford, was another Oxford student, this time at St Alban's Hall. He spent three or four years there where he was described as taking much more interest in romances, poetry and drama than in serious study – a criticism which has been levelled at writers, dramatists and actors ever since.

The latter years of the 1580s were to prove critical to the country but they also mark the beginning of the golden age of early theatre. In 1586 Philip Henslowe and Edward Alleyn founded the company which, although it would change its name and make-up several times, eventually became the Lord Admiral's Men and a magnet for every single dramatist of note between then and the end of the century. Between 1592 and 1600 alone Henslowe presented the staggering total of three hundred plays.

It was in 1587 that William Shakespeare suddenly disappeared from home.

5

Henslowe, Marlowe and the Rose

The brilliant young Queen had now become the ageing Gloriana, the jewelled icon so familiar from her portraits, her Court divided into ambitious and ruthless factions. The political situation grew steadily darker as she faced threats both at home and abroad.

The first major rebellion had come in 1569, followed by a plot involving her cousin, the Duke of Norfolk. She had forgiven him after he had pledged his loyalty, only to find that he broke his word by writing to Mary Stuart with an offer of marriage, an action which led to his execution. Throughout her reign, Elizabeth had tried to avoid open conflict with Rome but in 1570 Pope Pius V declared her to be excommunicated from the Church and that, as a heretic and bastard, she could be deposed. Her English subjects were told they were absolved from any allegiance to her and positively encouraged to plot and rebel and that such plots would meet with official approval.

The Pope's Bull, *Regnam in Excelsis,* proved catastrophic for those still faithful to the Catholic faith. If they obeyed the Pope they became traitors and if they refused they could be excommunicated. The Queen had been determined not to follow in her sister's footsteps telling her advisers that she 'would not have any of their [Catholic] consciences unnecessarily sifted to know what affection they had to the old religion'. All that was demanded was the acceptance of her sovereignty and the assurance of their allegiance. Now all that had to change.

Already heavily extended overseas assisting the Dutch in their struggle against Spain, the English government now found itself facing a subtler enemy as a steady stream of young priests, trained in the seminaries of Douai and Rheims, entered the country, many of whom were sent specifically to encourage the Queen's overthrow. The direct result was the introduction of repressive legislation for loyal and disloyal alike. It was no longer simply a question of fines for all those not attending Church on Sundays, the new Acts made it treasonable to attempt to convert a member of the Established Church to that of Rome, while those caught saying or hearing Mass received punitive fines. All 'seminary priests' were ordered to leave the country, any failing to do so would be suspected of high treason.

There were a whole series of plots, two of which, the Somerville and the Throgmorton in 1583, were designed to aid a Spanish invasion. That they both failed was due in no small part to Walsingham's intelligence gatherers. The last attempt was the Babington Plot in 1586. Its originator, Sir Anthony Babington, a naïve country gentleman, saw himself as some kind of knight errant setting out to rescue Mary Stuart and place her on the throne.

Although Elizabeth's two great advisers, Sir Francis Walsingham and William Cecil, the Lord of Burleigh, rarely agreed with each other, it is clear that they decided that the only way to remove the threat to the throne was to dispose of Mary once and for all. It was therefore decided to infiltrate the various Catholic factions using agents, or 'intelligencers' as they were known, to act as *agents provocateurs.* Step forward, therefore, Robert Poley, master spy and possible double agent, the doubt being that his part in the subsequent plot was so devious that there are grounds for thinking he might have been playing off both sides.

As Poley's path will later cross those of both Christopher Marlowe and Thomas Kyd, his earlier career is of interest. When he first joined Babington's circle he was greeted with some suspicion, for Babington himself wrote to Mary's secretary asking what opinion he had of Poley 'whom I find to have intelligence with her Majesty's occasions. I am private with the man and by that means therefore know somewhat, but suspect more.'[1] Thomas Morgan, a member of Babington's circle, warned that Poley might well be a plant but his advice not to send any letters through him went unheeded and soon all the conspirators' correspondence was being intercepted and government clerks kept busy reading it, making copies, deciphering those notes written in code before forwarding all of it on to its destinations, sometimes with added forgeries.

By March 1586 Poley had even convinced Morgan he was genuine, thanks to a well-honed cover story involving Sir Philip Sydney, and he was therefore employed as a courier between Paris, London and Mary Stuart's prison at Fotheringay. There are numerous accounts of what followed but suffice it to say that Poley played a crucial role, finally inviting the plotters to supper to aid in their arrest. For some reason they were not picked up immediately, although the priest, Father Ballard, was finally taken at Poley's lodgings. Right to the end poor Anthony Babington continued to believe in Poley's honesty, writing to him immediately before his arrest, 'take heed to your own part lest of these my misfortunes you bear the blame ... farewell, sweet Robin, if as I take thee, true to me ... return to me thine answer for my satisfaction, and my diamond and what else thou wilt. The furnace is prepared wherein our faith must be tried. Farewell till we meet which God knows when.' Among those involved with Poley in this enterprise was a part-time agent, Nicholas Skeres, and, it is said, Thomas Walsingham acting for his cousin.

The conspirators were indeed tried in the furnace. On 20 September Babington, Ballard and twelve others were dragged on hurdles to Tyburn. Ballard, under torture, had betrayed his colleagues but it did not help him. The first seven were duly hanged, drawn and quartered with all that entailed in prolonged suffering, but when the Queen heard what they had undergone, she sent word that the rest be shown mercy and simply hanged. In February 1587 Mary Stuart, Queen of Scots, was executed at Fotheringay.

* * *

In 1587 Marlowe finally came down from Cambridge and, like all the ambitious dramatists during the next forty years, made straight for London. His reputation had gone before him for he had already translated Ovid's poetry while at college, along with Virgil's *Tragedy of Dido.* More to the point, he had written a play which was already taking London by storm, the first part of a history of the ancient war lord and tyrant, *Tamburlaine,* a play which had already been eagerly snapped up by Philip Henslowe.

Henslowe was the true stuff of impresarios and that we have as much first-hand knowledge as we do about the world of Elizabethan theatre is due, in no small part, to the discovery in the eighteenth century of what is now known as *Henslowe's Diary* lying among some old papers in the library of Dulwich College. The manuscript started out in life as an accounts book, kept by Philip's brother, John, in which he detailed his income and outgoings from mining and smelting in the Ashdown forest during the years 1576–81. Then, when the book passed into Philip's hands, he used it first to detail the accounts of his timber business, then for details of his theatrical enterprises.

For from 1592 onwards he recorded which plays were in repertoire and how much was taken at the door, notes of advances made to dramatists on the acceptance of a 'plot' or storyline, inventories of costumes, scenery and props along with what had had to be paid out for what was needed to make the special effects. From this it is clear which plays proved most popular and which dramatists were writing for him and when. There are also a number of critical comments on his having had to bail dramatists and actors out of prison for various offences, mostly drunkenness or debt.

Henslowe was years ahead of his time. A self-made man, he had worked first for a timber merchant called Woodward then, when his employer died leaving behind a brisk young widow with a daughter, Henslowe promptly married the widow and took over the business. It was with that money behind him that he began his theatrical activities at the Curtain. It would, however, be foolish to see Henslowe as a man with a consuming passion for the arts in general and theatre in particular. He was a shrewd business man who grasped that putting on plays might be very profitable for those going into the new form of entertainment, as it were on the ground floor.

His early involvement with the talented and ambitious Edward Alleyn ensured his success and the dynasty was further secured in 1592 by the marriage of his stepdaughter Joan to Alleyn. The *Diary* is absolutely fascinating, not only because of its theatrical importance. It shows that Henslowe gave equal weight to running a bear pit, shamelessly manoeuvring to become the Queen's Bearward. He also fancied himself as an amateur physician and the *Diary* contains horrible remedies.

'Take ants and stamp on them,' he wrote, 'then strain them through a cloth then mix with swine's grease, then stamp on knot grass the same and take the juice and mix with the strainings of eggs and put in the ear which will help cure deafness.' Another deafness cure consisted of frying earthworms 'a dozen times at least' and pounding up the resultant mess to make an ointment. Other nostrums were more complicated and required more ingredients, such as that for eyestrain which entailed mixing fennel, rue, vervain, five types of grass, pimpernel, sage, celandine, then pounding them with pestle and mortar before boiling them all up in the 'urine of a boy'. This concoction was then painted on the eyes with a feather. There is also a section on spells to ward off everything from the evil eye and plague to 'making a fowl fall dead'. It would have been splendid had the Burbages kept such a record for posterity about life and work at the Globe in Shakespeare's day.

However, by 1587 Henslowe had more on his mind than medicines and magic. There was no end in sight to the constant battle between the City authorities and the theatres to the north of them. He therefore turned his eyes to the South Bank, an area which had much to commend it as it was outside the jurisdiction of the City with easy access, either by London Bridge or by the host of boats plying for trade across the Thames. There were gardens along the Bankside, bear-baiting was popular and there were already several bear pits there drawing plenty of trade. It was also notorious for its gaming houses, brothels and low life. Another plus was that he already had his timber warehouse on that side of the Thames and either then, or shortly afterwards, bought a house on the Bankside, along with the Bear Pit next to it.

So it was there, near to the old London Bridge with its houses and shops, that Henslowe built the theatre which was to be one of the most famous of the early playhouses, the Rose. There are records of the opening of both the Swan and later the Globe Theatre on the Bankside, but the dates of the building and opening of other playhouses have been a matter of much argument among academic experts.[2] Until recently it was thought the Rose was not built until the early 1590s but new research, not least the discovery of its foundations in 1989, points to it having opened in 1587 and then extended and improved in 1592. There was already another theatre on that side of the Thames, at Newington Butts, but hardly anything is known about it except that it did not seem to have a resident company but was used by those touring. It is thought to have stood roughly where the Elephant & Castle shopping centre is today. The new Rose needed new plays and Marlowe's *Tamburlaine* certainly fitted the bill.

So what of William Shakespeare? There are literally hundreds of theories as to how he spent what are known as 'the missing years', the years between the winter of 1586/87 and his emergence in London in the early 1590s as a promising theatrical talent. There is the hoary old myth that he had to leave Stratford in a hurry after poaching deer from the Lucy estate at Charlecote: it is a myth, for had he been brought up before the local magistrates and charged then there would be a record of it.

Then there is the military option: Shakespeare sympathised with soldiers, as is shown in the history plays, so he must have enlisted in the army and served in the Low Countries.[3] He knew all about the law too, so he must have studied at the Inns of Court. He was a tutor employed by Lord Strange at his home in Derby which is why he wrote roles for comic schoolmasters. According to this version, it was while he was in Derbyshire that his talent was discovered and he was then employed by Lord Strange to write plays for his own company which was based at the Rose.[4] He could write convincingly about voyages as instanced in *The Tempest* and *Pericles* and was able to do this because he had sailed to the New World. Then, of course, there is the other favourite tale, that Shakespeare, having run away to London, supported himself by holding the horses for those attending the theatre and so got a taste for it. It goes on and on. About the only claim not made for him so far is that as he wrote such wonderful parts for women, he must have spent the missing years as a woman.

There is another more prosaic possibility which is far more plausible. As has already been noted no less than five theatre companies visited Stratford in 1587. Mark Eccles points out that during the summer, the Queen's Men arrived in the town with one man short, for an actor, William Knell, had recently been killed in Oxford during a fight with a colleague, John Towne.[5]

A Coroner's Inquest at Thame reported that between 9 and 10pm on 13 June 1587, Knell came into a close known as White Hound Close and there ran into John Towne. There must already have been a running quarrel between the two actors for Knell, well primed with ale, drew his sword and attacked Towne. Towne, forced to defend himself, was soon driven on to a small mound from which he could neither get down nor cross to safety. His entreaties for the fight to be stopped fell on deaf ears and finally, 'fearing for his life', he struck out, hitting Knell in the throat. Knell died half an hour later and Towne was subsequently found not guilty of murder, but not in time to continue the tour.

So there were two vacancies in the company. If Shakespeare had fallen in love with the theatre, then here was his chance and he took it. Presumably he must have been deeply frustrated at the prospect of life as a small-town tanner and glovemaker, in spite of having major family responsibilities, a wife, a small daughter and the twins Judith and Hamnet, named after his close friends, the Sadlers. If it was a spur-of-the-moment decision, then it must have been a pretty desperate one as it was hardly an admirable thing to leave the burden of supporting his family to fall on his parents as it undoubtedly did for several years.

Perhaps he talked the Queen's Men into taking him on by offering to assist the Bookkeeper in copying out the 'rolls' on which each actor's part was written. Possibly they said they would give him a chance if he showed acting talent. There is another clue pointing to an early association with these particular players. Shortly before his fatal tour, Knell had married Rebecca Edwards at St Mary's Church, Aldermanbury. A year after his death in Thame his widow married another actor in the same company, John Heming, who was to become one of Shakespeare's closest friends. Knell's most successful role had been that of Prince Henry in *The Famous Victories of Henry V*, a play later rewritten by William Shakespeare.

However Shakespeare arrived in London, whether by himself on foot or on horseback, or riding in a cart belonging to the Queen's Men, it is very likely he was in town to see an early performance of *Tamburlaine*.

There would have been plenty of other plays to see too, at the Theatre, the Curtain, the Rose and, possibly, Newington Butts, and the standard of work was improving steadily, although Sir Philip Sydney, who had actually stood Godfather to Tarleton's son, continued to criticise the 'naughty playmakers'. The new playwrights, he complained, no longer always observed the 'rules of honest civility nor of skilfull poetry' set down by Aristotle, where all action took place within the compass of a single day and in one place.

> Now one side of the stage might be Asia, the other Africa along with so many underkingdoms that the

> Player, when he comes in, must ever begin with telling where he is, or else the tale will not be conceived [understood]. Then there shall be three ladies who walk to gather flowers, and then we believe the stage to be a garden.
>
> By and by we hear news of a shipwreck in the same place, and then we are to blame if we accept it not for a rock upon the back of which comes out a hideous monster, with fire and smoke . . . meanwhile two armies fly in, represented with but four swords and bucklers, and then what hard heart will not receive it for a pitched [battle]field? Now, of time they are much for liberal, for ordinary it is that two young princes fall in love. After many traverses she is got with child, delivered of a fair boy; he is lost, groweth a man, falls in love, and is ready to get another child; and all this in two hours space.

He reserved his main attack, however, for comedy.

> But besides these gross absurdities, now all their plays be neither right tragedies nor right comedies, mingling Kings with Clowns, not because the matter carries it, but thrust in clowns by head and shoulders to play a part in majestical matters, with neither decency nor discretion, so as neither the admiration and commiseration, nor the right sportfulness is, by their mongrel tragi-comedy, obtained.

In other, and less convoluted, words writing for the theatre was now open to all. Sydney did not mention a genre which was gaining popularity, the historical epic. An early example is *The Troublesome Reign of King John*, attributed to a writer called John Bale who had died in 1563. Bale, who was born into a poor Suffolk family, went to Cambridge, converted to Protestantism under Edward VI, married, and became Bishop during which time he wrote plays to be performed by children. When Mary Tudor came to the throne he attempted to flee the country, ending up shipwrecked on the Cornish coast where he was captured and imprisoned for heresy but he later escaped to continue writing but most of his work died with him.

But it was the first part of *Tamburlaine* that brought about the seachange in the way plays were written with the emergence of Marlowe's glittering, poetic, 'mighty line' of blank verse, which changed entertainment into an art form.

6

The World of Robert Greene

Popular as *Tamburlaine* undoubtedly was, there was a play which was an even bigger crowd-puller, remaining so well into the next century, Kyd's *The Spanish Tragedy.* This may have annoyed Marlowe though he might have been mollified to learn, had he lived long enough, that no play of Shakespeare's ever knocked it out of its prime position either.

If, as seems likely, Shakespeare did gravitate to the theatre immediately on his arrival in London and write his first plays for Henslowe, then he would have met his fellow-dramatists almost at once, among whom would have been Thomas Kyd. Compared to the rest of his theatrical colleagues, Kyd was a quiet and self-effacing soul, looked down on by the so-called 'University Wits', a group which now included Marlowe, as he continued his profession of scrivener. Yet *The Spanish Tragedy* provided the pattern for all the 'Revenge Plays' which followed: a story set in foreign parts, preferably Catholic Spain or Italy, characters who are royal or aristocratic and much dark intrigue which Elizabethans described as 'Machiavellian'. Such a play opens with a character, often the ghost of a wronged person, calling out for revenge and ends with the stage littered with corpses. Audiences particularly enjoyed the end of *The Spanish Tragedy* when Hieronimo, the protagonist, rips his tongue out to avoid confessing under torture.

Shakespeare would also have seen plays by the two notorious University Wits, George Peele and Robert Greene.

Weary of baling his son out of trouble at university, Peele's father had finally turned him out of the house, whereupon he immediately embarked on what nineteenth-century biographers describe primly as 'a life of dissipation', a course of action which left him with syphilis and a drink problem. He first joined Henslowe's company as an actor in the mid-1580s, during which time he returned to Oxford to 'stage' two plays, *The Rivals* and *The Tragedy of Dido.* The latter could not have been Marlowe's play of the same name as it is too early. Peele also began to write plays himself in between drinking bouts with Greene.

To a newcomer up from the country, like Shakespeare, Greene must have appeared quite outlandish; indeed, he would have drawn the eye at any time anywhere except, possibly, in the King's Road, Chelsea, at the height of the craze for punk. He liked to wear showy clothes, his favourite colour being a bilious shade of green, 'goose turd green', wore his red hair long and greased to a point a foot or so above his head and on occasion stiffened his beard likewise, hanging on its end a single pearl.[1]

Of himself and his background he wrote that his parents had been esteemed for their 'gravity and honesty' and were well known in Norwich.

> But as of one selfsame clod of clay there sprouts both stinking weeds and delightful flowers, so from honest parents often grow dishonest children. For my father had care to have me in my Nonage brought up at school, that might through the study of good letters grow to be the friend of myself, a profitable member to the commonwealth and a comfort to him in his old age. But as early pricks the tree that will prove a thorn, so even in my first years I began to follow the filthiness of my own desires, and neither to listen to the wholesome advertisements of my parents, nor be led by the careful correction of my Masters.
>
> For being at the University of Cambridge, I lit [moved] among wags as lewd as myself, with whom I consumed the flower of my youth, who drew me to

> travel in Italy and Spain, in which places I saw and practised such villainy as is abominable to declare.[2]

He was writing this, it should be pointed out, when he was terminally ill.

Greene lived a life of riotous dissipation on the Continent, assisted by funds from his 'sorrowing father', supplemented by money from his mother 'who pampered me so long'. He acquired the reputation of a braggart and practised 'sundry superficial studies' with his boon companions as well as drinking 'with ordinary spendthrifts'. He then went to Oxford to obtain a Master of Arts degree but there is no record of his having achieved it. However, all was not lost because 'I soon became famous as an author of plays and penner of love pamphlets'.

Sometime in his dissolute career he took time off to return to Norwich and marry 'a gentleman's daughter of good account, with whom I lived for a while; but forasmuch as she would persuade me from my wilful wickedness, after I had a child by her I cast her off, having spent up the marriage money which I obtained by her'. Whereupon he returned to London to meet his companions 'most particularly in the alehouses who commonly, for my inordinate expenses, would make much of me'.[3] At the very least Robert Greene could have introduced the young Shakespeare to the teeming life of the stews and taverns of the Bankside, with its countless traps for the unwary: a world light years away from that of a rural market town like Stratford-upon-Avon.

* * *

1588 was Armada Year and the whole country was swept with patriotic fervour, culminating in the defeat of the Spanish invasion force in July. Andrew Gurr puts some of the success enjoyed by the playhouses that year down to the fact that they all presented plays which although they were weak on plot, included battle scenes and spectacular sword fights, noting that Greene in *History of Orlando Furioso* provides the stage direction 'they fight awhile and then breathe', and that Tarleton, when he had achieved the title 'Master of Fence' the previous year, had demonstrated his skill by defeating on stage seven experts, one after another.[4]

This love of sword-play sometimes spilled out into the audience and in a letter to the Lord of Burleigh, William Fleetwood writes:

> Upon Wednesday, one Brown, a serving man in a blue coat, a shifting fellow having a perilous wit of his own, intending a spoil (fight) if he could have brought it to pass, did at the Theatre door, quarrel with certain poor boys, handicraft prentices, and struck some of them, and lastly he, with his sword, wounded and maimed one of the boys upon the left hand, whereupon there assembled near a hundred people. This Brown is a common cozener, a thief and horse-stealer, and colours all his doings here about this town with a suit he has, in law, brought against a brother of his in Staffordshire. He rests now in Newgate.[5]

The second part of *Tamburlaine* was presented that same year, alongside a further rash of indifferent historical plays, and the publication of *Pandosto,* by Robert Greene. Greene, who would go to his death decrying Shakespeare as a plagiarist, would have spun in his grave had he known that *Pandosto* would later furnish the plot for *The Winter's Tale.*

On 3 September Tarleton died suddenly at the house of a woman who had been his mistress, 'one Em Ball in Shoreditch, she being a woman of very bad reputation'. He is said to have been taken ill, made his will, died and was buried all on the same day, complaining on his deathbed that he was surrounded by sharks and sending word to Sir Francis Walsingham asking him to protect his small son, Philip, from harm.[6] It shows just what a special place Tarleton held in the affections of so many different people that Sir Philip Sydney had stood Godfather to his son and that he had felt able to petition Sir Francis in this way. Sorrow at his death was, however, marred by an unseemly wrangle between his mother, his brothers-in-law, his wife and his lawyer, over the contents of his will and the custody of little Philip, one matter of contention being a legacy of forty shillings left to Emma Ball. Tarleton lived on for years in memory, in his play *The Seven Deadly Sins*, his ballads and the many jokes attributed to him. He was also portrayed in the work of other dramatists including Henry Chettle's *Kind-Heart's Dream.*

Within a short time Emma Ball had taken up with Robert Greene. She seems to have been fascinated by theatre folk and might well in a later day have been an actress. As it was she continued whoring, in part to keep her extravagant new lover in funds. A tough woman, she and her brother had run wild on the streets of London since childhood after which she had turned to prostitution while her brother, Cutting Ball Jack, was now a notorious highwayman.

Emma's small house, where Tarleton died, was in Shoreditch, an area popular with theatre people because of its proximity to the Theatre and the Curtain. Lodgings were to be had in Hog Lane (now called Curtain Road), which ran between the Curtain Theatre and Norton Folgate, the latter later becoming part of Shoreditch High Street. It seems likely that both Marlowe and Shakespeare had lodgings in the vicinity at about this time.

* * *

Theatre as an entertainment was still continuing to attract critics. Stephen Gosson wrote:

> The argument of Tragedies is wrath, cruelty, incest, injury and murder either violent by sword, or voluntary by poison: the persons, Gods, Goddesses, juries, friends, Kings, Queens, and mighty men. The ground work of Commedies is love, cozenage, flatterie, bawdry, sly conveyance of whoredom; the persons, cooks, knaves, bawds, parasites, courtesans, lecherous old men, amorous young men . . .

In other words plots which have remained staple fare ever since. He continues:

> Sometime you shall see nothing but the adventures of an amorous knight, passing from country to country to love of his lady, encountering many a terrible monster made of brown paper, and at his return, is so wonderfully changed, that he cannot be known but by some posy in his doublet, or by a broken ring, or a handkerchief, or a piece of a cockle shell. What learn you by that? When the soul of your plays is either mere trifles or Italian bawdry or cursing of gentlewomen, what are we taught?

He goes on to repeat the common assertion that playhouses are 'snares unto fair women . . . and are as full of secret adultery as they were in Rome.'[7]

1589 brought a rash of new plays, Greene's funny pastoral piece, *Friar Bacon and Friar Bungay*, Lyly's *Midas* and *Mother Bombie*, Peele's *The Battle of Alcazar*, an anonymous version of *The Taming of the Shrew*, a version of *Hamlet* and Marlowe's *The Jew of Malta*. *Hamlet* is intriguing as there is no firm proof who wrote it but it is now generally attributed to Kyd in view of some satirical comments on his work by the poet Thomas Nashe:

> Yet the English Seneca, read by candlelight, yields many good sentences, as 'Blood is a beggar', and so forth; and if you entreat him fair in a frosty morning, he will afford you whole Hamlets, I should say handfuls of tragical speeches . . . the sea exhaled by drops will in continuance be dry, and Seneca, let blood line by line and page by page, at length must needs die for our stage, which makes his famished followers to imitate the Kyd in Aesop who, enamoured with the Fox's newfangles, forsook all hopes of life to leap to a new occupation.

Less poetic commentators speak of the play opening with a ghost, robed in a white sheet, clanking a length of chain while calling out 'revenge, revenge!' Since the text is long since lost there is no way of knowing how much Shakespeare took from it.

Marlowe's *Jew of Malta* stands as a major work in its own right but also brought a hint of things to come. Audiences loved the wicked Jew, who was presented in the typical fashion of the day as being greedy, mean, scheming, wicked, unfeeling and murderous. Yet there is far more to him than that. Like Shakespeare's Richard III he becomes irresistible because, as G.B. Harrison, editor of the old Bodley Head Quartos says, 'he is so completely master of himself, the perfect egotist, unhampered by those affections, creeds, scruples and moral laws which keep ordinary men in subjection.'[8] But the more thoughtful in the audience might also have pondered on who and what had made him that way. After all, he had done little harm until the Christians seized all his possessions and his hard-earned wealth merely because he was a Jew. At the end when contemporary audiences would have derived much amusement at his being boiled to death in a giant cauldron, while cheering on the Christians as the heroes of the piece, Marlowe, in a final twist, reveals that the only honourable men are the Muslims, betrayed, then murdered, by those very Christians to whom they have offered the hand of friendship.

It was in that same year that Marlowe became notorious for something other than satirical plays. While on his way down Hog Lane on the morning of 18 September he was accosted by a man called William Bradley. Bradley, the son of the landlord of the Bishop Inn which stood on the corner of Gray's Inn Road and High Holborn, was known for becoming aggressive in drink and had recently been bound over to keep the peace. Bradley was not actually looking for Marlowe but for his friend, the poet Thomas Watson, with whom he had picked a quarrel previously. However, he decided Marlowe would do just as well and following an exchange of insulting remarks, the two set about each other with rapier and dagger. They were soon going hard at it up and down Hog Lane. Marlowe was apparently getting the best of the exchange when Thomas Watson himself appeared, drawn by the sound of the fight.

Bradley immediately turned on Watson shouting out 'Art thou now come? Then I will have a bout with thee.' Ignoring Marlowe's pleas to leave Bradley to him, Watson, by far the poorest swordsman of the three, drew his weapon and began to fight. Bradley forced him foot by foot up Hog Lane to the ditch at the end, watched by an excited crowd happy to see a free show, by which time Watson was bleeding from two nasty wounds to his thigh. Then, at the last moment when his quarry had no way of escape, Bradley carelessly dropped his guard and Watson ran him through. He died almost immediately.[9]

It might well be that among the spectators were the intelligencer, Robert Poley, who had lodgings in the Lane and, possibly Shakespeare. It has been suggested that he later used the fight in *Romeo and Juliet* – indeed that he based the brilliant, articulate and misogynistic Mercutio on Marlowe. What the fight in Hog Lane does portray vividly is how close sudden death always was to the living, death from random sword fights or knifings in the street, death from epidemics in general, plague in particular and, for women, in childbirth or from puerperal fever.

Within minutes of Bradley's death a part-time constable, Stephen Wylde, 'tailor of Norgate', came panting up and he arrested Marlowe and Watson on the spot. They were then taken before Sir Owen Hopton, Lieutenant of the Tower and local Justice of the Peace, on a warrant 'upon suspicion of murder' before being incarcerated in Newgate prison.

The next day, 19 September, an Inquest was held by the Middlesex coroner, Ian Chalkhill, before twelve sworn men. The verdict was that Thomas Watson had slain William Bradley 'in self defence' and 'not by felony' and could therefore expect the Queen's pardon. Both men were then returned to gaol.

Thirteen days later Marlowe was allowed out on bail, his sureties being Richard Kytchine of Clifford's Inn, gentleman, and Humphrey Rowland of East Smithfield, horner, both of whom lodged £20 on his behalf. Marlowe was bound over in the sum of £40 to appear in person 'at the next Sessions of Newgate to answer everything alleged against him on the part of the Queen, and shall not depart without permission of the Court'. On 3 December he and Watson were brought before Sir Roger Manwood, chief Baron of the Exchequer and, coincidentally, one of Marlowe's sponsors for his Cambridge scholarship. Also present was the recorder of London, William Fleetwood, who shortly afterwards bought himself a copy of the script of *Tamburlaine.* The upshot was that Marlowe received his pardon and was immediately released, whereas poor Watson, who felt he had had no option but to fight, was returned to his stinking cell in Newgate where he remained, awaiting the Queen's pardon, for a further five months. Not surprisingly, the wounds in his thigh went septic and he was still suffering from their effects when he was finally released.

* * *

For young theatrical people there was plenty to do and no shortage of places to go, as Nashe wrote: '. . . whereas the afternoon being the idlest time of day, wherein men that are their own masters (as Gentlemen of the Court, the Inns of Court, and the numbers of Captains and Soldiers about London) do wholly bestow themselves upon pleasure and that pleasure they divide (how virtuously it skills not) either into gameing, the following of harlots, drinking or seeing a play . . .' While the young dramatists took a keen interest in the work of their rivals and visited all the playhouses to view each other's work, most social life would have taken place in the tavern and the nearest one to the Rose Theatre in Shakespeare's day, which still survives, is the Anchor on the Bankside.

But there was plenty of choice. William Harrison, in his *Description of England* published in 1587 says:

> In all our inns we have plenty of ale, beer, and sundry kinds of wine. Howbeit of all in England there are no worse inns than in London, and yet many are there far

> better than the best that I have heard of in a foreign country, if all circumstances be duly considered... And it is a world to see how each owner of them contends with other for goodness of entertainment of guests, as about fitness and change of linen, furniture of bedding, beauty of rooms, service at the table, costliness of plate, strength of drink, variety of wines, or well using of horses.

It is likely that indigent dramatists and actors patronised less splendid hostelries, but there is no better guide to the low life of the day than Robert Greene. Greene produced a number of popular journalistic pamphlets on what went on in the Elizabethan underworld of rough taverns, gaming houses and brothels, written rather in the manner of *News of the World* stories, the alleged purpose of which is to reveal the disgraceful and salacious activities people get up to in order to condemn them. It is unlikely, though, that Greene, after the manner of tabloid reporters, ever 'made his excuses and left', to avoid being compromised. Greene would undoubtedly have accepted anything he was offered.

In his *Art of Conney-Catching*[10] he dwells in great detail on the perils awaiting the innocent to the London scene, particularly where women are concerned. 'A shameless woman has honey in her lips,' he warns, 'and her mouth is as sweet as honey, her throat as soft as oil; but the end of her is more bitter than Aloes, and her tongue is more sharp than a two-edged sword, her feet go unto death and her steps lead to hell.' Here he was punning on words as Elizabethans loved to do. The 'end of her' might well mean she came to a bad one but it was also to be taken literally for while her mouth might well be sweet as honey, her 'end' was more than likely to give you at best 'the clap' (gonorrhoea) or at worst 'the pox' (syphilis).

He warned lengthily of the sin of lust (on which he was an expert) and the tricks of the whores, from the straightforward stealing of a purse and valuables as a client slept, to a variation where the client is set on and robbed by the whore's ponce or accomplice while she is busy servicing him. He particularly warned of 'cross-biting', a ploy still in operation centuries later known as the 'badger game'.

'Some unruly mates,' he writes, 'that place their content in lust, let slip the liberty of their eyes on some painted beauty, let their eyes stray to their unchaste bosom til their hearts be set on fire.' They then set about to court the fair one and 'alas, their loves need no long suit, for forthwith they are entertained and either go to the tavern to seal up the match with a bottle of Hippocras, or straight she carries him to some bad place . . . but once they shall be warm in their room, in comes a terrible fellow, with side hair and a fearful beard, as though he were one of Polyphemus cut, and he comes frowning in and says, "what has thou to do, base knave, to carry my sister or my wife or some such, to the tavern?"' The accomplice then turns on the woman, saying she is no better than a whore, and threatens to call a constable immediately and haul them both before the nearest Justice.

'The whore that has tears at command, immediately falls a-weeping and cries him mercy.' The luckless lover, caught in the act and terrified that his being brought publicly before the Justices will get back to his wife and family or his lord or his employer, had no option but to pay up.

In recent times it is not a man with a weapon who rushes in but a man with a camera on behalf of anyone with a vested interest from East End villains or the old KGB bent on blackmail to the circulation managers of the tabloid press.

Greene devotes considerable space in his pamphlets to the behaviour of whores rightly aware that sex will always sell journalism. He also warned against card-sharpers and how they operate, how cards are marked, games fixed, though adding, 'yet Gentlemen when you shall read this book, written faithfully to discover these cozening practices, think I go not about to disprove or disallow the most ancient and honest pastime or recreation of Card Play . . .' for Greene was a compulsive gambler, another reason for his always being in debt. As human nature changes little, it also comes as no surprise to learn that the Three Card

Trick or Find the Lady was as popular a way to part a fool from his money then as it is now. There is also information on how thieves operate and notes on the most common confidence tricks in vogue at the time.

He finishes on a warning note, pointing out that his stories of whores, gamesters, picklocks, highway robbers and forgers have been told only to show how such behaviour leads only to the gallows, but it is hard to believe this was the object of the exercise. For a young newcomer like William Shakespeare, a night out in the company of Robert Greene was likely to be a night to remember – if he were able to stay sober enough to recall it.

7

The Elizabethan Underworld

In the spring of 1590 Sir Francis Walsingham died, worn out, it was said, in the service of his Queen. His death was to have deep implications for at least two of the playwrights. As A. L. Rowse writes in *The England of Elizabeth*, the Privy Council, of which he had been Secretary, was the focus of government and the struggle for power at the top. Like its successor, the modern Cabinet, it was the permanent executive body dealing with government affairs but it was unlike the Cabinet in a number of fundamental ways. It was not answerable (or supposedly answerable) to Parliament as is our present system, had no popular base and was dependent on the will of the Queen. The great nobles of the day who were responsible for the major offices of State, the Lord Chancellor, the Lords Treasurer, Steward and Chamberlain, had little uniformity of outlook. They were held together solely by the fact that they were the Queen's servants, which is what enabled them to function at all. Otherwise it was every man for himself.

The office of Secretary of State to the Privy Council had greatly expanded its influence under Elizabeth and had become, by the time Walsingham died, a key position and one to which he had held on jealously during his last illness, for although he and Cecil, Lord of Burleigh, were among the Queen's oldest and most trusted advisers they had never got on and it was only after years of ill-concealed dislike and distrust that they had reached some kind of accommodation with each other the previous year. The Queen felt genuine grief at the loss of the man she had nicknamed her 'moon'.

Burleigh immediately began some busy politicking, having long coveted the post for his son. Robert Cecil was extremely ambitious and of that office he later wrote:

> All officers of State have a prescribed authority by patent, by custom or by oath, the Secretary only excepted. He has a liberty to negotiate at discretion at home and abroad, with friends and enemies, in all matters of speech and intelligence ... As long as any matter of what weight so ever is handled only between the Prince and the Secretary, those counsels are compared to the mutual affection of two lovers, undiscovered to their friends.

Robert had few illusions. He was undersized and humpbacked. The Queen liked to be surrounded by handsome, straight-limbed men, but while he and his father recognised that he would never become a favourite at Court, he and Elizabeth had a mutual need of each other, she for his Machiavellian mind and he for the power the office brought. Contemporaries spoke of his having 'handsome wits in a crooked body'. Even so, it seems that Elizabeth had doubts about conferring the office on Cecil for, so desperate was he to achieve it, that he undertook it unpaid and unrecognised for the next six years.

One of the first tasks he set himself was to examine and re-organise Walsingham's secret service.

* * *

Another crop of new plays were produced in 1590. A less successful piece by Marlowe, *The Massacre at Paris* dealing with the events leading up to the Massacre of St Bartholomew's Eve and its aftermath; Greene's *The Pinder of Wakefield*, Lyly's *Love's Metamorphosis*; a stringing together of old fairy tales and legends by Peele called *The Old Wives' Tale* and several whose authors are now unknown. They include *Edward III*, at one time attributed to Shakespeare but possibly written by Peele, *Fair Em*, likewise part of the so-called 'Shakespeare Apocrypha' but bearing nothing at all of his mark and the play of *King Leir and His Three Daughters*, the forerunner of his own *King Lear*. There was also the first production of *Henry VI Part I*. While scholars may quarrel as to how much of this can be directly attributed to Shakespeare, there is no doubt that at the very least he had a major part in its writing.

The updated and expanded edition of Holinshed's *Chronicles* had provided playwrights with a positive treasure chest of stories about Kings which they were to plunder for many years.

It has been suggested that Marlowe had a hand in the *Henry VI* trilogy[1] – not to mention those who think he somehow managed to write the entire Shakespeare canon – and it is a possibility as both were closely involved with Henslowe. At the very least so successful and brilliant a dramatist must have influenced the inexperienced Shakespeare in his early days as a writer.

Nor is it surprising that more than one hand is seen to have been at work in many of the plays for time was short, scripts desperately needed. Old texts were thrown to a new writer with instructions to improve them, and several writers might well get together to rush a script to the actors. Later they would all put their names to it, much in the way screenwriters did in Hollywood in the 1930s. But flawed as the first part of *Henry VI* undoubtedly is, the voice of the early Shakespeare comes through clear and unmistakable.

There is much confusion too as to who wrote what for which company.[2] It was not until later that the two major companies, the Lord Chamberlain's and Lord Admiral's, emerged supreme. Strange's, Pembroke's, Derby's, the Lord Admiral's players and many others formed and reformed themselves, actors moving between them playing first a few months with one, before moving on to another. Burbage continued to be based north of the Thames at the Theatre, while Henslowe operated out of the Rose.

Robert Greene was quick to take advantage of the confusion caused by the lack of consistency in the fragmented companies and in 1591 he succeeded in selling his new play, *History of Orlando Furioso,* twice. Thomas Nashe accused him of being no better than one of the 'conney-catchers' about which he wrote, suggesting that he 'ask the Queen's Players, if you sold them not Orlando Furioso for twenty nobles, and when they were in the country, sold the very same play to the Lord Admiral's Men for as much more. Was this not plain Conney-Catching Master R.G.?'[3]

In fact Greene seems to have offended just about everyone by the end of the year, including the low-life villains he had described in his pamphlets, for he wrote:

> All the crew have protested my death, and to prove they meant good earnest, they beleaguered me about in the St John's Head within Ludgate, being at my supper. There were fourteen or fifteen of them met, and thought to have made that the fatal night of my overthrow but that the courteous Citizens and Apprentices took my part, and so two or three of them were carried to the Counter [a local gaol], although a gentleman in my company was sore hurt. I cannot deny but they begin to waste away about London and Tyburn since the setting out of my book hath eaten up many of them, and I will plague them to the extremity, let them do what they will with their blades. I fear them not . . .[4]

It is clear that historical plays remained popular and there were productions of an anonymous play of *The True Tragedy of Richard III,* which again must have been noted by Shakespeare, and *The Life and Death of Jack Straw,* possibly written by Peele.

A play of an entirely different genre was *Arden of Faversham,* one of the first in the line of what today we would call drama documentaries or 'faction'. Nobody has yet come up with a satisfactory explanation as to who wrote it and it is likely it was the work of several hands.

Sex scandals and murders were as popular then as they are now and this play tells of the murder of Thomas Arden. The actual event took place on 15 February 1551 and it rapidly became a *cause célèbre.* There was ample factual material readily available to the dramatist in the form of two detailed accounts, as the story had caught the popular imagination because not only was the wife involved in the crime (and she an adulteress), but no less than six attempts were made on Arden's life before he was successfully done to death. Just as the Victorian melodramas of *Maria Marten and the Murder in the Red Barn* and *Sweeney Todd, the Demon Barber of Fleet Street* pulled in the crowds in their day, *Arden of Faversham* remained popular for years.

The 'Brevist Chronicle' of 1551 notes 'This year on Valentine's day at Fav. in Kent was committed a shameful murder of one Arden, a gentleman, who was by the consent of his wife murdered whereof she was burned at Canterbury 14 March 1551.' Henry Machyn, a London Merchant Taylor, recorded the execution of Alice's lover, Mosby, and Mosby's sister, as well as the sentences of the other accomplices, and notes he was 'fascinated by the horribleness' of that domestic crime. It is worth giving the details as the story paints a fascinating picture of the seamy side of life among the better off in rural England.

The first full account appears in the *Wardmote Book of Faversham.*[5] It tells what took place in the living-room of Arden's house at seven o'clock on the evening of 15 February, and the events leading up to it. Arden was chief controller of HM Customs at Faversham and, in 1548, the Mayor. He does not seem to have been well liked, in fact he is described as being grasping and avaricious. He had acquired much land from the local Abbey on the Dissolution and his handsome house (which still exists) is built out of part of the Abbey gatehouse. He made many enemies by wresting land off them by doubtful means – harsh leases, fore-closed mortgages, etc. He even insisted the annual fair be moved from the still existing Abbey lands to his own so he could take the profits from it.

At the age of fifty-six he married Alice Morfyn, stepdaughter to Sir Edward North, the translator of Plutarch. She was twenty-eight and had long been involved in an affair with the family steward, Thomas Mosbie. The *Wardmote Book* says 'it was felt desirous by her friends and family to marry her off', that Arden knew all about the ongoing affair but 'was so greatly given to seek his advantage and cared so little how he came by it that in hope of attaining some benefits from Lord North by means of this Mosbie, he winked at that shameless disorder'. Alice is said to have told a friend her future husband was so mean that his old mother was forced to beg in the streets for a crust. It was obviously not going to work out well.

Alice was soon bored with life as Mrs Arden and was still continuing her affair with Mosbie. Arden, she decided, had to go. Her first attempt was to poison him using a powder procured from a local artist which she put in his gruel. He did not eat much of it as he disliked the taste. He was sick but that was all. Alice then cast about for an accomplice and found a man called Greene, who had been badly treated by Arden over some land – indeed the two men had come to blows – and offered him £10 to kill her husband.

He agreed but did not know how to set about it. The true sequence of events, later portrayed in the play, is worthy of black farce. Greene first involved a man called Loosebag (alias Shakebag!), then, searching round for a more experienced conspirator, a neighbour called Mr Bradshaw introduced him to a villain known as Black Will. The trio then made a number of attempts on Arden's life, most of them taking place on a journey he made to Gravesend. They included an ambush, a shooting and a variety of staged 'accidents'. Nothing worked.

In desperation, Alice brought Mosbie and his sister in on the scheme and finally a plot was hatched involving Black Will, Mosbie and one of Alice's servants. Will hid in a closet while Arden was out. When he came home he found Mosbie there, who challenged him to a game of chess. As the two men played, Black Will crept out of the closet and attempted to strangle Arden but bungled it. During the ensuing struggle Mosbie finally 'stroked him on the head' with a fourteen-pound weight, before Will eventually cut Arden's throat.

They all then lugged the body out into a field, arranging

it to look as if Arden had been attacked by footpads on his way home. Alice wiped up the blood and, after a suitable time-lapse, made enquiries as to her 'missing' spouse. His body was found at once and the whole crew arrested almost as quickly. It had been snowing when the body was removed and the conspirators had assumed the snow would continue and cover up their footprints, but it had stopped and their tracks led directly to the Arden home. Also rushes of a kind used to strew the floor of the Arden kitchen were found between his foot and his shoe, while a bloody knife and cloth were discovered stuffed in a barrel by the well.

The aftermath was grim. Alice was burned at the stake in Canterbury, her unfortunate maid suffering a similar fate in Faversham, 'pitifully bewailing her case and crying out on the mistress who had brought her to this end'. Alice was burned because the murder of a husband was classed as a crime of 'petty treason' and punished accordingly. Greene fled and was picked up in Cornwall years later and hanged at the roadside; poor old Mr Bradshaw, whose sole crime was to have introduced the gang to Black Will, was hanged at Canterbury, Mosbie and his sister were hanged at Smithfield and Loosebag, alias Shakebag, and Black Will, were never seen again. A nasty note in the Canterbury town record says 'for the charges of burning Mistress Arden and the Execution of Geo. Bradshaw – thirteen shillings'.

So bizarre was this tale that it even tempted Holinshed to set aside his chronicling of the Kings to write up a second and more flowery version of the story and many of the fictional speeches he gives to the protagonists appear in the subsequent play. He also quotes superstitions, such as that the grass never grew on the ground where the body had lain, and that its shape could be clearly seen. Another is that the corpse's wounds bled when Alice touched it, a dramatic touch used to effect by Shakespeare in his own *Richard III.* Holinshed makes Alice a tall and elegant blonde, although this is probably poetic licence. There was even a ballad made about her at the time called 'the Complaint and Lamentation of Mistress Arden of Faversham sung to the tune of *Fortune my Foe*'. It is not surprising then that the unknown playwright or playwrights could hardly go wrong putting such a story on to the stage.

* * *

Two major historical events were to catch the imagination of the population during the year: the desperate fight to the death of Sir Richard Grenville who took on a number of Spanish ships of Flores in the Azores in the little *Revenge*; and the expedition led by the Earl of Essex to France to assist Henry of Navarre in his fight against the Catholic Medicis.

The latter assured the popularity of the *Henry VI* trilogy, especially the exploits of the great English hero, Talbot, on the battlefields of France during the Hundred Years War. Shakespeare's portrayal of Talbot thrilled those who saw it, including Nashe, who wrote:

> How it would have joyed brave Talbot, the terror of the French, to think that after he had lain to hundred years in his tomb, he should triumph on the stage, and have his bones new embalmed with the tears of ten thousands spectators at least, [at several times] who, in the Tragedian that represents his person [Burbage], imagine they behold him fresh bleeding![6]

By the end of 1590 Shakespeare was becoming a name to be reckoned with for he had captured the popular mood, Emma Ball had presented Greene with a frail and sickly son to whom he gave the inappropriate name Fortunatus, and Marlowe had acquired a generous and affectionate patron in Thomas Walsingham, who had inherited his older cousin's estate and fortune. He had also been taken up by a strange esoteric circle of gallants founded by Sir Walter Raleigh and the mathematician Thomas Harriot, who called themselves the School of the Night, where many topics considered extremely dangerous were discussed, such as the authenticity of the Bible stories and the nature of the universe. It seemed there was no end to his popularity and success.

However, the year ended on an ominous note: the number of deaths from plague was rising steadily.

8

Deaths and Entrances

Over the next two years the story of the early professional theatre unfolds against a background of ever-darkening shadow, culminating in a series of events which, by the end of 1593, would effectively draw a line under its first phase.

First there was plague. Plague was endemic in Europe in the sixteenth century and there were always a few cases in the country at any one time, but there were also cyclical epidemics of devastating virulence. As it was to be several centuries before the discovery was made that it was carried by the fleas which infested black rats, apart from being feared as a punishment for the sins of mankind, there seemed no logic behind its regular appearance and no knowledge as to how it spread.

Acute epidemics could last months or even as long as a year, but this particular affliction continued throughout the years 1592 and 1593. Whether it attacked the lungs as in its thirteenth-century manifestation, which became known as the Black Death, or settled in the lymph glands producing lumps or 'buboes' in the groin or armpit, the outlook was bleak for all who caught it. It was particularly terrifying as it could strike at speed, killing whole families within hours. Prayer and a variety of nostrums were tried in vain; those who could fled from the towns and cities to the countryside, all too often taking the infection with them.

However, while it was not known how or why plague spread, the authorities considered a sensible precaution was to prevent large numbers of people congregating together in close contact in one place and therefore, throughout those two years, the playhouses and bearpits were closed down for months at a time. The result was that the theatre companies, unable to make a living in London, were forced to take to the road and tour the provinces, both Alleyn and Burbage leading their respective companies out of the city on a number of occasions.

Marlowe and Shakespeare were fortunate in that they had ways of supporting themselves other than writing plays. Thomas Walsingham continued to be Marlowe's generous patron and his splendid mansion at Scadbury in Kent was always open to him, while Shakespeare toured the country with his colleagues, earning his bread as an actor. Presumably Kyd could always find work as a scrivener, while Greene continued writing his pamphlets on the Elizabethan low life.

Marlowe's involvement with the School of the Night continued and he took a leading role in the hours of intense discussion which took place in Sir Walter Raleigh's London home. The new learning was truly exciting; science and mathematics were not just fascinating in themselves but were forcing those who studied them to totally reappraise the very foundations of accepted religious belief. It is scarcely surprising that such studies were considered dangerous and that at about this time Robert Cecil placed an informer in Raleigh's household to discover the nature of these discussions.

Marlowe's own venture into the popular genre of historical plays, *Edward II*, had certainly caused a stir. Unlike the other epics which offered brave kings (*Edward III* and the early version of *Henry V*), weak kings (*Henry VI*), bad kings (*The Troublesome Reign of King John*) and Machiavellian schemers (*Richard III*), here was a King shown as having had not just one, but two, homosexual lovers, a man murdered by having a poker thrust up his anus in a dungeon through which a sewer flowed.

Was Marlowe homosexual? From what we know of him and through his own writing it seems very likely, even though it is also true that it was a charge later used to effect by his enemies, his notorious remark that 'all those who love not boys and tobacco are fools' being widely quoted. Certainly in his own work, apart from being unable to write believable roles for women (a failing he shared with such robust heterosexuals as Ben Jonson), he appears to luxuriate in descriptions of male beauty, as instanced in his unfinished long poem, *Hero and Leander*:

> His dangling tresses that were never shorn,
> Had they been cut, and unto Colchos borne,
> Would have allured the venturous youth of Greece
> To hazard more than for the Golden Fleece . . .
> His body was as straight as Circe's wand,
> Jove might have sipped out nectar from his hand.
> Even as delicious meat is to the taste,
> So was his neck in touching, and surpassed
> The white of Pelops' shoulder; I could tell you
> How smooth his breast was and how white his belly,
> And whose immortal fingers did imprint
> That heavenly path with many a curious dint
> That runs along his back . . .

Homosexuality was not only a mortal sin but officially a crime in the sixteenth century and a major government cover-up had taken place in 1586 when no lesser person than Antony Bacon, brother of the famous Sir Francis, had been charged with sodomy while living in France and supplying information to Sir Francis Walsingham's office. Bacon, as well as sharing his house with his close friend, Thomas Lawson, had filled it with pretty pages, one of whom left his employment with corroborative physical details of an alleged assault. The accusation was taken extremely seriously by the French authorities – the penalty for being found guilty was burning at the stake – and Bacon only escaped prosecution through the personal intervention of Henry of Navarre, under pressure from the English government.

The story only came to light when Daphne du Maurier, researching her history of the Bacon family, discovered it in a French archive.[1] 'It is remarkable,' she writes, 'that among the State documents of Queen Elizabeth for the years 1586/87, there is not a single one referring to the charge brought against Antony Bacon. If any ever existed, it must have been destroyed.'

It is safe to assume that penalties or not, there were as many gay men and women in the population in the sixteenth century as there are now, although it is also likely that they were either discreet about it or suppressed it. However, strong emotional and loyal friendships between people of the same sex were not only accepted but highly regarded. There are numerous examples of such relationships both in real life, as instanced by that of Sir Philip Sydney and Fulke Greville, and in the plays of the time. In Shakespeare's early *Two Gentlemen of Verona*, Valentine actually offers to hand over his fiancé to his best friend, Proteus, even though he knows his friend has tried to seduce her; while Beatrice in *Much Ado About Nothing* calls on Benedict to kill Claudio for having jilted her friend Hero at the altar.

It is known that at some time during 1591 or 1592 Marlowe shared a room with Thomas Kyd, presumably to enable both to have a place where they could write uninterrupted. Quietness and privacy were luxuries even for the rich, let alone indigent writers. Like any other young men without families, living and working in London, they would have lived in cheap lodgings, eaten out at the ordinary and conducted their social life in the taverns. Therefore a haven of comparative quiet in which to work without distraction was obviously valuable and it would also have made sense for them to share the rent. They could scarcely have guessed the decision would prove fatal to both of them.

It looks as though it was at about the same time that Marlowe's public behaviour became increasingly erratic. He was drinking hard and drink brought out all his natural aggression. On 9 May he was bound over in the sum of £20 by Sir Owen Hopton, JP at the Middlesex Sessions for what would now be called 'threatening behaviour' towards a Constable, Allen Nicholls, and his assistant, after they had approached the poet in the street for being offensively drunk.[2] In the autumn, while visiting Canterbury on a family matter, he was involved in a fight with a tailor, William Corkine, at the Chequers Inn, during which he pulled a knife. He was arrested, put in the local gaol for the night, then fined.[3]

While it is likely that words were put into Marlowe's mouth by those seeking to destroy him, he enjoyed a reputation for saying dangerous and shocking things when drunk. The authority of the scriptures, the divinity of Jesus Christ, patriotism, the stupidity of those who believed everything they were told, all became subject matter for the taproom or ordinary. There was also the exciting subject of his next play, based on the German *Faustbook*, where a man sells his soul to the devil in exchange for unlimited forbidden knowledge.

For those around them, it must have seemed that during the early years of the 1590s Marlowe and Greene were vying with each other in excess. But by the early summer of 1592 it is clear that Marlowe's behaviour was actually beginning to alarm Greene.

* * *

Shakespeare attracted no such notice and from what we know seems to have lived his working life in London with great discretion. It was said of him that in his early days when he lived in Shoreditch, he 'was the more to be admired in that he was not a company-keeper . . . that he would not be debauched and, if invited to, writ – he was in pain'.[4] Money earned was spent not on riotous living but carefully saved to be invested in property back home. Shakespeare would remain, at heart, a member of the Stratford bourgeoisie.

If, as is now accepted, Shakespeare's sonnets date from the years 1592–93, then he, too, had found a patron, the most likely candidate being the Earl of Southampton. It was at this point in his life that he became involved with the woman known as the Dark Lady of the Sonnets, whose identity has been the subject of intense speculation.

For years the prime favourite was Mary Fitton,[5] yet anyone taking the trouble to visit Arbury Hall in Warwickshire, the home of the Newdigate family, would see at once that this is highly unlikely. Mary Fitton was related to the Newdigates and her portrait hangs in the picture gallery. Mary Fitton bears no resemblance whatsoever to Shakespeare's description of his lady, who had hair like 'black wires', dark eyes and dun-coloured skin. Mary Fitton has red-gold hair, pale blue eyes and a white complexion – though she was certainly promiscuous enough, taking several lovers at Court before finally running away to Plymouth to live with a one-legged pirate. The Arbury portrait is quite eerie for it shows her wearing, over a wide farthingale, a magnificent brocade dress which appears to be crawling with spiders, beetles and other insects.

While Dr A.L. Rowse's notion that the woman in question was Emilia Lanier, née Basano, was at one time greeted with derision the case now seems a strong one.[6]

Her family, the Bassanos, originally came from Venice and had been picked out by Henry VIII, towards the end of his reign, to become Court musicians. Emilia was the daughter of Baptisto Bassanio and his common-law wife, Margaret Johnson. We do not know why they did not marry, but it is possible that one or other of them had a spouse living elsewhere. The family lived in the parish of St Botolph, Bishopsgate, in the area popular with theatre people. Baptisto had died in 1576, leaving two daughters, Angela and Emilia, who was only six. By 7 July 1586, when Margaret Johnson died, Angela had long been married to Joseph Holland, 'a gentleman', and Emilia was just seventeen.

At his death Baptisto had left to Emilia,'the daughter of Margaret Bassany, alias Margaret Johnson my reputed wife, the sum of £100 . . . to be paid in her full age of twenty-one years or day of marriage', but there was still up to four years to go and so it was necessary for Emilia to make her own way in the world. There were few opportunities for intelligent and ambitious young women without means who did not wish to go into service. A hundred years later she might have become an actress but that career was not open to her. So she did what many had done before her and countless others have since, made full use of her undoubted gifts – dark good looks, fluency in Italian and talent as a musician – and found herself a rich keeper.

However she set about it, she was quickly taken up at Court, for she wrote later that she had soon found favour with the Queen. She also took the eye of the elderly Lord Chamberlain and if she had not known the members of Burbage's company before she became involved with Hunsdon, she must certainly have met them afterwards. Emilia remained the Lord Chamberlain's mistress for some considerable time until, after she had finally become pregnant by him, he arranged a suitable marriage for her 'for colour', much after the manner of Henry VIII who married off his mistress, Mary Boleyn, Anne's older sister and mother of the Lord Chamberlain, to a Henry Carey whom he then ennobled. The man chosen was another Court musician, Alfonso Lanier, three years younger than Emilia, and neither pretended it was anything other than a marriage of convenience. The Lord Chamberlain's child was called Henry after its real father and later became a Court musician to Charles I.

Emilia later wrote something of her early life in a preface to a book of poems.[7] She also confided in her doctor, Simon Foreman, and is recorded in his casebook.[8] Foreman, a remarkable man, was a fashionable physician (though not recognised as such by the College of Physicians) and also a surgeon, alchemist and astrologer. He was much sought after by the gentry and merchants of the day and was consulted by a number of actors, but specialised in 'women's complaints', treating, among many, Shakespeare's Bankside landlady. Details of his consultations and cases and his diary are held in the Bodleian Library in Oxford. Emilia, consulting him about a possible pregnancy, told him that not only had she been the Lord Chamberlain's mistress, but had had other noblemen as lovers. If, as has often been suggested, Southampton was both

Shakespeare's patron and his rival with the Dark Lady, then possibly Emilia was referring to the Earl.

Emilia visited Foreman a number of times, mainly on gynaecological matters. Foreman also had his own method of treatment for barren wives. If, for any reason, it was thought the fault might lie with the husband, then Foreman would secretly undertake the task for him. He would also, if given half a chance, go to bed with any patient he fancied. His code word for sexual intercourse was 'haleking'.

It is clear from what Emilia said and wrote that she knew many of those in the theatre community well. It can never be proved that she was *the* Dark Lady but there is no doubt that she could well have been.

Lovelorn or not, Shakespeare was now turning his talents to comedy and *The Comedy of Errors,* based on a story from Plautus of the misadventures of two sets of identical twins, was a great success. Indeed, when it was put on at the Inns of Court in 1594 for the entertainment of the students it resulted in a court case due to 'the great disorders and abuses done and committed during the evening by a company of base common fellows under the leadership of a sorcerer or conjuror'. Towards the end of the play a conjuror, brought in to cast out devils from one of the unfortunate twins who has been mistaken for his brother and is thought to have gone mad, succeeds only in causing even more chaos. Presumably it was the actor playing this part who was accused of causing mayhem after the show, for he successfully defended himself and the other actors by accusing the attorney and solicitor who brought them to court of 'knavery and juggling' in presenting the case. It was promptly dismissed.

Commenting on the incident, one Henry Helmus noted that as an evening out the entertainment 'was not thought to offer much of account, save Dancing and Revelling with Gentlewomen and after such Sports a *Comedy of Errors,* like to Plautus his *Menechmus* was played by the Players. So that night was begun, and continued to the end, in nothing but confusion and errors. Whereupon, it was ever afterwards known as The Night of Errors.'

He then adds: 'Grays Inn Hall, Innocents Day, December 28 1594. There was such a row and such crowding by gentlewomen and others on the stage, that the Temple visitors to Gray's Inn went away disgusted. And so the Grays Inn Men had only Dancing and Shakespeare's play.'

* * *

Meanwhile, Robert Greene had parted from Emma Ball and was living in lodgings with a cobbler and his wife. It must have been a wretched year for Emma, already struggling to bring up the sickly Fortunatus, for her brother, Cutting Ball Jack, had finally paid the price for highway robbery and was hanged at Tyburn.

Among the harshest critics of the playwrights and playhouses were the Harveys, a family of academics from East Anglia, in particular Gabriel Harvey who intensely disliked Greene. Of Greene, Harvey wrote:

> Who in London has not heard of his dissolute and licentious living; his fond disguising of a Master of Arts with ruffianly hair, unseemly apparel, and more unseemly company: his vainglorious and Thrasonical bragging; his piperly extemporising and Tarletonising: his apish counterfeiting of every ridiculous and absurd toy; his fine cozening of jugglers, and finer juggling with cozeners; his villainous cogging and foisting; his monstrous swearing and horrible forswearing; his impious profaning of sacred texts; his other scandalous and blasphemous ravings; his riotous and outrageous surfeitings; his continual shifting of lodgings; his plausible mustering, and banqueting of roisterly acquaintance at his first coming; his beggarly departing in every hostess's debt; his infamous resorting to the Bankside, Shoreditch, Southwark, and other filthy haunts; his obscure lurking in the basest corners; his pawning of his sword, cloak and what not, when money came short; his impudent pamphletting, fantastical interluding and desperate libelling, when

> other cozening shifts failed; his employing Ball (known as Cutting Ball), til he was intercepted at Tyburn, to lend a crew of his trustiest companions to guard him in danger of arrest; his keeping of the aforesaid Ball's sister, a sorry ragged quean, of whom he had his base son, Infortunatus Greene; his forsaking of his own wife, too honest for such a husband: particulars are infinite: his condemning of superiors, deriding of others, and defying of all good order?

What a critique!

Greene promptly responded to Harvey's invective with a pamphlet in his series against social abuses, *Quips for an Upstart Courtier*, in which he called Harvey's father, a well-to-do rope maker, a 'halter-maker', and followed this up with rude gossip about the three Harvey sons, the eldest of whom was a Divine, 'which comforts his father's soul though he be a vainglorious ass' and who, according to Greene, chased after his parishioners' wives. He described the second son as a 'physician or fool', who dabbled in astrology, while the third, a 'civilian' given to academic study, had only recently been 'clapped in the Fleet Prison'.

Given his reputation, it is hardly surprising that Greene never found a regular patron, although over the years he approached a whole raft of Earls – those of Arundel, Oxford, Leicester, Essex and Derby – in an attempt to find a sponsor. In 1591 he gave up chasing the nobility and dedicated his *Farewell to Folly* to a mere gentleman, Robert Carey, Esq., to whom he wrote:

> Having waded (noble minded Courtier) through the censures of many both Honourable and worshipful, in committing the credit of my books to their honourable opinions, as I have found some of them not only honourably to patronise my works, but courteously to pass over my unskilled presumption with silence, so generally I am indebted to all Gentlemen that with favours have overslipt my follies: Follies, I term them, because their subjects have been but superficial.

Yet most of those who knew him had a soft spot for him however badly he behaved. Henry Chettle, who published the works of a number of playwrights as well as writing indifferent plays himself, described him at about this time as 'a man of indifferent years, of face amiable, of body well proportioned, his attire after the habit of a scholarlike gentleman, only his hair is somewhat long'.

While Nashe, having given the graphic description of Greene's hairstyle, with its 'jolly long peak of hair, like the spire of steeple', gave him full marks as a popular writer, saying 'in a day and a night he would have yanked up a pamphlet as well as in seven years, and glad was that printer that might be so blest as to pay him dear for the very dregs of his wit. He made no account of winning credit by his works . . . his only care was to have a spell in his purse to conjure up a good cup of wine at all times.'

But his health was failing, whether due to his heavy drinking, past venereal infections or a combination of both and he was to write no more plays. Indeed, with the exception of Shakespeare, there are few records of productions of any new plays, in part because the plague continued to close the theatres, although *John of Bordeaux*, attributed to Chettle, and two popular anonymous pieces, *Fair Em* and *Rosamund of Woodstock*, both at one time attributed to Shakespeare, are noted as having been performed during the period.

Shakespeare was rapidly establishing himself as London's most prolific playwright and while dating the early plays is notoriously difficult and the subject of much contention, as well as *The Comedy of Errors* plays attributed to the early 1590s include *Two Gentlemen of Verona*, the blood-spattered *Titus Andronicus*, *The Taming of the Shrew* and *Richard III*, both of the latter based on earlier dramas on the same subjects. Tudor propaganda or not, Shakespeare's history of crook-backed Richard soon equalled *Tamburlaine* and almost rivalled *The Spanish Tragedy* in popularity. It is now thought that *Love's Labour's Lost* also dates from 1593 or 1594 and that the sharp-tongued Rosalind is a portrait of the Dark Lady – whoever she was.

During the summer of 1592 Marlowe suffered two blows. The first was emotional. Thomas Watson, poet and wit, the friend of the fatal fight in Hog Lane, died of the plague. The second had more worrying implications: Sir Walter Raleigh, so long one of the Queen's favourites, was sent to the Tower in disgrace for seducing one of the Queen's Maids of Honour, Elizabeth Throckmorton, and then persuading her into a hasty and secret marriage.

So far as Elizabeth was concerned he had sinned on two accounts: first, she did not like her favourites to marry and secondly, Maids of Honour were not supposed to do so without her express permission. To make matters worse, Bess Throckmorton was the daughter of a powerful family who were outraged and mortified in equal proportion. Raleigh was promptly sent to the Tower.

Scandalous stories about the affair were soon common currency, later repeated with relish by that great gossip, John Aubrey:

> He loved wench well; at one time getting up one of the Maids of Honour up against a tree in a Wood, who seemed at first boarding to be something fearful of her Honour, and modest, she cried, sweet Sir Walter, what do you me ask? Will you undo me? Nay, sweet Sir Walter! Sweet Sir Walter! Sir Walter! At last, as the danger and the pleasure the same time grew higher and higher, she cried in her ecstasy, Swisser Swatter Swisser Swatter. She proved with child and I doubt not but this Hero took care of them both, but also that the Product was more than ordinary mortal.[7]

So popular was this anecdote that a madrigal was written about it, the chorus of which goes 'Swisser, Swatter, Swisser, Swatter'.

The disgrace and imprisonment of his powerful protector left Marlowe exposed, for while Raleigh had remained in the royal favour, the members of the School of the Night were relatively safe. For Marlowe, adder-tongued, now dangerous in drink and writing plays which increasingly dealt with contentious topics, powerful friends were essential to his survival.

* * *

By the end of August Robert Greene lay dying, hounded by creditors and pursued by Gabriel Harvey who was threatening to sue him for defamation of character. He was also a desperately frightened man. As death drew closer he became fearful of damnation, and in his last pieces of written work, his *Groatsworth of Wit bought with a Million of Repentance* and *The Repentance of Robert Greene*, he turned on his friends, the players and writers among whom he had lived and worked. He reserved special venom for Shakespeare, in the famous passage:

> . . . for unto none of you, like me, sought these burrs [actors] to cleave; those puppets, I mean, that spake from our mouths, those antics garnished in our colours. Is it not strange that I, to whom they have all been beholding, shall – were that ye were in that case as I am now – be both at once of them forsaken? Yea, trust them not: for there is an upstart crow, beautified with our feathers, that with his 'Tiger's heart wrapped in a Player's hide', supposes he is well able to bombast out blank verse as the best of you, and being an absolute Johannes Factotum, is, in his own conceit, the only Shake-Scene in the country.

For Marlowe, so long his rival in the theatre and companion in drink, blasphemy and enjoyment of the low life, there is now condemnation, especially of 'unnatural vice', and he ends with the warning:

> I know the least of my demerits merit this miserable death but wilful striving against known truth exceedeth all the terrors of my soul. Defer not with me till this last point of extremity, for little knowest thou how, in the end, thou shalt be visited...

One can only shiver at so prescient and chilling a prophecy.

Greene staged his deathbed as theatrically as he had

everything else in his life, complaining loudly to those gathered around it that he was dying only as a result of eating pickled herrings washed down with Rhenish wine. He unkindly brushed aside Emma's plea that he should formally recognise little Fortunatus as his son and, finally wrote to his wife 'from whose sight and company I have refrained these six years: I ask God and thee forgiveness for so greatly wronging thee, of whom I seldom or never thought until now. Pardon me, I pray you, wheresoever thou art, and God forgive me all my offences.' He then added: 'Sweet Wife, as ever there was good will or friendship between thee and me, see this bearer (my Host) satisfied of his debt. I owe him ten pounds and but for him, I had perished in the streets. Forget and forgive my wrongs done to thee, and Almighty God have mercy on my soul. Farewell till we meet again in heaven, for on Earth thou shall never see me more. This second of September 1592. Written by thy dying husband, Robin Greene.[10] He died the next day.

At the first whiff that the illness was fatal, Gabriel Harvey was knocking up Greene's neighbours to learn all about it. Hearing from them that Greene 'had played his last part and was gone to Tarleton', went directly to Greene's landlady, who met him 'with tears in her eyes and sighs from a deeper fountain (for she loved him dearly) and told me of his lamentable begging of a penny pot of Malmsey . . .'

He also added, bitchily, that Greene's only deathbed visitors were two women, Emma Ball, 'sister to the rogue, Cutting Ball, lately hanged at Tyburn, demanding a name for her bastard, and her woman associate'. Whatever Harvey might have thought, there is a tradition that Greene was buried in style, accompanied to his grave by his fellow writers, his corpse strewn by his landlady with garlands of bay as befitted a poet.[11]

The anonymous 'R.B.' in Greene's *Funerals* published in 1594, writes:

> Greene is the pleasing object of an eye:
> Greene pleased the eyes of all that looked upon him.

Greene is the ground of every painter's dye:
Greene gave ground to all that wrote upon him.
Nay more, the men that so eclipsed his fame
Purloin his plumes: can they deny the same?

Of those writing in the early days of the theatre, he and Marlowe had been the most colourful. Rivals and drinking companions, their outrageous behaviour had dominated the society in which they moved. Now, with Greene's death, Marlowe was left alone centre stage.

9

The Reckoning

Two weddings were celebrated in the autumn of 1592. The first, that of Joan Woodward, Henslowe's stepdaughter, to Edward Alleyn had been long anticipated. The second was that of a young soldier, Ben Jonson, recently home from the wars in the Low Countries, to an Anne Lewis, a London girl.

The first was a match of great affection as is shown in the correspondence which passed between the two whenever Alleyn was on tour in which he always refers to Joan as his 'mouse'. His own portrait in the Dulwich Gallery is that of a grave gentleman in a long gown, who might be a wealthy merchant or scholar, very suitable for one who later went on to endow Dulwich College. Joan's portrait, showing a plain and round-faced young woman wearing an unflattering tall black hat, is flat and amateurish compared to those painted by unknown artists of Burbage and other Elizabethan actors. It looks almost as if it could have been the work of a scenery painter from the Rose.

Henslowe noted the wedding in his diary:[1] 'Edward Alleyn was married unto Joan Woodward the 22nd day of October 1592 in the 35th year of the Queen's Maj. reign, Elizabeth by the Grace of God of England, France and Ireland, Defender of the Faith.' The entry appears among a welter of accounts for work carried out on his own house, that of Edward Alleyn next door and improvements and enlargements to the Rose Theatre. Items include nails, boards, hinges, spikes, laths, loads of sand and lime, elm planking and wages for painters, carpenters and builders. There are also scribbled fragments, some of which appear to be useful sayings, e.g. 'for when I lent I was a friend, and when I asked I was unkind' and 'a man without mercy of mercy shall miss, and he shall have mercy that merciful is'.

We know little or nothing of Ben Jonson's marriage to Anne, except that he was to say of her later that 'she was a shrew, but honest'. He had returned from the wars in Holland penniless and full of tall stories of his war record. These included how he challenged a crack swordsman from the enemy side to face-to-face combat in front of the opposing armies and how, in spite of his enemy's sword being a foot longer than his own, killed him and took his armour from him; typical Jonson.

He did not, however, settle tamely back into bricklaying. He must have arrived home fired with an ambition to become an actor, for later his colleague, Thomas Dekker, was to remind him 'have you forgot how you ambled in leather pilch [breeches] by a play-wagon in the highway and took mad Hieronimo's part to get service among the Mimics?' It would seem that he was never more than a mediocre actor and soon turned his attention to writing plays, but at this stage in his career he was trudging the roads with an unknown company of players which must have had Kyd's *The Spanish Tragedy* in its repertoire.

* * *

The plague raged on, even during the winter of 1592–93 when the colder weather might have been expected to dampen it. The death carts continued their deadly rounds, carrying victims to the plague pits, but records show that Henslowe did open the Rose for performances whenever possible. When it was not he made use of the time to continue the work of improving and enlarging it, as can be seen from the accounts for the building materials used. At one period in 1592 Burbage's company also came south of the river, forsaking the Theatre for that at Newington

Butts, but we have no record of its repertoire.

We do know from Henslowe's careful accounting of his box office takings the titles of many of the plays put on at the Rose in the 1590s and which were the most popular: Greene's *Friar Bacon and Friar Bungay*, the old play of *Henry V*, *The Jew of Malta*, the comedy of *Donnaricio*, *Pope Joan*, *The Spanish Tragedy* (consistently), *Titus and Vespasia*, *The Looking Glass*, *Tamburlaine*, *A Knack to Know a Knave*, possibly *Titus Andronicus*, and the first part of *Henry VI*. Takings varied from a few shillings for *Titus and Vespasia* to thirty-six shillings for *Tamburlaine* in May 1592 and forty-four shillings for *The Spanish Tragedy* on 8 June. These two were definitely top earners at the Rose.

The first performances of *Dr Faustus* were given outside London, presumably because the London playhouses were closed, but it soon acquired a sensational reputation. Rumour had it that the spell used by Faustus to conjure up Mephistopheles was a real one and that Alleyn, when he played the part, would always wear a surplice and hang a cross around his neck. Word got around that on some occasions the conjuring resulted in 'the visible apparition of the Devil on stage.'[2] A first-hand report from Devon affirmed that in Exeter: 'Certain players acting upon the stage the tragical story of Dr Faustus the Conjurer, as a certain number of devils kept every one to his circle there, and as Faustus was busy in his magical invocation, on a sudden they were all dashed, every one harkening the other in the ear, for they were all persuaded that there was one devil too many among them. And so, after a little pause, desired the people to pardon them, they could go no further in this matter; the people also understanding the thing as it was, every man hastened to be first out of doors. The players, as I heard it, contrary to their custom, spending the night in reading and in prayer, got them out of town the next morning.'

From the list of props and materials used for special effects listed in *Henslowe's Diary*, it is clear that when the play was finally presented at the Rose, Henslowe pulled out all the theatrical stops in the way of special effects, which included thunder, lightning, red smoke, and a gaping Hell

Mouth through which Faustus was finally dragged by a team of devils.

If those in high places had already been made uneasy by a play about a King of England, ruling by Divine Right, portrayed as an effete weakling madly in love with two men, then *Dr Faustus* must have reinforced their fears. For here was a man, who though he goes to Hell in the end, challenges God himself: a man who states 'this word damnation terrifies not him' and means it. Faustus is Marlowe's ultimate over-reacher and it is hard not to see in him the author himself. Faustus's thirst to push back the frontiers of knowledge to the very limit resonates into our own century and it is not for nothing that the splitting of the atom is often referred to as 'a Faustian bargain', though even Marlowe was unlikely to have dreamed up the unleashing of such demons.

* * *

As the plague dragged on into 1593 without any apparent cessation, those who could spared no expense in a desperate attempt to find a nostrum and there were plenty of cozeners happy to profit from their distress. In 1593 Simon Kellaway published his *Defensative Against the Plague*, which lists a number of supposed prophylatics, the most effective of which was 'fugi locu!' Customers parting with good money to buy his pamphlet and unable to read Latin found, when it was translated to them, that they had parted with good money to be told the best way of avoiding infection was to flee the place![3]

Thoroughly frightened, those unable to take such advice began to cast around for a cause, a scapegoat to blame for the continuation of the scourge. They found one close to hand. For years the country had received a steady stream of Protestant refugees from the Continent: Huguenot silk weavers from France, Dutch silversmiths and hatters escaping from the Spanish invasion of the Low Countries, all skilled in crafts and able to earn a living. They had been tolerated, even welcomed, but now they found themselves on the receiving end of abuse, even violence. Stones, wrapped round with unpleasant messages, were thrown through windows, workshops were set on fire, men and women attacked late at night in the street. It all has a familiar ring.

It is against this background that one of the playwrights, very possibly Kyd, was given the old play of *Sir Thomas More* to revise, one of those sometimes attributed to Shakespeare. In fact there are the marks of three or four different hands in the messy surviving text.

Just as Marlowe's over-reachers strike chords today, so also do the words given to Sir Thomas More when he castigates the population for refusing sanctuary to those fleeing persecution abroad, with their vivid picture of the 'wretched strangers, their babies on their backs and their poor luggage, plodding to the ports and coasts for transportation ...' More points out that if insolence, tyranny and lack of humanity are allowed to prevail not one of those so prejudiced against the refugees could guarantee their own old age.

> . . . you'll put down strangers?
> Kill them, cut their throats, possess their houses,
> And lead the majestie of law in liam [leash],
> To slip him like a hound?
> Suppose they too became refugees. To what country
>   would they flee?
>
> Why, *you* must needs be strangers; would you be
>   pleased
> To find a nation of such barbarous temper,
> That breaking out in hideous violence,
> Would not afford you an abode on earth?

Whoever wrote the speech and expressed such sentiments, Kyd, Shakespeare or a writer quite unknown, these are fine sentiments and it seems they were needed, for in April 1593 there was a further outbreak of violence against the immigrants, coupled with the flyposting of an unpleasant verse:

You strangers that inhabit this land,
Note this same writing, do it understand,
Conceive it well for safeguard of your lives,
Your goods, your children and your dearest wives.[4]

The Privy Council, acting with exemplary haste, issued an Order to the effect that the publishing of such malicious libels must cease forthwith and that anyone found doing so would be punished with the utmost severity. In order to hunt such persons down and bring them to justice, officers of the law would, from now on, be entitled to search the house, workplace or lodgings of anyone suspected of this or similar crimes. Should there be any cause, however slight, to think that such a person had been discovered, then they must be arrested.

It ends on a chilling note ' . . . and after you shall have examined this person, if you shall find them to be suspected and they shall refuse to confess the truth, you shall, by the authority hereof, put them to the torture in Bridewell and by the extremity therefore, draw them to discover the knowledge they have. We pray you use your utmost travail and endeavour.'

* * *

By the beginning of May, Marlowe was at Scadbury working on *Hero and Leander* while Kyd remained in London alone in the workroom they had once shared.

In spite of the plague, the great spring festival of May Day was celebrated in the usual way even in London and in one of the earliest existing letters from Ned Alleyn to Joan, his 'good sweetheart and loving mouse', he teases her about gossip which had reached him while on tour in Chelmsford, that

> you were, by my Lord Mayor's officer, made to ride in a cart [in the May Day procession], you and all your fellows. I am sorry to hear that those supporters, your strong legs, would not carry you away but let you fall into the hands of such termagents, but mouse, when I

> come home, I'll be revenged on them, till when, mouse, I bid thee farewell and prithee send me word how thou dost, and do my hearty commendations to my father, mother, and sister and so sweetheart the lord bless thee – from Chelmsford the 2nd day of May 1593, thine and nobody else's by God of Heaven, Edward Alleyn. Farewell mouse ...[5]

* * *

We are unlikely ever to know why the authorities finally decided to move against Marlowe in the spring of 1593, although the 400th anniversary of his death in 1993 provoked a host of possible theories.[6] What is certain is that during 1593 an informer, Richard Baines, had been assigned to note down what Marlowe was doing and saying. It would only require visits to the taverns where he drank to find instances where he had made outrageous, possibly blasphemous, remarks.

No doubt Kyd, working away in London, had also watched the May Day processions. Fortune was finally about to smile on him for, as he informed those who knew him, he had finally found a patron although he did not reveal who it was. It is now thought the most likely candidate was Lord Strange, Earl of Derby. So he was quite unsuspecting when, on 12 May, officers bearing a warrant burst in on him and began turning his room over in search of – what? The authority given was the Order regarding the publishing of malicious libels against immigrants. It is highly unlikely that the quiet and reticent Kyd could seriously have been suspected of publishing such stuff and the explanation, in view of what came next, is that the Order was used to search the premises with the aim of finding anything which might be used against Marlowe.

It did not take the searchers long. They soon discovered a pamphlet, considered heretical, written half a century earlier by a man called Arrian.

From then on the events of that May are lit with a lurid

glow. Kyd was dragged to Bridewell, protesting that the pamphlet was not his but one of a number of papers left behind by Marlowe when he had shared the room. Questioned on his attitude to blasphemy, he swore he loathed it and, no, he had never said anything which might be construed to the contrary and that anyone who knew him could vouch for that. When the interrogation turned next to treason he was bewildered and had no idea what his questioners were talking about. It was then the real nightmare began for Kyd as his interrogators, using the power given to them under the special Order, ordered him to be taken below and put to the rack.

Six days later on 18 May a warrant was issued for Marlowe's arrest at Scadbury: 'Warrant to Henry Maunder one of the Messengers of Her Majesty's Chamber to repair to the house of Mr. Thomas Walsingham in Kent, or to any other place where he shall understand Christopher Marlowe to be remaining, and by virtue hereof to apprehend and bring him to the Court in his Company. And in case of need to require aid.'

By this time poor Kyd had signed (as well as he could after having his limbs dislocated), the first of the two statements he had been forced to make.[7] It is a pathetic document in which he had obviously raked together everything he had ever heard Marlowe say, drunk or sober, when ranting on of an evening in a tavern, or backstage at the theatre. Marlowe had jested at the divine scriptures, jibed at prayers, had argued against much of what had been written by prophets and other such men. He had said that St Paul was little better than a juggler, that the prodigal son's portion was but four nobles which did not seem very much, that things deemed to have been done by divine power could just as well have been done by men and probably were; and, more damning, that Marlowe had said that St John was Jesus' Alexis. 'I cover it with reverence and trembling: that is that Christ did love him with an extraordinary love.'

On 20 May Marlowe, having been arrested at Scadbury, was brought to London to appear before the dreaded Star

Chamber: 'This day Christopher Marlowe of London, gentleman, being sent for by warrant from their Lordships, has entered his appearance accordingly for his Indemnity herein, and is commanded to give his daily attendance on their Lordships until he shall be licensed to the contrary.'[8] He was then released, most remarkably in view of the fact that the charges against him included blasphemy and treason. There has never been an official satisfactory reason for this. Ten days later, on 30 May, he was dead in Deptford 'stab't with a dagger' through the eye, the received wisdom being that it had come about following a quarrel in a tavern as to who should pay the bill, 'the reckoning'.

That doubt has been cast on the official version is due almost entirely to a brilliant piece of detective work carried out in 1925 by the American scholar Henry Hotson. Marlowe had been hastily buried in the churchyard of St Nicholas, Deptford, and even the name of his killer wrongly transcribed as 'ffrancis archer' instead of Ingram Frizer.

Hotson learned of a tradition that Marlowe had been killed by a man called 'Ingram', and began searching through documents in the Public Record Office until he came across a reference to an Ingram Frizer, but this merely documented a property transfer. He set out to hunt in earnest. Neither the Inquisitions of Post Mortems or the Rolls of Assizes yielded anything; then it suddenly occurred to him to look under 'Pardons' for the relevant date and there he found a brief entry 'granted to Ingram Frizer (sc. for homicide) in self-defence'. If this was what he was looking for then there had to be a cross-reference to an Indictment or Inquest but by then it was the end of the day and the office about to close. After a sleepless night, Hotson was outside the door when the office opened next morning, ready to follow his clue through every possible avenue 'until by examining every item listed under Kent, I found at length what I wanted. The Writ and Inquisition were preserved and in a legible condition.'

The translation from the original Latin first lists the names of the members of the jury called to Deptford on 1

June 1593 'upon the view of Christopher Morley [sic] there lying dead and slain.' The Inquisition then gives the version of what happened as presented to the coroner: that Marlowe, accompanied by three friends, Ingram Frizer, Nicholas Skeres and Robert Poley, had met in the room of a widow, Eleanor Bull, passed time together and later, walked in the garden before returning to the room for supper. After supper, without warning and after angry words about the reckoning, Marlowe had attacked Frizer.

Frizer, we are expected to believe, was sitting on a bench eating his supper between Poley and Skeres when Marlowe wrenched 'Frizer's dagger from his belt and cut him on the head. The three men were sitting so close together that Frizer could not properly defend himself but, without moving from his seat, he somehow managed to grasp Marlowe's dagger hand and, in pushing hand and arm away, inadvertently drove the dagger into Marlowe's eye socket '. . . and so it befell in the affray that the said Ingram, in defence of his life, with the dagger aforesaid to the value of 12d gave the said Christopher then and there a mortal wound over his right eye to the depth of two inches and the width of one inch; of which mortal wound the aforesaid Christopher Morley then and there instantly died.' The document is signed not by the ordinary Deptford coroner but by the Queen's coroner, Sir William Danby.

Whether the jury believed what they were told or had it made known to them that they had better appear to do so, they duly cleared Frizer of murder on the grounds that he had only acted in self-defence.

Immediately after Marlowe's death a number of rumours had circulated – that he was struck down blaspheming in the street, that he had died in a quarrel over 'a lewd wench' with a serving man, that he was killed in a street brawl – but the story of the reckoning was the one that came down the centuries.

Until Hotson's dramatic discovery the identity of Marlowe's assailant had not been known, nor the companions of his last day, who had sat by and done nothing while a member of their party fought for his life.[9]

Robert Poley, as we now know, was a senior agent, or intelligencer in the secret service, Skeres a part-time agent who had worked with him in infiltrating the Babington Plot,[10] while Ingram Frizer actually lived on the Scadbury estate, was used by Thomas Walsingham for such work as debt-collecting and had recently been involved in a court case in which he had defrauded a young man out of a substantial sum of money using a confidence trick worthy of television's Arthur Daley.[11]

As to the 'tavern' of legend, there is no record of an Eleanor Bull keeping any tavern in Deptford at that date and the Inquest Indictment specifically describes the venue of the murder as 'a room in the house of a certain Eleanor Bull, widow'. Recent research has revealed that Eleanor Bull had friends in very high places, being related both to Blanche Parry, the Queen's Chief Gentlewoman of the Privy Chamber, and Robert Cecil, then running the secret service.[12] The most logical explanation is that she ran what we would now describe as a 'safe house'.

Meanwhile, Kyd still languished in the Bridewell dungeons after making a second statement which adds little to the first except that he alleges Marlowe had once told him it was all one to him whether he served Elizabeth of England or James of Scotland and in which he pleads with the governor to believe that he neither condoned blasphemy nor spoke treason. Richard Baines, the informer set up to monitor Marlowe's activities, came up with the famous 'Note', a lengthy document much of which repeats information already given by Kyd, with few additions: that 'one Ric Cholmley has confessed he was persuaded by Marlowe's reasons to become an Atheist' (Cholmley was the spy placed in Raleigh's circle); that 'the Indians and many authors of antiquity have assuredly written about 16,000 years ago, whereas Adam is proved to have lived within 6,000 years' and notoriously, 'all that love not tobacco and boys are fools'.[13]

So, if the story over the tavern quarrel does not ring true, particularly as we now know that Marlowe had been arrested and was out on bail, why was he killed?[14] His death raises far more questions than answers. Was he still working for the secret service? And, even if he wasn't, had he somehow become a danger to those who were? Did he hold information that might have fingered others had he been brought to trial? Was it thought that he might blurt out in drink details of that secret world of which he had once been part? We have had plenty of twentieth-century examples of heavy-drinking, homosexual, Cambridge-educated spies.

Charles Nicholls in *The Reckoning* reasons convincingly that Marlowe, whose own hands were possibly far from clean, was used as an unwitting agent by Essex in an attempt to destroy his rival, Raleigh, and that Marlowe no doubt did say much that was attributed to him but that there were those who blackened and smeared him and ensured his words were widely known and used against him. He believes Skeres to have been Essex's man and the prime mover of the events in Deptford.

Another possibility is that Marlowe had run foul of Robert Cecil, not least because of his relationship with Raleigh and the School of the Night. Cecil, cold, ruthless and desperately ambitious, was still insecure in his position as only Acting Secretary to the Privy Council. Did he see Marlowe not only as a dangerous ex-spy but as a persuasive playwright, exposing ignorant audiences to a whole range of new, and deeply subversive, ideas?

Then there is Thomas Walsingham. Had he had enough of his friend and erstwhile lover? One supposition is that while he did not directly have a hand in it, he turned a blind eye to what he knew was to happen, taking Frizer back into his service after he had been pardoned.

And why did Marlowe go to Deptford in the first place? The theory offered by the American writer Calvin C. Hoffman in 1960, and believed by some, rests on Marlowe having written all Shakespeare's plays.[15] This meant that he had to be smuggled out of the country to live the rest of his life in Holland or France, while a substitute corpse was found for the Inquest. A large sum of money remains in trust for the scholar who can prove beyond a shadow of doubt that Marlowe did survive and wrote the works of Shakespeare.

But it is not too farcical to suppose that Marlowe was persuaded into believing, or hoping, that he could go abroad until things had quietened down and what better person to entice him to where he met his death than his old secret-service colleague, Robert Poley, who regularly travelled as a courier between Deptford and Holland.

* * *

On 28 June 1593 Ingram Frizer received his official pardon from the Queen, was released from prison and returned at once to Scadbury. Within a comparatively short time he was given a gift of lands and rents belonging to the Duchy of Lancaster and, in 1611, was made one of two certified assessors for Eltham and an officer of various charities, being described as 'one of the sixteen good and lawful men of the county'. He had come a long way from the shady cozener who had been awaiting trial shortly before the Deptford affair.

A warrant for payment, made out to Robert Poley and signed by the Vice Chamberlain at the Court on 9 June 1593, is for 'carrying of letters on her Majesty's special and secret affairs of great importance from the Court at Croydon on 8 May 1593 to the Low Countries to the town of The Hague in Holland and for returning back with letters of answer to the Court at Nonsuch on 8 June 1593 *being in her Majesty's service all throughout the aforesaid time*' (my italics). But, as we know, Poley was already back in England on 30 May and at Eleanor Bull's house in Deptford. Poley continued in the secret service into the next century until he either died or retired.

In March 1595 Nicholas Skeres was arrested at the house of a man called Williamson, who had testified against Robert Poley. He was imprisoned first in the Counter Prison to await further examination, transferred then to Newgate, and finally to Bridewell after which, 'he was never seen again'.

A man called Richard Baines, who may have been the informer, was hanged at Tyburn on 6 December 1594.

10

End of Act One

We simply do not know what impact the arrests of Kyd and Marlowe, and the latter's subsequent death, had on those among whom they had worked and been so closely associated, as it is not recorded, though it is hard to imagine that, in such a close-knit world, their respective fates were not the subject of intense speculation. But whatever those nearest to Kyd and Marlowe must have thought or surmised, it is hardly surprising that nothing was said publicly: anyone seeking to defend Kyd or Marlowe or investigate the events surrounding their misfortunes would almost certainly have shared their fate.

1593 dragged itself out with London still beset by the plague while the players' companies continued to tour. On 5 July Henslowe wrote to Alleyn, who was in Worcester, telling him how the rebuilding work was going on his (Alleyn's) house and sending the good wishes of John Griggs, the carpenter, and his wife.[1] The company was travelling the road as the Lord Strange's Men and Alleyn wrote back from Bristol on 1 August exhorting the Henslowe household to take every care against the plague, advising strewing the floors and windowsills with fresh herbs and throwing water on to the dust outside both front and back doors every day.

The country tours were proving increasingly unsuccessful financially. Burbage's company had found itself in such dire straits after some time on the road that the actors had had to sell their costumes and props to pay their bills and were left only with what they stood up in. Possibly Alleyn feared a similar fate, for he sent home to Joan, via a kinsman of Thomas Pope, one of the other actors, his best white waistcoat to be carefully put away until his return. Future letters, he told her, should be sent to Shrewsbury, c/o Lord Strange's Men.

He ended: 'Mouse, you send me no news of anything. You should send of your domestic matters, such things as happen at home, as how your distilled water proves this or that or any other thing that you will . . . and, jug, I pray you let my orange tawny stockings of wool be dyed a good black against I come home to wear them in the winter. You send me no word of my garden but next time you will remember this, in any case, that all the bed which was parsley in the month September you should sow with spinach for then is the time. I would do it myself but we shall not come home 'til All Hallows tide, so farewell sweet Mouse.' It was addressed to 'Mr. Hinslo . . . on the Bankside, right over against the Clink.'

Obedient to his wish to have news of her domestic concerns, Joan replied to Alleyn that she had seen to the dyeing of his stockings, had bought them a good new bedstead and was busy planting out the spinach, but had been unable to buy the cloth he had asked for as the plague had shut down the shops of the merchants. Nor had she been successful in selling his horse as he had also asked her to do. The best offer she had received had been only £4, 'so I have sent him into the country until your return'.

The correspondence continued into the late autumn. Aware of his son-in-law's anxiety for the safety of his family, Henslowe kept him up-to-date with the progress of the plague, while thanking God for their own good health. They had much to be thankful for, he tells Alleyn, for during the last week of August alone, 1,603 people had died, including the actor Robert Brown's wife, in Shoreditch, and all her children which would be grievous news to Brown, when he returned home from a tour in Germany.

There are a number of instances during this period of theatre companies touring in Europe and in Gdansk in

Poland there has long been a tradition that Shakespeare's plays were performed there before the end of the sixteenth century, a legend which came nearer to being proved true when, in 1993, the foundations of an 'Elizabethan' theatre, similar to the Fortune, were found in Gdansk.

The letters exchanged between the Henslowe household and Alleyn as he toured the countryside, are touching, bringing us into direct contact with the domestic concerns of a real Elizabethan theatrical family. Nor was Ned Alleyn kept out-of-touch about professional matters for Henslowe, busy with his renovation of the Rose, enclosed in one of his letters a little drawing of the new stage.

In December, a broken, limping figure was pushed out into the street from Bridewell Prison. It seems likely that in his desperate efforts to absolve himself from any taint of blasphemy or treason and to ensure an end to his torment, Thomas Kyd had signed his name to some of the allegations against Marlowe when the latter was already dead. There is no record of when he discovered, or was told, that his erstwhile colleague was long past any further harm that could be done to him, but when Kyd did find out, he wrote that while he did not like slandering the dead 'thus much have I dared in the greatest cause which is to clear myself of being thought an Atheist which some swear he was'.

Kyd was never charged with any offence but he came out into a cold world, spurned and ignored by his old colleagues. Whether this was due to his betrayal of Marlowe becoming known or whether they were bent on self-preservation is not clear; perhaps it was a combination of the two.

His play *Pompey the Great, his Fair Cornelia's Tragedy,* translated from the French of Robert Garnier, was registered at Stationer's Hall on 26 January 1594, nine months after his arrest. It was dedicated to the Countess of Sussex with a dedication which speaks of the afflictions of mind, the misery, the 'bitter times and privy broken passions' of his sad life.

While a consensus of opinion does suggest that Lord Strange was the unknown patron who had taken Kyd up shortly before his arrest, Arthur Freeman in *Thomas Kyd:*

Facts and Problems suggests that it was the Countess, as in his dedication Kyd reminds her 'of honourable favours past', and that he will 'ever spend one hour of the day in some kind service to your Honour, and another of the night wishing you happiness', these phrases suggesting a personal acquaintance with the lady. But if he had known her before, then it must have been a very young girl for she was still only nineteen at the time of Kyd's dedication, having become Countess on her marriage three years earlier.

If, as seems more likely, Kyd's patron was indeed Lord Strange then it is hardly surprising that he made no effort to rescue his protegé, for during Kyd's imprisonment, Strange had been both taken ill and had found himself under investigation by Robert Cecil.

Kyd died on 15 August 1594 aged thirty-six, just sixteen months after Marlowe. He had never married and left behind no reputation as a womaniser, so no mistress, wife or child was left to mourn him. His mother, Anna, formally renounced the administration of his estate in the name of her husband, Francis. One explanation is that this might have been a way of preventing their being pursued by their son's creditors. Another, that they were desperate to distance themselves from their son and his disgrace, is an even less happy one.

At the end of Kyd's *The Spanish Tragedy*, Hieronimo, who has already fully explained why he embarked on the series of terrible deeds which end the play, is then threatened with torture to make him tell more, at which point he tears out his tongue after announcing he has nothing more to say. It is a black irony that seven years after writing the play its author was to undergo such torment to make him tell what he did not know. Innocent and in his own words 'utterly undone' by what happened to him, he might well have echoed the words of his own protagonist: 'Justice is exiled from the earth'.

The last word on the plague years of 1592–93 and their aftermath goes to the poet Thomas Nashe, who had been so closely associated with Robert Greene, Thomas Kyd and Christopher Marlowe. Nashe wrote his cycle of verses *Sum-*

mer's Last Will and Testament towards the end of 1593, although it was not published until eight years later.

It is dedicated to all the victims of the plague, of 'King Pest', who had ruled so savagely for so long, but he must also have had in mind those close colleagues who had so recently perished:

> Beauty is but a flower,
> Which wrinkles will devour,
> Brightness falls from the air,
> Queens have died young and fair.
> Dust hath closed Helen's eye;
> I am sick, I must die,
> Lord have mercy on us.

The poem ends:

> Haste therefore each degree
> To welcome destiny,
> Heaven is our heritage
> Earth but a player's stage.
> Mount we unto the sky.
> I am sick, I must die,
> Lord have mercy on us.

* * *

The deaths of Greene, Kyd and Marlowe bring to an end the first great phase in the history of the English theatre, drawing a line under an era. Left alone, in the spotlight, stands the single towering talent who was to dominate the English stage for the rest of his life and for centuries to come – William Shakespeare.

Part Two

11

Shakespeare Centre Stage

As the plague finally died away, life returned to some kind of normality. The players' companies came back to London from the country and, yet again, set about re-organising themselves, but this time with a difference for the two major companies, those of Burbage and Henslowe and Alleyn, acquired the major patrons which would enable them to dominate the theatre scene until the end of the century. In 1594 Lord Hunsdon, the Lord Chamberlain, became patron to Burbage, while the Lord Admiral fulfilled the same function for Henslowe and Alleyn.

Lord Hunsdon was directly related to the Queen, being the son of Anne Boleyn's sister, Mary. Mary had preceded Anne as Henry VIII's mistress but when Henry fell passionately in love with her younger sister, he arranged a good marriage for Mary with one of his gentlemen-in-waiting, William Carey. Mary had a son by Carey, who was dutifully christened Henry after the King, shortly after which Carey died, leaving behind a merry widow; Mary certainly fared considerably better than her unfortunate sister. The young Henry, later created Lord Chamberlain by Queen Elizabeth, was a man of considerable influence at Court.

The principal companies of the day were set up in a similar manner: a fixed number of sharers ran both playhouse and company, made the decisions as to the repertoire, hired and fired actors and writers, took on apprentices and shared the profits of the enterprise.[1] The sharers might be the builder of the theatre, the founder of the company, senior actors, dramatists or others of vital importance such as the Bookkeeper or Bookman. This latter position was crucial for, when a new play was to be put on, the actors were not given the entire play text from which to rehearse. Each individual part was copied out on to a roll of paper (hence the term roll-call) and handed to the actor, his appearance in the relevant scenes and his words marked only by the cues, the last words of the character before him and the first of the one who came after. Then the Bookman would call the cast together and read the whole play to them from his master copy – that was the last time they would hear it in its entirety until all had learned their parts and were well into rehearsal.

It was also the responsibility of the Bookman to look after the play scripts and rolls, see the copying was kept up to date and try to ensure that pirated versions did not get into the hands of rival companies, an almost impossible task.

The original sharers of the Lord Chamberlain's Men were Richard Burbage, Shakespeare, Will Kempe (the company comic), Thomas Pope, John Hemmings (or Heminge), William Sly, Henry Condell, George Bryan and Augustine Phillips. The average size of an acting company was fifteen and included senior sharers, 'hirelings' – actors hired for a set length of time from a part in one play to a whole season – and the apprentices who played the female roles. Apart from the actors there were the 'servants', those we would now call stage management staff: scenery builders and painters, prop and costume makers, technicians and front-of-house people to show the better class of audience to its seat. There was also the Gatherer, who collected the entrance money and kept the accounts.

It seems that the first theatre to re-open after the plague months was that at Newington Butts, during which time it was shared by the Lord Admiral's and the Lord Chamberlain's Men, but by June 1594 it was not only the actors who were getting restive and pressing for the re-opening of all the playhouses. The prolonged closure of the Rose had caused particular hardship to the watermen who relied on the money they could earn ferrying people back and forth from the Bankside.

In the middle of the month, the Privy Council received several petitions on the subject, the first in the name of the Lord Strange's Men:

> To the right honourable, the Lords of Her Majesty's Most Honourable Privy Council
>
> Our duties in all humbleness remembered to your honours, for as much as our Company is great and thereby of charge intolerable in travelling the country, and the continuance therefore will be a means to bring us to division and separation, whereby we shall not only be undone, but also unready to serve Her Majesty, when it shall please her to command us. And by that reason also the use of the playhouse on the Bankside, by reason of the passage to and from the same by water, is a great relief to the poor watermen there. And our dismission thence now in this long vacation, is to those poor men a great hindrance, and in manner an undoing, as they generally complain. Both ours, and their, humble petition and suit therefore to your good honours is that you will be pleased of your special favour to recall this restraint and permit the use of the said Playhouse again. And not only ourselves but also a great number of poor men shall be especially bound to pray for your honours.
>
> Your honours' humble supplicants, the right Hon. the Lord Strange's servants and players.[2]

To this was added a petition by the watermen themselves to the Lord Admiral, the Lord Howard, (presumably before he became official patron to the company at the Rose), some of which is hard to decipher. The watermen, it says,

> in the most humble manner complain and sue unto your good lordship, your poor supplicants and, daily, the orators [of] Phillipp Henslo (sic) . . . so it is if it

> please you that we, your said poor watermen, had much help and relief for us, our poor wives and children, by means of the resort of such people to the said Playhouse. It may therefore please your good lordship, for God's sake and in charity, to respect us your poor watermen and give leave to the said Phillipp Henslo to have playing in his said house during such time as others have according as it has been accustomed. And your honours, by doing so, shall not only do a good and charitable deed but also bind us all according to our duties, with our poor wives and children, daily to pray for your honour in much happiness and long life.

It is signed by William Dorret, Master of Her Majesty's Barge, and a number of other watermen who were unable to write but made their respective marks.[3]

The petition bore fruit for the Privy Council issued a warrant:

> Whereas not long since upon some considerations we did restrain the Lord Strange his [actors] from playing at the Rose on the Bankside, and enjoined them to play three days at the Butts, now, for as much as we are satisfied that by reason of the tediousness of the way, and that of long time plays have not been used on working days, and for that a number of poor watermen are relieved, you shall permit and suffer or any other there to exercise themselves in such sort as they have done heretofore. And that the Rose may be at libertie without any restraint, so long as it shall be free from infection or sickness . . .

* * *

The defeat of the Spanish Armada had removed the immediate threat of a Spanish invasion, but hostilities continued with the successful sacking of the port of Cadiz by the English and, in France, the Protestant Henry of Navarre was crowned Henry VI, although he later became a Catholic for pragmatic reasons.

The political *cause célèbre* in 1594, however, was the trial and execution of the Queen's own personal physician, Dr Rodrigo Lopez, a Portuguese Jew. The charge was that he had conspired with Spanish agents to poison the Queen, the grounds being that he had accepted the gift of a jewel from them. Lopez protested to the end that he had had no intention of doing any such thing, pointing out that he had presented the jewel in question to the Queen herself, but he had made a powerful enemy of the Earl of Essex, having let it be known that he was treating the Earl for venereal disease.

The interrogators worked on the unfortunate doctor but without success. While he was unable to offer any satisfactory explanation as to why he had become involved with the Spaniards in the first place, there was no proof that he had ever agreed to carry out their demands. Indeed, there were strong reasons for believing him when he said that there were those in high places who had encouraged him to appear to accept their overtures in order to gain knowledge of what they were up to. Finally, still unable to convince the authorities, he was brought to trial before Essex himself, sentenced to death and hanged, drawn and quartered. Presumably it was this incident that prompted Henslowe to revive Marlowe's *Jew of Malta*, which received at least fifteen performances between Lopez's execution and the end of the year. It may also have inspired Shakespeare to write *The Merchant of Venice.*

It was also during 1594 that Robert Cecil finally moved against the School of the Night, setting up an official inquiry at Cerne Abbas in Dorset (close to Raleigh's country home) under the auspices of the High Commission in Causes Ecclesiasticus. Its brief was to make inquiry 'concerning blasphemous and atheistic matters' and the charges have a familiar ring – that members of the School doubted the truth of the Bible, practised atheism, dabbled in black magic and alchemy and showed interest in science and mathematics – but the evidence of any actual wrongdoing was slim. All the High Commission could come up with after its deliberations was that one of those attending the School was said to have dried tobacco leaves on pages torn from his Bible, that Raleigh had denied the immortality of the soul saying, when told he should prepare it for God, that he would carry it up to the top of a hill then 'run God, run Devil, fetch it that will', and a few other minor pieces of hearsay in a similar vein.

There is no record of who actually belonged to the School; it may well not have had any formal membership, apart from Raleigh himself, his half-brother Carew, and the mathematician Harriot who had particularly befriended Marlowe. Others mentioned include the antiquary Thomas Allen, Richard Cholmley (Cecil's man who claimed Marlowe had persuaded him to atheism), the playwright George Peele, Thomas Walsingham and Ferdinando, Lord Strange, Earl of Derby.

During the time the High Commission was taking evidence, Strange died. There was much gossip of poisoning, possibly by government agents, for Strange was a Catholic, though completely loyal to the Queen. A modern reading of his symptoms suggests some kind of acute kidney failure following prolonged dysentery. They could have come about by poison but are just as likely to be caused either by disease or food poisoning. (Sixteenth-century poisoners are given more credit than is their due: sheer lack of hygiene in the preparation of food often did their job for them without outside assistance.)

The inquiry into the School of the Night dragged on after Strange's death. Despite a number of depositions taken on oath, nothing came of it and there is no record of anyone being brought before either the Star Chamber or Privy Council as a result, nor was any action taken against either Raleigh or any of his circle. That round definitely went to Raleigh.

* * *

It is popularly believed that we know hardly anything of Shakespeare's theatrical career but already, by the age of thirty, he was receiving a considerable amount of recognition which was recorded by those among whom he lived and worked. Between 1594 and 1596 he was to write *Love's Labours Lost* (as already mentioned) and almost certainly *Romeo and Juliet, A Midsummer Night's Dream, King John* and *The Merchant of Venice.*

It seems he was well liked. Following the publication after his death of Greene's *Repentance*, its publisher, Henry Chettle, felt he owed Shakespeare an apology for the reference to him as an 'upstart crow'. Therefore, in the preface to his own play, *Kind Heart's Dream,* he apologises for circulating Greene's scurrilous criticisms of Shakespeare, while defending what had been written about Marlowe:

> With neither of them that take offence was I acquainted, and with one of them I care not if I never be. The other, whom at that time I did not so much spare as since I wish I had; for that I might have used my own discretion, especially in such a case, the author being dead. That I did not, I am sorry as if the original fault had been my fault: because myself have seen his demeanour no less civil than he excellent in the quality he professes. Besides, divers of worship have reported his uprightness of dealing, which argues his honesty, and his facetious grace in writing that approves his art.[4]

There is also Richard Field, who published *Venus and Adonis.* Field's apprenticeship papers still exist[5] in which he is described as 'Richard, son of Henry Field of Stratford-upon-Avon in the County of Warwickshire, tanner' who 'hath put himself apprentice to George Bishop, Citizen and Stationer of London for Seven Years – 29 September 1579.' In a place as small as Stratford and with fathers who were both in the same trade, it is impossible that William and Richard had not known each other at home and what better person to entrust with the publication of his poem than a printer, now in London, whom he had known since childhood?

In 1594 a tribute to Shakespeare appeared in the book of poems *Willobie, his Avisa,* a work devoted to the praise of

Avisa, a constant wife, by her admirers:

> Though Collatine hath dearly brought,
> To high renown a lasting life,
> And found that most in vain have sought
> To have a fair and constant wife,
> Yet Tarquin plucked his glistering grape,
> And Shakespeare paints poor Lucrece rape.

In 1595 there is a record of payments 'To William Kempe, William Shakespeare and Richard Burbage, servants to the Lord Chamberlain, upon the Council's Warrant dated at Whitehall 15 March 1594 for two several comedies or interludes showed by them before her Majesty in Christmas time last . . . upon St Stephen's Day and Innocent's Day and by way of her Majesty's reward.'[6]

So through Chettle we have a portrait of a pleasant enough man and, from contemporary records, that of one busy enlarging his reputation as a poet and playwright. As to his involvement with women we can only guess. So far as we know, Shakespeare had seen little of his wife and family during his early years in London and he had certainly been through a gruelling emotional experience with the Dark Lady of the Sonnets.

The only contemporary reference to Shakespeare and women is in the form of a standing joke which was widely circulated at the time and is noted in his diary for 13 March 1602 by John Manningham, law student in the Middle Temple:

> Upon a time when Burbage played Richard III there was a citizen grew so far in liking with him that before she went from the play, she appointed him to come to her that night by the name Richard III. Shakespeare, overhearing their conclusion, went before, was entertained and at his game e'er Burbage came. The message being brought that Richard III was at the door, Shakespeare caused return to be made that William the Conqueror was before Richard III.

* * *

By 1595 Burbage was feeling the need to expand his operation. He still did not contemplate moving over the river to the Bankside but he was having trouble with the freeholder of the ground which he had leased to build the Theatre. He decided therefore to buy a large and imposing building in the extremely fashionable district of Blackfriars, which had once been used for Parliamentary meetings, and convert it into a covered or 'private' theatre. Although inside the City walls, the enclave did not fall under the jurisdiction of the City.

It seemed an astute move to put a new playhouse in an area where the majority of the residents were comparatively wealthy: as Andrew Gurr says in *Playgoing in Shakespeare's London* it was 'an emphatic shift up market'. He would also be able to charge more for admittance as, although the theatre would be smaller than either the Theatre or the Rose, its being enclosed ensured that the audience would be protected from the weather and could be seated more comfortably. So it seemed well worth investing the huge sum of £600.

Then he came unstuck. Apparently the wealthy and fashionable inhabitants of Blackfriars did not appreciate the new amenity in their midst. On the contrary, they petitioned the Privy Council to forbid its use on the grounds that:

> It will grow to be a very great annoyance and trouble, not only to all the noblemen and gentlemen here inhabiting but also a general inconvenience to all the inhabitants of the same precinct, both by reason of the great resort and gathering together of all manner of vagrant and lewd persons that, under colour of resorting to the players, will come thither and work all manner of mischief, and also to the great pestering and filling up of the same precinct . . . and besides, that the

same playhouse is so near the Church that the noise of the drums and trumpets will great disturb and hinder both the ministers and parishioners in time of divine service and sermons.

It has the familiar ring of those who oppose the opening nowadays of night clubs, restaurants or discos.

Further, the petitioners pointed out that Burbage's own patron, the Lord Chamberlain, Lord Hunsdon, also lived nearby. Burbage must have assumed he would have the support of the company's patron but in this he was wrong, for Hunsdon, who was the Privy Councillor responsible for all the playhouses and players, actually signed the Order preventing the opening of the new theatre. As Gurr writes: 'It was either betrayal, or a total failure of consultation. Burbage miscalculated disastrously the willingness of the nobility and especially that of his own patron to tolerate adult players in that vicinity.' It was to be some years before the Blackfriars Theatre opened its doors.

However, another new theatre had opened on the Bankside. The reason we have at least some idea of what an Elizabethan playhouse looked like is because a Dutchman, Johannes de Witt, drew a detailed picture of the Swan Theatre and its stage. The opening of the Swan also provides us with more information on Shakespeare.

In 1596 in the Michaelmas term of the Law, a Court order was issued for the arrest of William Shakespeare, Francis Langley, Dorothy Soer and Anne Lee, in the Controllment Rolls of the Queen's Bench.'Be it known that William Wayte craves sureties of the peace against William Shakespeare, Francis Langley, Dorothy Soer, wife of John Soer, and Anne Lee, for fear of death and so forth. Writ of attachment issued directed to the Sheriff of Surrey . . .'[7]

There are thousands of such orders in the records of the day issued by people who were concerned that they might be the object of violence: those so summonsed were then bound over to keep the peace. Yet we know that Shakespeare was no Marlowe with a reputation for violence, being variously described as 'friendly' (Antony Scholoker), 'peaceful' (Chettle) and 'gentle' (Ben Jonson). So what was it all about?

Gurr offers an explanation.[8] Francis Langley was the builder of the Swan and the Order might have had something to do with the Lord Mayor of London who was totally against playhouses. He was outraged that a licence had been granted for the building of yet another one and wrote to the Lord of Burleigh, urging him not only to refuse the granting of any more licences but to pull down all the existing theatres, including the newly built Swan. He followed this up with another petition, also signed by his Aldermen, calling for the abolition of all stage playing. Thomas Nashe, in a letter to a friend, wrote: 'now . . . the players are piteously persecuted by the Lord Mayor and Aldermen, and however in their old Lord's time they thought their stole [fate] settled, it is now so uncertain that they cannot build upon it.'

Without waiting for an official response, the Lord Mayor ordered the Justice of the Peace, William Gardiner, to suppress all theatres on the Bankside and tear down the Swan. This, not surprisingly, provoked a violent quarrel between Langley and Gardiner. Wayte, who was often employed in Gardiner's affairs, was also his stepson and the likelihood is that Langley, supported by Shakespeare and others, refused to allow him anywhere near the Swan, threatening him with dire consequences should he lay a finger on it. As all the players were equally under threat, they must have supported each other – though who Dorothy Soer and Anne Lee were and what their role was in the business is not clear.

What makes all this likely is that in the autumn of that year Francis Langley took out an order against Gardiner and Wayte: 'Be it known that Francis Langley craves sureties of the peace against William Gardiner and William Wayte for fear of death and so forth, returnable upon the morrow of All Souls.'

The players obviously succeeded in keeping their theatres for Burleigh did not order their removal and the Lord Mayor was unable to proceed with his plans.

* * *

Shakespeare was now successful both artistically and financially. His plays packed the Theatre and he would shortly have enough money to buy himself the finest house in Stratford. At home his father, now out of debt, was once again taking his place in the affairs of the town and was considered to be of sufficiently good standing in the summer of 1596 to apply to the College of Heralds for a coat of arms. It was not necessary to be a member of the nobility or to have been knighted to do this, so long as you had the right to call yourself 'gentleman'. The arms were to be 'gold, on a bend sable, a spear of the first point steeled proper; for his crest or cognizance a falcon, his wings displayed argent, standing on a wreath of his colours, supporting a spear, gold, set upon a helmet, mantelled and tasselled. It was duly signified that it should be lawful for the said John Shakespeare, gentleman and for his children, issue and posterity.'[9]

However, in August 1596 Shakespeare suffered a grievous blow – the death of his small son, Hamnet, at the age of eleven. It is not recorded whether he had been a sickly child, had died of a childhood ailment or whether he was the victim of an epidemic. Nor is it known if Shakespeare was present at his son's death or even at his funeral on 11 August. He might well not have been for Burbage's company was playing in Faversham at the time and the news could have taken weeks to reach him. What must his surviving children have made of a father who had left them in their infancy, returned home only infrequently and must hardly have known his own son?

Shakespeare left no word of his feelings at Hamnet's death, unlike Ben Jonson who wrote most movingly on the early deaths of his children, but it is possible that he had the boy very much in mind when in *King John* he puts into the mouth of a grieving mother the words:

Grief fills the room up of my absent child,

Lies in his bed, walks up and down with me,
Puts on his pretty looks, repeats his words,
Remembers me of all his gracious parts,
Stuffs out his vacant garments with his form . . .
I have heard you say
That we shall see and know our friends in heaven:
If that be true, I shall see my boy again.

12

How to Survive in Elizabethan England

London in the mid-to-late 1590s was a city of contrasts. Those living in Hog Lane, scene of the Marlowe and Watson encounter with the drunken Bradley, could still walk out to open fields and, although housing was steadily encroaching on them, the overall impression was that of a rural landscape. The sails of the windmills on the high ground turned above flocks of grazing animals and the butts for archery practice. Nearby Moorfields was the resort of housewives and laundresses, who brought their wet washing to hang on bushes or spread on the grass to dry. (When we go to the theatre today and see a beautifully dressed Elizabethan or Jacobean play, it is worth remembering that in reality the outer clothing even of the rich was only rarely washed, even if their shirts, smocks, petticoats and stocks received a more frequent rinse. The poor changed their clothing only when necessity demanded.)

Down the middle of the streets ran the 'kennels', the open drains in the middle of the road full of all kinds of disgusting matter: the contents of chamber pots emptied out from bedroom windows to the cheerful shout of 'gardez loo!', refuse that had collected over several days, rotting odds and ends of food, dirty water, rats (dead and alive) and the corpses of dogs and cats. Those wanting a more detailed description of this nauseating effluent can do no better than read Ben Jonson's description of it when it arrived in the Fleet River where:

. . . hot cooks do dwell,
That with still-scalding steams, make the place hell.
The sinks run grease and hair of meazled hogs,
The heads, houghs, entrials and the hides of dogs . . .[1]

A pedestrian could walk in no time from the open fields north of the city to the narrow lanes and alleyways of the overcrowded poor. In 1596 the Privy Council had drawn the attention of the Middlesex Justices to the state of the 'multitudes of base tenements and houses of unlawful and disorderly resort in the suburbs' and the 'great number of dissolute, loose and insolent people harboured in such and the like noisome and disorderly houses, namely poor cottages, and habitations of beggars and people without trade, stables, inns, alehouses, taverns, garden houses converted to dwellings, ordinaries, dicing-houses, bowling alleys and brothels'.[2]

On the other hand, foreign visitors to the capital were immensely impressed by the streets where the wealthy had their houses. One such, Paul Hentzner, visiting London at about that time notes: 'The streets in this city are very handsome and clean but that which is named from the goldsmiths, who inhabit it, surpasses all the rest; there is in it a gilt tower, with a fountain that plays.'[3]

The area opposite the playhouses on the Bankside was dominated by the great Church of St Paul's with its huge, square tower, rising high above the splendid old mansions of the nobility, each set in a fine garden with flowers and fruit trees. Fronting the river at Blackfriars were the fine houses of the upwardly mobile who had protested so strongly at having a theatre in their midst.

The ditches, rivers and creeks from Chelsea down to Deptford poured their detritus into the long-suffering Thames, yet the women would fill their pails with its water for domestic use and wild radishes still grew in the joints of the stone wall by the Savoy, to be picked by housewives for their 'salats' when the tide was out.[4]

But the river was also the main artery and means of transport for Londoners. Boats could be hailed from the many flights of watersteps, the watermen competing for trade as taxis do today, though their passengers needed to be thick-skinned as they had a reputation for being foul-mouthed.

Or, if you wanted to reach the Surrey side of the river, you could cross by London Bridge, its portal crowned with the rotting heads of traitors, and push through the narrow passageway between the crowded merchants' shops. Old drawings show a small projecting cupboard-sized attachment projecting from the back of each bridge dwelling or shop: this was the lavatory, its contents dropping straight into the Thames. The supports of the bridge were built on boat-shaped bases known as 'starlings', a protection against the pressure of the savage tidal flow.

For those seeking entertainment on the Bankside, there was a choice of the Rose or Swan Theatres or Henslowe's Bear Pit. The same people who enjoyed an afternoon watching *Romeo and Juliet* or *Orlando Furioso* would just as happily go to a bear-baiting or push to the front of the crowd at Tyburn to ensure a good view of the latest executions.

* * *

Among those just emerging on the London theatre scene was Thomas Dekker. As well as writing plays both on his own account and jointly with others, he wrote a number of pamphlets, some journalistic on social issues, others simply to amuse. For a first-hand picture of a day in the life of an indigent young man in the London of that time, there is no better guide than Dekker's *The Gull's Hornbook*, in other words a child's primer for the naïve.[5] While the trade of the young man (and the reader) to whom it is addressed is not specified, it is clear that the guide and mentor is closely associated with poets, writers and players – not to mention drinkers – and therefore the 'gull' could well be a young, would-be actor, come to London to seek his fortune.

The newcomer, invited by the author to meet him at his lodgings in the morning, finds him still in bed, thus leading to a discourse on the pleasures of sleep:

> Do but consider what an excellent thing sleep is. It is an estimable jewel, a tyrant would give his crown for an hour's slumber. It cannot be bought. Of so beautiful a shape is it that even when a man lies with an Empress, he cannot be quiet until he leaves her embracements to rest with sleep. So indebted are we to this kinsman of death, that we owe the better tribute of half our lives to him. He is the golden chain that ties health and our bodies together.

Those who cannot sleep must avoid doctors and their noxious draughts for 'Derrick the Hangman of Tyburn cannot turn a man off his perch as fast as one these breeders of purgation.'

Next comes dress and toilet:

> It is well to try and dress in fashion. For instance, one's boots should always be as wide as a wallet and so fringed as to hang down to the ankles. One's doublet of the showiest stuff one can afford. Never cut your hair, nor suffer a comb to fasten his teeth there. Let it grow thick and busy, like a forest or some wilderness. Let not those four-footed creatures that breed in it and are tenants to that crown land, be put to death so that the delicate and tickling pleasure of scratching be not taken from you. Long hair will make you dreadful to your enemies, manly to your friends; it blunts the edge of sword and deadens the thump of the bullet; in winter a warm nightcap, in summer a fan of feathers.

The first port of call for the fashionable is St Paul's, where the gull is informed that

> before entering, you must plant your feet in a Stationer's Shop where instruction will be given you as to what books to call for (to show you are a man of learning and fashion), how to censure all new books (as do our critics), how to despise the old, and how to inquire for such-and-such in Greek, French, Italian and Spanish.

Of the building the guide comments: 'Is it not more like a market place than a great house of God?', before leading his charge inside where he is told it is essential that he choose the right part of the building in which to be seen. The aisle known as the 'Mediterranean' is a good one as it is 'the only gallery wherein the pictures of your truly fashionable gulls are caught and hung up. Into that gallery carry your neat body, but pick out such an hour when the main shoal of flounders are swimming up and down and make your entrances as do the players in the theatre.'

The two walk among the sellers of fine velvets and taffetas, and discuss with them the making of a new doublet. A good ploy is to ask if there is not something finer to be had before ordering several yards to be paid for and collected later. When the goods remain uncollected they will soon be sold on to another customer. If, while circulating around the church, the gull should recognise someone rich or famous he should 'salute him not by his name of Sir Such-a-One but call him Ned or Jack. This will set off your estimation with great men', following this up by 'shouting out loud where he will know to find you at two o'clock, tell him in such-and-such an Ordinary . . .' By greeting him in such a friendly or public manner 'all may marvel at the breadth of your acquaintance'.

No visit to St Paul's would be complete without a trip up the Great Tower, which costs two pence. 'As you go up you must count all the stairs to the top and, when you reach it, carve your name on the leads, for how else will it be known that you have been here? Fear not, there are more names carved there than in Stowe's Chronicle.' The visitor should take care, however, for 'the rails are as rotten as your great-grandfather', and only recently one, Kit Woodroffe, tried to vault over them and so fell to his death.

It is now time for lunch and a visit to the ordinary.

> Always give the notion you have arrived by horse. Then push through the press, maintaining a swift but ambling pace, your doublet neat, your rapier and poniard in place and, if you have a friend to whom you

> might fling your cloak for him to carry, all the better. Let him, if possible, be shabbier than yourself and so be a foil to publish you and your clothes the better. Discourse as loud as you can – no matter to what purpose – if you but make a noise and laugh in fashion and promise for a while, and avoid quarrelling and maiming any, you shall be much observed.

Remind your friend loudly how often you were in action as a soldier,

> of the hazardous voyage you took with the Great Portuguese Navigator, besides your eight or nine small engagements in Ireland and the Low Countries. Talk often of 'his Grace' and how well he regards you, how frequently you dine with the Count of this and that and, if you perceive this is going down well with the assembled company, ply them with more of such stuff, such as how you interpreted between the French King and the great Lord of Barbary . . . By all means offer assistance to all and sundry, ask them if they require your good offices at Court? Are there those present bowed down and troubled with holding two offices? A vicar with two church livings? You would be only too happy to purchase one.
>
> At this point the guide steps forward and, as he does so, pulls a handkerchief from his pocket, bringing with it a paper which falls to the floor. When it is picked up and handed to him the response should be 'please, I beg you, do not read it!' Try without success to snatch it back. If all press you as to if it is indeed yours, say, 'faith, it is the work of a most learned gentleman and great poet'. This seeming to lay it on another man will be counted either as modesty in you, or a sign that you are not ambitious and dare not claim it for fear of its brilliance. If they still wish to hear something, take care you learn by heart some verses of another man's great work and so repeat them. Though this be against all honesty and conscience, it may very well get you the price of a good dinner.

So to the playhouse and advice as to how to ruin a performance from one who must have suffered it. First the would-be wrecker must ensure he does not stand with the

> common groundlings and gallery commoners, who buy their sport by the penny . . . Whether you visit a private or a public theatre, arrive late. Do not enter until the trumpet has sounded twice. Announce to all that you will sit on the stage, and then haggle loftily over the cost of your stool. Let no man offer to hinder you from obtaining the title of insolent, overweening, coxcomb. Then push, with noise, through the crowds to the stage.

Once seated

> ask loudly whose play it is. If you know not the author, rail against him and so behave yourself as to enforce the author to know you. By sitting on the stage, if a knight, you may haply get a mistress; if a mere Fleet Street gentleman, a wife; but assure yourself by your continual residence, the first and principal man in election to begin the number 'we three'. By spreading your body on the stage and being a Justice in the examining of plays, you shall put yourself in such authority that the poet shall not dare present his piece without your approval.

Before the show begins, play cards with others seated on the stage, shout insults at the gaping 'ragamuffins' and then throw the cards down in the middle of the stage just as the last sound of the trumpet rings out 'as though you had lost'. As the 'quaking prologue rubs his cheeks for colour' and gives the trumpets their cue for him to enter,

> point out to your acquaintances a lady in a black-and-yellow striped hat, or some such, shouting to all that you had ordered the very same design for your mistress and that you had it from your tailor but two weeks since and had been assured there was no other like it . . . then, as the Prologue begins his piece again, pick

> up your stool and creep across the stage and sit on the other side.

After some more chat and fidgeting and as soon as the actors appear 'take from your pocket tobacco, and your pipe and all the stuff belonging to it and make much of filling and lighting it.' As the leading actor commences his speech

> comment loudly on his little legs, or his new hat or his red beard. Take no notice of those who call out 'Away with the fool!'. It shall crown you with rich commendation to laugh aloud in the midst of the most serious and saddest scenes of the terriblest tragedy, and to let that clapper, your tongue, be tossed so high the whole house may ring with it.
>
> Lastly you shall disgrace the author of this piece worst, whether it is a comedy, pastoral or tragedy, if you rise with a screwed and discontented face and be gone. No matter whether the play be good or not, the better it is the more you should dislike it. Do not sneak away like a coward, but salute all your gentle acquaintance that are spread either on the rushes or on the stools behind you, and draw what troop you can from the stage after you. The Poet [the author] may well cry out 'a pox go with you!' but care not you for that; there's no music without frets.

When hunger strikes in the evening, the gull should make his way to a tavern where

> you will need to find, to pay your reckoning for you, some young man lately come into his inheritance who is in London for the first time; a country gentleman who has brought his wife up to learn the fashions, see the tombs at Westminster, the lions in the Tower or to take physic; or else some farmer who has told his wife back home he has a suit at law and is come to pursue his lechery – for all these will have money in their purses and good conscience to spend it.

On entering all the drawers should be called familiarly

by their names, Jack, Will or Tom, and asked if they still attend the fencing or dancing school to which you recommended them.

> Then clip mine hostess firmly around the waist and kiss her heartily, so calling to the Boy 'to fetch me my money from bar!', as if you had left some there, rather than you owed it. Pretend then that the reckoning they give you is but an account of your funds. Aim to have the gulls tell each other 'here is some grave gallant!'

Make a show of visiting the kitchen to see what is cooking and return extolling the virtues of this or that dish, recommending them to the 'gulls', who are then made to feel grateful for your trouble, before sitting down and dining 'in as great state as a churchwarden among his parishioners at Pentecost or Christmas.'

> For your drink, let not your physician confine you to any one particular liquor, for as it is required that a gentleman should not always be plodding at one art, but rather be a general scholar (that is, to have a lick at all sorts of learning, then away), so it is not fitting a man should trouble his head with sucking at one grape, but that he may be able to drink any strange drink . . .

Next enquire which great gallants sup in the next room and if you know them, then, whether you do or not, send them up a bottle of wine saying it is at your expense. Round off your meal by announcing to the whole room

> what a gallant fellow you are, how much you spend yearly in taverns, what a great gamester, what custom you bring to the house, in what witty discourse you maintain a table, what gentlewomen or citizen's wives you can, at the crook of a finger, have at any time to sup with you and such like . . .

This sort of behaviour should greatly impress those who do not know you but 'who will admire you and think themselves in paradise but to be in your acquaintance'. If any of your close friends are in the house then they should be encouraged to praise you to all and sundry 'so that you may join company and be drunk together'. After further loud discourse and, possibly, a game or two of dice (which you must take care to win), and the time comes to leave 'give your hostess a hearty kiss, down a last flagon, dowse your face with sweet water and when the terrible reckoning bids you hold up your hand, and you must answer it at the bar, you must not abate one penny in any particular, no, though they reckon beef to you when you have neither eaten any, nor could every abide it, rare or toasted.' You do not argue over the amount as that would make you look 'as if you were acquainted with the rates of the market', after which you reel off into the night leaving those you have entertained with your talk to pay your bill.

Then,

> after the sound of pottle-pots is out of your ears and that spirit of wine and tobacco walks in your brain, the tavern door now being shut on you, cast about to pass through the widest and goodliest parts of the City. If you approach any night walker who is up late, as yourself, curse and swear in a lofty voice that your man has used you as a rascal by not waiting on you, and that you will pull his cap about his ears in the morning.
>
> If you smell the Watch (and that you might easily do, for commonly they eat onions to keep themselves from sleeping, which they account a medicine against the cold), if you are with a friend, say loudly within the ears of the constables, 'come Sir Giles, or Sir Abram, turn this way' or 'let us take that street'. It matters not that there is no dubbed knight in your company, the Watch will wink at you for the love they bear to arms and knighthood.
>
> If you have no sweet mistress to whom you may retire, then continue speaking loudly how you and your shoal of gallants have swum through an ocean of wine, that you have danced out the heels of your

> shoes, and how happy you are to have paid all the reckoning . . . so that this may be published; the only danger in this is that if you owe money, your creditors might get it by the ears which, if they do, you will look to have a peal of ordnance thundering at your chamber door next morning demanding what you owe.

Should this misfortune befall you then you should appear 'to them in your nightshirt, clutching a glass in your hand and saying that only today have you been purged of your terrible sickness . . . this should drive them quickly back to their holes."

With that the writer bids the gull, and the reader, goodnight, promising on the morrow an introduction to the barber's, fencing school, a dancing master 'and the best tricks for gallants to acquire themselves fine mistresses, how to teach grave country squires by familiar demonstration how to spend their patriarchy and get themselves names when their fathers are dead and rotten . . .' but enough is enough, at least for that night. 'Yet if, as I perceive, you relish this first lesson well, the rest I will soon prepare for you.'

13

Trouble with the Law

In 1597 Shakespeare returned home to Stratford and bought its finest property, New Place, for the sum of £140, although at the time he was being pursued by the City Authorities for not having paid his rates. A certificate submitted by the London Tax Commissioners, dated 15 November 1597, shows that his goods were valued at £5 and that he owed five shillings for the second installment of 'the subsidy'. He still had not paid either that or a further subsidy by 1 October 1598, when again his goods were valued at £5 and the total sum now owed was 13s.4d. It was noted that he lived in the parish of St Helen's, Bishopsgate and that he might be among those who 'are either dead, departed and gone out of the said ward or their goods conveyed out of the same or in such private or covert manner kept, whereby the several sums on them assessed neither might nor could be levied of them'.[1]

A later note lists the debt as the business of the Sheriff of Surrey and Sussex under the jurisdiction of the Bishop of Winchester. As the only area in either county where the Bishop had jurisdiction was the liberty of the Clink in Southwark, it is clear that by that time Shakespeare had moved his London lodgings to the Bankside.[2]

In 1598 Shakespeare returned again to Stratford and began to add further property to his purchase of New Place.

On 24 January 1598 Abraham Sturley of Stratford wrote to a fellow townsman, Richard Quiney, a mercer:

> It seemeth that our countryman, Mr. Shakespeare, is willing to disburse some money upon some ... land or other at Shottery or near about us; he thinketh it a very fit pattern to move him to deal in the matter of our tithes. By the instructions you can give him, therefore, by the friends he can make, therefore, we think it a fair mark for him to shoot at, and not impossible to hit. If obtained, it would advance him in deed and would do us much good.[3]

A letter dated that same year is the only one in existence actually addressed to Shakespeare and it is from that same Richard Quiney. There was great hardship in Stratford. First, in 1594 there had been a terrible fire which had burned down 120 houses and left over 400 people homeless, a disaster from which the town had not recovered, then, more recently, taxes had been raised. Quiney was sent to London on behalf of the town to petition the Queen for a more favourable Charter and for tax relief. By the time he wrote to Shakespeare he had been negotiating with the authorities for four months and had run out of money. So he wrote to his fellow townsman:

> Loving Countryman, I am bold of you as of a friend, craving your help with thirty shillings . . . you shall friend me much in helping me out of all the debts I owe in London, I thank God, and much quiet my mind which would not be indebted. I am now towards the Court, in hope of an answer for the dispatch of my business. You shall neither lose credit nor money by me, the Lord willing, and now but persuade yourself, so as I hope, and you shall to need to fear but with all hearty thankfulness I will hold my time and content your friend and if we bargain further you shall be the paymaster yourself. My time bids me haste to an end and so I commit this your care and hope of your help. I fear I shall not be back this night from the Court. Haste. The Lord be with you and with us all amen. From the Bell in Carter Lane the 25 October 1598, yours in all kindness, Richard Quiney.[4]

It seems Shakespeare obliged and the two men must have remained on good terms for later Richard Quiney's son married Shakespeare's daughter, Judith.

There is another odd Shakespeare footnote in that year. At the same time he was acquiring further property at home, he was brought to court there for hoarding grain. Stratford people, still coping with the after-effects of the fire and asked to pay higher taxes, had also suffered two bad harvests. There was a scarcity of wheat barley, forcing prices up, and those caught hoarding them and waiting for prices to rise were deeply unpopular. On 4 February 1598 dozens of local people, including the Quiney family, were brought to court for hoarding corn. Among the thirteen people of the Chapel Street Ward fined for doing so is William Shakespeare.[5] There is no record as to whether or not he put in an appearance.

For four years Shakespeare had had the London theatre scene almost to himself but now the younger group of playwrights were coming up fast behind. The deaths of Greene and Marlowe had long left a vacancy for a colourful, dominant theatrical personality and Ben Jonson was the obvious candidate. We know more about him than any other dramatist of his day in part because he lived longer than his contemporaries but also because he wrote about himself at length and ensured his own works were properly published in his lifetime while he was there to oversee it.

An evening with Ben Jonson was once described as being like listening to the beating of a loud drum in a small room.

Jonson did not have much to say about his earliest days in the theatre although he must have soon recognised that he had no skill as an actor. He and his honest shrew set up home in London and had several children, the first a daughter who died in infancy, and for whom he wrote the touching epitaph, *On My First Daughter*:

> Here lies, to each her parents ruth,
> MARY, the daughter of their youth;
> Yet all heaven's gifts being heaven's due,

It makes her father less to rue.
At six months end she parted hence
With safety of her innocence;
Whose soul heaven's Queen, whose name she bears,
In comfort of her mother's tears,
Hath placed amongst her virgin-train:
Where while that, severed, doth remain,
This grave partakes the fleshly birth;
Which cover her lightly, gentle earth!

As ever, the dating of plays is difficult but in Jonson's case this is exacerbated by the fact that he spent much of his working life going from company to company, involved in constant wrangles. He was a man who both gave and took offence easily.

Much of what both he and Thomas Dekker wrote in their early careers was collaborative, sometimes with each other, sometimes with other up-and-coming talents. The only survivor now of those brilliant university wits of the early 1590s was Thomas Nashe and it was with him, probably in July 1597, that Jonson wrote *The Isle of Dogs*. The play itself has long been lost but its notoriety lives on, for it caused a mighty scandal.

It would need the discovery of the missing text to know what all the fuss was about, but what is clear is that it upset the Privy Council, for it contained, it said, 'very seditious and slanderous matter.' It ordered the play to be taken off at once and called in all copies of existing scripts, even those actors had lent to their friends. Not content with that, it ordered the actors to be rounded up and imprisoned along with the two authors, Nashe and Jonson.

Jonson was arrested straight away but Nashe, considering he had spent enough time in gaol for debt, swiftly departed for Yarmouth. In a sinister echo of the past, on the orders of the Privy Council a search was made of his lodgings for seditious papers, but none was found. Possibly recalling the fates of Kyd and Marlowe, Nashe circulated the information that he had only written Act I, the other four having been completed by Jonson without either his knowledge or consent. Thus it was that the new playwright found himself in the Marshalsea Prison, sharing a cell with two actors, Robert Shaw and Gabriel Spencer. Jonson's crime was considered particularly heinous since he was 'not only an actor but a maker of part of the said play', albeit he is thought to have been released from prison in the October.[6]

The furore over *The Isle of Dogs* took place against a background of rising food prices and popular discontent and, possibly because of its content, orders were sent yet again to the Justices of the Peace in Surrey and Middlesex asking that they superintend 'the wrecking of all stages and that the buildings be so spoiled that they can never be used again'. Happily, as on earlier occasions, this drastic measure was not carried out.

Henslowe's Diary is crowded with information about this period. In July, shortly before the *The Isle of Dogs* affair, Henslowe recorded that he had lent Jonson £4, to be paid on demand, and on 2 December a *Diary* entry reads: 'Lent unto Bengemen Jonson upon a book he was to write for us before Christmas next after the date hereof, which he showed the plot unto the company, I say lent in ready money the sum of twenty shillings, I say lent.'[7] (The Warwickshire poet, Michael Drayton, must also have arrived in London at about this time for there are notes of advance payments made to him around the same date as well as to Dekker.

Henslowe also provides us with numerous details of his expenditure on costumes and materials for costumes. It is obvious that these were very fine indeed. There is money 'laid out' for cloaks of silk and velvet, embroidered in silver and gold thread, lengths of copper lace, 'laid out for my company of the Lord Admiral's Men to buy taffeta and tinsel to make a pair of bodices for Alice Pearce, which I delivered to the little tailor in ready money – 15s'. According to Marchette Chute in *Ben Jonson of Westminster*: 'The taffeta for a single gown cost as much as the salary of a hired actor for fifteen weeks, and even a robe "for to go invisible" represented a considerable investment.'

The *Diary* contains numerous inventories of costumes,

props and scenery:

> Orange tawny satin doublet, laid thick with gold lace; 1 blue taffeta suit; Green coats for Robin Hood; Green hats for Robin Hood and one hobbyhorse; Trumpets and drum and treble viol; 1 rock, 1 cave, and 1 Hell-mouth [presumably for *Faustus*], 1 tomb of Guido, 1 tomb of Dido, 1 bedstead, 8 lances and a pair of stairs for Phaeton; 1 chime of bells and a beacon; 1 globe, 1 gold sceptre and the City of Rome; 1 golden fleece and a bay tree; Old Mahommet's Head; 1 tree of golden apples, Tamburlaine's bridle and wooden matock; 1 head of Serberosie [Cerberus?] and eight other heads; Sign for Mother Redcap's; Mercury's wings and dragons, 1 chain of dragons; Imperial crowns and ghosts' crowns; Cauldron for the Jew [presumably of Malta], Silver hose with satin and silver panels; French hose of cloth of gold, Tamburlaine's coat with copper lace, Peach colour satin doublet, Black satin doublet layered thick with black and gold lace, Carnation satin doublet layered with gold lace, Flame-coloured doublet, pinked . . .

and so on and on.

It does give some idea of the outlay involved for Henslowe, Burbage and others, not to mention the cost of commissioning playscripts and paying the actors. All the adult actors and apprentices would need numerous changes of costume even though they were expected to provide some of their stage clothing themselves.

The appetite for new plays was now voracious, hence the need to secure scripts by advancing money to the writers, the system pioneered by Henslowe. There are several notes of payments out to Thomas Dekker in 1597 and 1598. In 1597 Henslowe had paid 'Mr. Dikker' – (his spelling was nothing if not creative) the sum of £4 for a book of his called *Fayeton* (Phaeton). Then comes 'Lent unto the company the 4 February 1598 to discharge Mr. Dikker out of the Counter in the Poultry, the sum of forty shillings.' The Counter was the debtors' prison and Dekker was to get to know it very well indeed, later spending the three years from 1613 to 1616 in it.[8]

1598 was to prove a crucial year for Jonson and it depends which source you read as to which came first for him, the bad news or the good. As there is no specific date for the latter it cannot be said which came first. An allusion to Jonson's brush with the scaffold first comes in a worried letter from Henslowe to Alleyn, who was on tour and, somewhat rarely, accompanied by Joan.

> . . . therefore I rather desire to have your company and your wife's, than your letters . . . I assure you I do not forget now to let you understand the news and I will tell you some, but it is for me hard and heavy. Since you were with me I have lost one of my company, which hurts me a great deal, that is Gabriel, for he is slain in Hogsden Fields by the hands of Bengemen Johnson, bricklayer. Therefore I would fain have a little of your counsel if I could . . . this, with hearty commendations to you and my daughter and likewise the rest of our friends, I end from London the 26 September 1598.[9]

'Gabriel' was that very Gabriel Spencer who had gone to prison with Jonson the previous year and he was an important member of the Lord Admiral's Men, being one of the sharers. He was talented but, like Jonson, hot-tempered. Two years earlier he had quarrelled with a goldsmith's son in Shoreditch and, when the young man had picked up a copper candlestick and threatened to throw it, Spencer had attacked him with his undrawn sword, scabbard and all, hitting him on the head and making a gash six inches deep. The unfortunate goldsmith's son died three days later.

What caused the quarrel is not clear or who attacked who, whether it was a spur-of-the-moment fight or a more formal meeting in Hogsden Fields. According to Jonson later, Spencer fought him with a sword ten inches longer than his own (which bears a striking similarity to the story he told of his duel in the Low Countries) which seems rather unlikely, but whatever the truth of it, Spencer wounded Jonson on the arm and Jonson reacted by running him through, 'for which he was imprisoned and almost at the gallows'.[10]

Unlike the Watson and Marlowe fight with Harvey in Hog Lane, and Ingram Frizer's attack on Marlowe, the jury on this occasion did not consider Jonson had acted in self-defence but that the 'aforesaid Benjamin Jonson, feloniously and wilfully slew and killed the aforesaid Gabriel Spencer at Shoreditch aforesaid, with a three-shilling rapier'. The verdict was, therefore, murder, the punishment for which was death by hanging at Tyburn.

There was a way out, however, for first offenders or rather *male* first offenders, through an anachronism in the law dating from medieval times designed to protect those in Holy Orders. It was called 'benefit of clergy' and harked back to the time when only the better off and better educated clergy were expected to be literate. In the event it was taken advantage of by any first offender who could read an appropriate verse from the Bible before throwing themselves on the mercy of the court. Women had no such option, literate or not, since they could not be ordained.

As soon as he heard the verdict, Jonson pleaded 'benefit of clergy', and a clergyman handed him a psalter from which to choose a passage. He chose the most popular 'neck verse', so called for obvious reasons, the first verses of Psalm 51 and read, (in Latin):

> Have mercy upon me, O God, according to thy loving kindness: according unto the multitude of thy tender mercies blot out my transgressions.
>
> Wash me thoroughly from mine iniquity, and cleanse me from my sin.

The judge then asked the representative of the church if he had read it like a clerk, 'legit ut clericus?', to which the clergyman replied, 'legit'. However, punishment had to be seen to be done and Jonson was duly trundled to Tyburn in a cart and there his thumb was branded with the letter 'T' for Tyburn by the public executioner. Later, when visiting William Drummond of Hawthornden Jonson told him that, while serving his sentence, he 'took his religion, by trust, from a priest who visited him in prison, thereafter he was twelve years a Papist'. There is still a great deal of argument as to whether or not this was indeed the case or just another of Jonson's stories.

There is no doubt though that *Every Man in his Humour* had its first performance that year because Jonson noted it down himself: 'This comedy was first acted in the year 1598, the principal comedians were: Will Shakespeare, Ric. Burbage, Aug. Phillips, John Heminges, Henry Condell, Thomas Pope, Will Sly, Chris. Beeston, Will Kempe, and John Duke.'[11] Shakespeare's name is put against the character of Mr Knowell, the father of the poet-hero.

The original script was probably written for Henslowe. Whether it was turned down either because Alleyn did not like it or Henslowe refused to touch anything from Jonson after what had happened (he could not have found a more insulting epithet for him than to describe him as a 'bricklayer' in a letter to Alleyn), we do not know but the end result was that it was taken up by the Lord Chamberlain's Men. Jonson originally set the play in Italy, even though it was obviously a very English comedy, but he was persuaded to revise it and move the action to London.

There is a tradition that the Lord Chamberlain's men had rejected the piece at first but that after Jonson came out of prison, Shakespeare felt so sorry for him that he read it, liked it and then persuaded the company to put it on. Whatever the truth of the matter, the play was a success and established Jonson as a dramatist and poet of note. Shakespeare could well afford to be generous. By this time he had added *Richard II* and the two parts of *Henry IV* to his canon.

Jonson, like his colleagues, cut his teeth on revising other people's scripts, one of which was Kyd's *The Spanish Tragedy*, and had most likely had another play, *The Case is Altered* (a comedy of a missing son) produced before *Every Man in his Humour* but it is the latter we know more about. He believed in going back to the old classical theory that the story of the play should take place in one timespan, in one place and, regarding comedy, he agreed with Cicero that it should be 'a copy of life, a mirror of custom, a representation of the truth'.

Therefore the action of *Every Man*, however complex, takes place within the framework of a London day, even though it begins in the country. So strong is the feeling of a real place and real people that when John Caird directed the play for the Royal Shakespeare Company at the Swan Theatre in 1987 Michael Billington remarked that it was like going through a tavern door at the bottom of Ludgate Hill and emerging in Elizabethan Cheapside. When the actors walk off at the end, we imagine the day still going on, the water-carrier still trundling his fresh water through the streets, the merchants buying and selling, the maids busy in the households. The plot is slight – two country idiots and a town fool are hoodwinked by the streetwise people with whom they come into contact; a jealous husband is put in his place; a servant takes the place of his master for a day – nothing original in any of it, but written with enormous energy and zest.

It also brings in a character who, in a variety of guises, was to appear in a number of Jonson's London comedies. In *Every Man* he is called Captain Bombadil, in *The Poetaster*, Captain Tucca; but he is, in almost every respect the same person, a swaggering roysterer who exaggerates about his prowess in any field mentioned, continually draws attention to himself and sees the whole of life as a mammoth epic in which he always stars. Those who were kind thought Jonson had been influenced by Falstaff, those who were not saw a clearly drawn self-portrait, an analogy which was later to stoke the fires of what would become known as the Poet's War.

* * *

1598 marked the death of Elizabeth's great elder statesman, William Cecil, the Lord of Burleigh, he she had nicknamed her 'Spirit'. 'Indeed,' writes Dr A.L. Rowse, in *The*

England of Elizabeth,

> he was the very spirit of her administration. We can read his character very clearly from his actions and the abundant evidence he left us: a penetrating intelligence, a shrewd tactical eye, a cool nerve, audacity combined with prudence and unsleeping watchfulness . . . Temperance, self-control, probity, a fantastic capacity for work, these were the clues to his success. He was a most secret man, none being admitted to his inner confidence – not his greatest friend; but, we remember, though he was affable and cheerful, he *had* no greatest friend. His household chaplain writes of him: 'He was delighted to talk and be merry with his friends, only at meals; for he had no more leisure. He never had any favourite, as they are termed, nor any inward companion as men commonly have. Neither made any man of his counsel, nor did ever any know his secrets: some noting it for a fault, but most thinking it a praise and an instance of his wisdom. For by trusting none with his secrets, none could reveal them.'

That spinner of webs of intrigue, his son Robert (finally confirmed in his appointment as Secretary to the Privy Council) had learned very well the precept given to him by his father: 'Trust not any man with thy life, credit or estate. For it is mere folly for a man to enthral himself to his friend, as though, occasion being offered, he should not dare to become the enemy.'

Burleigh's death was an enormous loss to Elizabeth, the very last link with her own youth. Old, tired, suffering from depression, obsessed with the Earl of Essex and increasingly isolated, there was little left of that brilliant, fiery young woman who had refused to walk through Traitor's Gate. Burleigh had continued his work for her almost to the end, even after his sight failed him: 'I am become a monoculus,' he said, 'because of a flux in my eye.'

When he was dying Elizabeth not only visited him continually but sat at his bedside feeding him with her own hand and he was openly and deeply touched. After his death she could not hear his name without breaking down in tears. 'She wept,' writes Rowse, 'for the years that were over, for herself and the few years that remained without him: the years that brought her greatest grief in the death of Essex, who should have been her son, whose stepfather was Leicester.' We are unlikely ever to know just what the relationship really was between Elizabeth and Leicester, the great love of her life, when both were young. There was no Elizabethan equivalent of the tabloid press to broadcast their secrets to the world.

* * *

In 1598 James Burbage, now an elderly man, came to a decision which would have far-reaching consequences. For three years the Burbage family, James and his sons, Richard and Cuthbert, had been wrangling with Giles Allen, the owner of the land on which the Theatre had been built, over the terms, conditions and the cost of a new lease. One had been drawn up as long ago as 1595 but Allen had refused to ratify it, assuming, it is said, that the Burbage family had made a fortune out of the Theatre and could therefore afford to pay an enormous sum for a new agreement.

This was not the case, for in order to be able to lease the land and build the Theatre in the first place, James had borrowed the enormous sum of a thousand marks (about £660) from his father-in-law, and the repayments, plus interest, had been a continual drain ever since. For months he argued with Allen, but to no avail. He either accepted a new lease for a greatly increased ground rent or he could go elsewhere. Allen felt satisfied that Burbage would realise there was nothing he could do and would give in to the ultimatum.

He did not know his man. Taking advantage of the clause he had had inserted into the original lease which stated that, if he spent more than £200 on the building, he was free to dismantle it and remove it, 'overnight', towards the end of the year, James Burbage did just that. He had the building taken down and the materials shipped over to the Bankside and there, a stone's throw from the Rose and much to Henslowe's chagrin, he began to rebuild. The litigation with Allen rumbled on for years, but for Burbage it was a blessing in disguise. From the ruins of the old Theatre there arose the biggest and best playhouse of its day. It was called the Globe.

14

The Wooden O: The Opening of the Globe

Whether out of pique or the fear that the Globe might severely affect box office takings at the Rose, Henslowe promptly built another theatre, the Fortune, on the north side of the Thames in Golden Lane, Cripplegate, and from then on the Lord Admiral's Men made it their base with the Rose fulfiling the purpose of what we would now describe as a 'touring-in' house. There were now at least three theatres north of the river, the old Curtain, the Fortune and another amphitheatre, the Red Bull, a playhouse with a reputation for having a rather more downmarket audience with rougher tastes.

There is no shortage of evidence that theatre audiences gave short shrift to plays that bored them and one such incident is recounted by one of the lesser known playwrights, William Fennor, whose work failed to please a Fortune audience:

> Yet to the multitude it nothing showed,
> They screwed their scurvy jaws and look't awry,
> Like hissing snakes adjudging it to die:
> When wits of gentry did applaud the same,
> With silver shouts of high loud-sounding fame,
> Whilst understanding grounded men contemned it,
> And wanting wit (like fools to judge) condemned it,
> Clapping, or hissing, is the only mean,
> That tries and searches out a well-writ scene,

So it is thought by *Ignoramus* crew,
But that good wits acknowledges untrue,
And stinkards oft will hiss without a cause,
And for a bawdy jest will give applause,
Let one but ask the reason why they roar,
They'll answer, cause the rest did so before.

Not long after they opened the Globe, Burbage and Shakespeare lost an important member of the company and a sharer, their clown or comedian, Will Kempe. Like his predecessor Richard Tarleton, he was famed for his after-performance 'jigs'. He was also a notable ad-libber and there is a suggestion that he exasperated Shakespeare by refusing to stay within the script as written and that Hamlet's speech to the players, in which he complains of actors speaking more than is set down for them is aimed at Kempe.[1] Whether because of a dispute or because he was bored with appearing in productions saying other people's words, Kempe left the company to undertake what became known as 'Kempe's Jig', dancing a morris dance from London to Norwich. He seems to have spent the rest of his professional life in stunts of a similar sort.

By the end of the 1590s, references to London playwrights were being made well outside the capital. Between 1597 and 1601 the students of St John's College, Cambridge, wrote and acted in three Christmas plays, *The Pilgrimage to Parnassus*, in which there are references to Shakespeare and Jonson (the latter being described as 'the wittiest fellow of a bricklayer in England'). Interestingly there is also a mention of Marlowe's demise.

Marlowe was happy in his buskinned muse,
Alas, unhappy in his life and end,
Pity it is that wit so ill should dwell,
Wit lent from heaven, but vices sent from hell.

This is obviously a reference to one or other of the legends surrounding the poet's lifestyle and violent death. No one had overtly broken the silence which followed it, at least in print, but it must have remained a subject of interest to those who had known him, but there do appear to be some allusions to his demise. Shakespeare in *As You Like It* has his clown, Touchstone, say:

When a man's verses cannot be understood, nor a man's good wit seconded with the forward child, understanding, it strikes a man more dead than a great reckoning in a little room.[2]

There is also a fascinating reference to Poley, whose name must have struck a sufficient chill in the theatre for Ben Jonson to warn his readers against making a friend of him. In his poem 'On Inviting a Friend to Supper', Jonson, who loved his food, lists the delights awaiting those invited to his supper party, mutton served with capers and olives, 'hen', with salad served with a lemon and wine sauce, rabbit pie, followed by cheese and fruit, the whole washed down with canary wine; but then he ends, enigmatically:

Of this we will sup free, but moderately,
And we shall have no Poley nor parrot by,
Nor shall our cups make any guilty men.
But at our parting, we will be as when
We innocently met. No simple word,
That shall be uttered at our mirthful board,
Shall make us sad next morning; or affright,
The liberty, that we enjoy tonight.

It has also been suggested that Thomas Nashe, the only remaining close associate of Marlowe, had written about him in the guise of an Italian poet, Pietro Aretino 'who valued liberty of speech above his life'.[3] Handsome, witty and talented, Nashe died in 1601 most likely cut down by the very King Pest whose ravages he had immortalised in *Summer's Last Will and Testament.*

In 1600 Burbage was finally given permission to open the Blackfriars Theatre, giving him the enormous advantage of flexibility, for while the Globe with its large standing space could pack in an audience of up to 3,000, the Blackfriars offered its smaller audience the comfort of a covered auditorium. The new enclosed 'private' theatre changed the pattern of admission fees for while those groundlings standing in front of the stage in the open theatres paid the least, at the Blackfriars, where everyone had a seat, those near the stage paid the most. It was also possible for them to achieve greater comfort by hiring a cushion but other facilities still left much to be desired: those desperate to relieve themselves during the performances still had to do so in handily placed buckets.

* * *

By 1600 a steady stream of young would-be playwrights were trying their luck in the theatres. John Marston, who would remain at the Inns of Court for a further eight or nine years, had published his first work in 1598, a long erotic poem in the style of Ovid called *The Metamorphosis of Pygmalion's Image*, which, not surprisingly, had proved very popular. He followed it up with two satirical works, *Certain Satires* and *The Scourge of Villainy*. Marston senior did not approve of his son's works, more importantly neither did the authorities who threatened him with prosecution for obscenity, causing Marston hastily to issue a statement that *Pygamalion's Image* had been 'misunderstood by an ignorant public and that it was actually designed as a parody of the lubricious genre to which their concupiscent imaginations had assigned it'. Modern readers can make what they will of the sincerity of this claim.

The Scourge of Villainy proved equally repugnant to the authorities and both it and *Pygmalion's Image* were burned by the public hangman, following a ban on such writing announced by the Archbishop of Canterbury and the Bishop of London. Nothing daunted, Marston turned with enthusiasm to writing for the theatre, producing two plays in 1599, *Antonio and Mellida* and *Historiomax*, following them up in 1600 with a sequel to the first, *Antonio's Revenge*.

Thomas Heywood, who once said he had written, or had a part in writing, some two hundred plays, had been taken on by Henslowe for whom he wrote *Four Apprentices of Lon-*

don, which was put on about the same time as Dekker's delightful comedy of life among the London artisans, *The Shoemaker's Holiday*. Jonson followed *Every Man in his Humour* with *Every Man out of his Humour*, while continuing to work in association with others. He collaborated with Dekker on the play *Page of Plymouth*, based on the true story of the lurid murder of Page by his wife, Ulalia, and her lover, George Strangwidge, who were executed for the crime in 1589. Unfortunately no copy of the script exists.

Meanwhile, the young Thomas Middleton was up at Queen's College, Oxford, on one occasion having to rush up to London to support his mother in her continuing battle against his stubborn stepfather, but he never took his degree. Like Marston he spent time writing long poems, including one, *The Ghost of Lucrece*, obviously influenced by Shakespeare. In it the lady's ghost warns in graphic detail of the dangers of sexual depravity. Condemned like Marston for publishing titillatory verse, Middleton also affirmed he had intended it only as a terrible warning. In 1600 it was said of him that 'he remaineth here in London daily accompanying the players', which could explain why he did not graduate. Indeed he may have become an actor for a short while, for he appears in the cast list of a play called *Caesar's Fall*, on which he collaborated with Dekker.

Shakespeare's character of Sir John Falstaff had proved enormously popular, so much so that when the dramatist finally decided to kill him off, the Queen herself had demanded his resurrection resulting in the comedy *The Merry Wives of Windsor*. Yet the portrayal of the fat knight had not been without considerable controversy. Among the plays once attributed to Shakespeare is *Sir John Oldcastle*, written in 1599, commissioned by Henslowe (from a posse of writers) almost certainly in response to Falstaff's undoubted success. An entry in his company's accounts for 16 October 1599 reads: 'received Thomas Downton, of Philip Henslowe, to pay Mr. Monday, Mr. Drayton [the Warwickshire poet, Michael Drayton], Mr. Wilson and Mr. Hathway for the first part of the *Lyfe of Sir John Ouldcasstel* [sic], and in earnest of the second part for the use of the company, ten pounds, I say received.'

The performance of the Oldcastle play revived the controversy surrounding Shakespeare's original texts of the *Henry IV* plays in which he had actually called his great comic creation Oldcastle, thus inadvertently becoming caught up in the power struggle between Robert Cecil and the Earl of Essex. The appearance of 'Sir John Oldcastle' on stage had led to an immediate objection from Lord Cobham who demanded the playwright change the name at once, the reason being that there had been a real Sir John Oldcastle who had lived during the reign of Henry IV and had taken the name Cobham by virtue of his marriage. He had ended up disgraced after turning Protestant and then compounding it by taking refuge in Wales where he supported Owen Glendower in his rising against the English.

How much of this Shakespeare knew is not clear but he must have known some of it for Oldcastle, when captured and brought to trial, confessed that he had been much given to pride, gluttony and lechery and had later been cast off by the King to whom he had once been very close. This was not considered a sufficient excuse to avoid execution either by the gallows or at the stake for heresy, depending on which source you accept.

Cobham was personally incensed at the portrayal of the ancestor he considered a Protestant martyr as a roystering, bragging, ale-swilling monster, but that was as nothing compared to the offence given to his brother-in-law, none other than Robert Cecil. The portrayal of 'Oldcastle' gave Essex and his followers a rich seam for ridicule and they picked on the family connection with glee even after Shakespeare had hurriedly changed his character's name, to the fury of both Cecil and Cobham. Essex went so far as to write to Alexander Ratcliffe that 'Cecil's sister is married to Sir John Falstaff'. Soon it became an Essex family joke and indeed while the Earl was away on his fatal visit to Ireland, his wife wrote to him: 'All the news I can send you that I think will make you merry is that I read in a letter from London that Sir John Falstaff is, by his mistress, Dame Pintpot, made father of a goodly miller's thumb, a boy that's all head and very litte body; but this is secret.'[4]

As a result of all this Shakespeare had to insert the words 'For Oldcastle died a martyr and this is not the man' at the end of the first Quarto of *Henry IV Part 2*; but for years the older name of Oldcastle lingered on in the memories of those who had seen the first productions of the plays.

Some time in the late 1590s, the youngest son of John and Mary Shakespeare decided to follow in his brother's footsteps and try his fortune as an actor in London. If he joined Will's company at the Globe, there is no record of it. Indeed there are only two references to his having ever worked in the theatre and both are sad ones and appear in the Register of Burials of the church of St Saviour's, Southwark, now Southwark Cathedral: '12 August 1607 – Edward, son of Edmund Shakespeare, player, baseborn'; and '31 December 1607 – Edmund Shakespeare, a player, buried in the Church with a forenoon knell of the Great Bell twenty shillings'. This would have been a very expensive funeral for a mere player and was presumably paid for by William, the burial taking place on a day so cold that the Thames had frozen over. So all we know of Edmund is that he went to London, became a player and had a liaison which resulted in a bastard son.

B. Roland Lewis in *The Shakespeare Documents* writes:

> In view of the silence which obtains concerning village and home life in Elizabethan England, and particularly with respect to the boyhood of the great genius, William Shakespeare, it is not surprising that history and tradition alike have little to say about Edmund, except that he was born and that he died. What individuality the sons of Mary Shakespeare showed in youth, what experiences they had, what vicissitudes they survived, we do not know – we cannot even conjecture with any degree of certainty. Time and the customs of Shakespeare's era – including the lack of literacy, appreciation of the actual, the contemporary world – have obliterated much which would be extremely welcome to Shakespearean students.

Shakespeare was now at his most prolific. Between 1598 and 1600 he produced *Henry V, Much Ado About Nothing, Julius Caesar, The Merry Wives of Windsor* and *Twelfth Night. Julius Caesar* was popular and in 1599 a certain Thomas Platter notes in his *Travels in England*: 'On September 21st, after lunch, about two o'clock, I and my party crossed the water and there in the playhouse with the thatched roof witnessed an excellent performance of the tragedy of the first Emperor, Julius Caesar with a cast of some fifteen people; when the play was over, they danced very marvellously and gracefully together as is their wont, two dressed as men and two as women.'[5]

He goes on to describe another theatre visit when he saw a comedy

> in which they presented diverse nations and an Englishman struggling together for a maiden; he overcame all except the German who won the girl in a tussle . . . Thus daily at two in the afternoon London has two, sometimes three, plays running in different places, competing with each other, and those which play best obtain most spectators. The playhouses are so constructed that they play on a raised platform, so that everyone has a good view. There are different galleries and places, however, where the seating is better and more comfortable and therefore more expensive. For whoever cares to stand below only pays one English penny, but if he wishes to sit he enters by another door, and pays another penny, while if he desires to sit in the most comfortable seats, which are cushioned, where he not only sees everything well, but can also be seen, then he pays yet another English penny at another door.
>
> And during the performance food and drink are carried around the audience, so that for what one cares to pay one may also have refreshment.

Platter was pleased to see that

> Good order is kept in the city in the matter of prostitution, for which special commissions are set up, and

> when they meet with a case, they punish the man with imprisonment and fine. The woman is taken to Bridewell, situated near the river, where the executioner scourges her naked before the populace. But although close watch is kept on them, great swarms of these women haunt the town in the taverns and playhouses.[6]

* * *

The end of the decade was enlivened by what came to be known as 'The Poets' War', which starred Ben Jonson, John Marston and Thomas Dekker. When in 1599 John Marston resurrected the old play, *Histriomastix*, he rather admired Jonson, so he gave the character of Chrisoganus some of Jonson's well-known characteristics and habits which he later swore was intended as a compliment.

To say that Jonson did not take it as such is to put it mildly; he was absolutely enraged. *Every Man out of his Humour* was playing at the time and, with no more ado, Jonson added various sentences and phrases to the dialogue he had written for the character he had originally called 'Carlo Buffone' to suggest to those in the know that Buffone was Marston, thinly-disguised. He then added insult to injury by having another character refer to Buffone, disparagingly, as 'a public, scurrilous and profane jester' and who could scent a good meal three miles off.

Marston struck back. His next play, *Jack Drum's Entertainment*, offered a much more recognisable portrait of Jonson, this time with malice aforethought, in the person of Master Brabant Senior. While the character still showed vestiges of Jonson's more likable traits, he was also portrayed as being extremely pompous, forever pontificating on the correct way to write comedies, exactly as Jonson did. Jonson considered it an insulting parody.

Quick as a flash, he riposted with *Cynthia's Revels*, ridiculing Marston in the role of Hedon and, for no apparent reason, dragging in his old colleague Dekker, who had done nothing whatsoever to draw Jonson's fire. Soon theatres began to fill with audiences eager to discover who was going to be insulted next.

In retaliation Marston and Dekker combined their efforts in an over-the-top portrayal of Jonson as the swaggering and bombastic character Lampatho Doria in *What you Will*, which drove Jonson to finish his next play, *The Poetaster*, at top speed. In it the barely disguised Marston and Dekker appear as two terrible hacks, Crispinus and Demetrius, in a Roman gallery of poetic fame in which they are rated at the very bottom of the literary scale. Points in this round are generally awarded to Jonson.

There is some proof that even Shakespeare was eventually dragged into it for, before he left for Norwich, Will Kempe, notwithstanding what he might have thought of his insistence on sticking to the script, wrote: 'Few of the university men pen plays well, they smell too much of the writer, Ovid, and that writer Metamorphosis . . . whereas here's our fellow Shakespeare puts them all down, aye, and Ben Jonson too. O that Ben Jonson is a pestilent fellow, he brought up Horace, giving our poets a pill, but our fellow Shakespeare has given him a purge that made him betray his credit.' The 'purge' might well be the character of the swaggering lout Ajax in *Troilus and Cressida.* In his Preface to *The Poetaster*, spoken by 'Envy', Jonson takes a number of swipes at his critics and their 'spy-like suggestions' and 'petty whisperings', but in his 'Apologetical Dialogue' at the end of the play after describing how some with better natures had been drawn into the quarrel, he announces that he is now fed up with the whole business and intends turning his considerable talents to writing tragedy.

That, very nearly, was that. But Dekker was determined to have the last word and his play *Satiromastix*, put on a few weeks after *The Poetaster*, includes one of Jonson's own characters, Captain Tucca. To compound the insult, Dekker says it would have been impossible for anyone to invent such a swaggerer, leaving his audience in no doubt as to his meaning. As *Satiromastix* was staged by the Lord Chamberlain's Men, presumably it had Shakespeare's blessing.

After this Jonson faded away from the public scene for a

while and turned his attention to tragedy, but eventually he must have made it up with Marston for by 1605 both of them were in very serious trouble over a joint collaboration, *Eastward Ho!*

15

Death of the Queen

The bright dawn when the Queen stated she would have no windows into men's souls was long past. Years of Catholic plots, the Pope's excommunication and the abortive Spanish invasion had led to a regime almost as intolerant and oppressive as that of her sister Mary. Catholic recusants who could not convince the authorities of their unswerving loyalty were no longer given the benefit of the doubt, Catholic priests caught entering the country were shown no mercy. Every kind of appalling torture, including what we would now consider to be contemporary methods such as sleep and sensory deprivation, was inflicted on the victims before their final execution, under the dreadful expertise of the appaling Richard Topcliffe. But by 1601 Elizabeth was finally sickened with it all and it is noted in the *Calendar of State Papers* for that year that she said if the Council wanted to convert Catholics to Protestantism then they should do it by the example of their lives, 'for I will persecute no more as I have done'.

It is against this background that the final dramas in the life of Robert Devereux, Earl of Essex, were played out,[1] the last act of all also involving Shakespeare's likely former patron, the Earl of Southampton. It was the nearest Shakespeare would ever come to political danger even though he and his company were very much on the periphery of it all, but the sequence of events was dramatic enough to have provided subject matter for a play, a suitable title for which would be *The Reckless Earl or Pride Before a Fall.*

Essex's good looks, his apparent devotion to the Queen, and, above all, the fact that he was the stepson of Robert Dudley, Earl of Leicester, the man she had loved, had allowed him almost unlimited licence, a licence which had made him powerful enemies at Court from which the Queen's favour had always protected him.

Raleigh's disgrace and imprisonment because of his marriage had removed an intensely disliked rival, which made it all the more remarkable that when Raleigh was released from prison the two men should join forces in the venture known as 'the Island Voyage', whose object was to capture a Spanish treasure fleet off the Azores. Essex, as was his wont, refused to take any advice even from the more experienced Raleigh and the result was a fiasco in which the venturers missed the fleet and so accomplished nothing. The two men returned blaming each other while the Queen informed them she would never back such a foolhardy excursion again.

Essex's temper was further soured when he discovered that Elizabeth had finally ratified Cecil's appointment as Secretary to the Privy Council and that she also planned to send his own uncle, Sir William Knollys, to Ireland to negotiate with the wily Hugh O'Neil, Earl of Tyrone. Essex wanted his uncle to remain at Court to assist him in his intrigues, but Elizabeth was adamant and told Essex her mind was made up. Whereupon, theatrically and in full view of the Court, he turned his back on her and flounced off, at which appaling piece of *lèse-majesté* she ran after him and smacked him on the head. Enraged, he roared that he would not have put up with such treatment even from her father, Henry VIII, a sentiment which must have amazed bystanders as Henry would undoubtedly have had his head off in no time at all. He had to be physically restrained from drawing his sword on all and sundry, a major offence in the Queen's presence, compounded by the fact that, as Lord Marshall of England, his duty was to keep the peace in the presence of the Sovereign.

Time passed without his sending any apology to the Queen but, for a while, she had more important matters on her mind, not least the serious illness of the Lord of Burleigh. However, finally she weakened and within a few months Essex was back at Court, as cocky as ever and begging her to make him commander of the army she was proposing to send to Ireland, as the negotiations with O'Neil had broken down, and the Queen agreed.

As had been the case with the Azores venture, Essex immediately surrounded himself with favourites and it was his announcement that he would make his closest friend, the Earl of Southampton his Master of Horse, which brought him once again into conflict with the Queen. Southampton had disgraced himself in her eyes for the same reason as had Raleigh: he had got one of the Maids of Honour pregnant.

His familiarity with Elizabeth Vernon had caused gossip three years earlier but had died away after he had made it known that he did not intend to marry a girl with no dowry to speak of. She did, however, finally become his mistress and was eventually seen around Court red-eyed, her face 'washed with too many tears'. Angry scenes were witnessed between the two, followed by public quarrels between Southampton and members of the Vernon family. In the words of a squire, Ambrose Willoughby:

> Mistress Vernon is from Court and lies at Essex House; some say she hath taken a venue under her girdle and swells upon it, yet she complains not of foul play but says the Earl of Southampton will justify it. And it is now bruited underhand that he was lately here four days in great secrecy of purpose to marry her and effected it accordingly.[2]

Shortly afterwards Essex set out for Ireland accompanied by Southampton, staging, as he had when he had gone to the assistance of Henry Navarre, a tremendous procession through the London streets; after which the Lord Chamberlain's Men gave a special performance of Shakespeare's *Henry V.* As soon as he reached Ireland he made Southampton his Master of Horse, bringing about a furious exchange of letters between himself and the Queen who ordered the appointment to be cancelled immediately which provoked from the Earl a hysterical and emotional defence of Southampton.

Not only did Essex refuse to obey Elizabeth's order, he deliberately ignored that of the Privy Council that he should take on O'Neill's army as soon as possible. Instead he did nothing, prompting more correspondence from the Queen to the effect that she appeared to be paying him £1,000 a day to embark on a progress. She wrote, says historian Elizabeth Jenkins, 'a series of letters, not indeed abusive, but making a bitingly accurate criticism of his incompetence, his disobedience and the stark failure in which they resulted. The legend of a young man pursued by a shamefully infatuated old woman is exploded for anyone who cares to read them.'[3]

When Essex and O'Neil finally met at the Battle of Yellow Ford, O'Neil inflicted on the English army its greatest ever defeat in Ireland. Essex lost 12,000 men, by which time he had spent the astronomical sum of £300,000. Already smarting from Elizabeth's rebukes and aware that this was the second overseas fiasco in which he had been in command, Essex foolishly decided to start secret negotiations with O'Neil, who could run rings round the Earl politically, and the two held a secret meeting known only to Southampton. The newly married bisexual Southampton had taken an enormous fancy to one of Essex's captains, Piers Edmund, who 'ate and drank at his table and lay in his tent where he would cull and hug him in his arms and play wantonly with him'. It was possibly during these affectionate exchanges that Southampton passed on to Edmund what Essex was up to. Edmund was not slow to use the information.

As soon as the report of the defeat reached Elizabeth, she demanded an explanation and ordered him to stay in Ireland until he had saved something from the disaster. But while considering his next move he was warned that the Queen had been told of his secret meetings with O'Neil. He left for London at once, taking with him a handful of his remaining troops. As Dr Rowse says in *William Shakespeare*: 'He left for Ireland like Henry V but returned from it a Richard II, to stumble on disaster', a reference to the scene in Shakespeare's play when the unlucky Richard also returns from defeat in Ireland.

Essex arrived in London to discover the Queen was at Nonesuch and, realising his only hope was to tell her his side of the story first, he and his party raced off, seizing horses from some astonished riders, and set off hell-for-leather for the palace. En route they ran into Lord Gray of Wilton who informed them, ominously, that he had urgent business with Cecil, at which one of Essex's friends threatened to kill him if he did not get out of their way.

Gray arrived first and was already in conclave with Cecil by the time Essex, covered in mud and panting for breath, arrived. He pushed everyone out of his way as he made for the Presence Chamber, stormed through that to the Privy Chamber and then, finding it empty, forced his way into the Queen's own bed chamber. She was sitting at her mirror, half-dressed, her grey hair falling about her shoulders, surrounded by her astonished Maids. Essex at once fell on his knees, passionately kissed the Queen's hands and begged that she would listen to his side of the story before that of anyone else.

His totally unexpected arrival left Elizabeth at a disadvantage. She sent him away to wash himself and change his clothes, while she finished dressing, after which she called the Privy Council together for an emergency meeting. A preliminary investigation into Essex's expedition to Ireland was set in train the same day while he was sent to York House in the custody of Lord Egerton.

Although there was ample grounds, he was not charged with treason. Ireland even then was regarded as a special case, its people untrustworthy, those who set foot in it dogged with misfortune. Essex still thought he could win. He had *always* brought the Queen round in the end and he saw no reason why this time should be any different. He refused to apologise and alleged he was ill, sending word to the Queen that he was close to death. She responded that she would visit him if it was consistent with her honour. Lady Essex, who had recently had a baby, rose from her bed and, dressed all in black, appeared at Court to beg the Queen for permission to visit her husband. Daily visits were granted and, for the last time, Elizabeth softened towards Essex.

But he still had not learned sense. Crude insults concerning Cecil were scrawled on the walls of Whitehall Palace. A pamphlet was published referring to an earlier play by Shakespeare on the subject of the deposition of Richard II and the subsequent triumph of Henry IV. A copy was sent to the Queen with a note to the effect that Devereux women had twice married Plantagenet princes. She said she had not needed to have this pointed out.

In June Essex was brought before a special Commission and charged with disobedience to the Queen's commands, after which he was ordered to remain at his home until the Queen's wishes were known. Elizabeth agonised for weeks over what action she should take. At a wedding party for Lord Herbert, eight Maids of Honour, wearing dresses of cloth-of-silver and cloaks of carnation taffeta, danced a masque for her. Foremost in the troop was Mary Fitton who, when asked who she represented, told the Queen it was 'Affection'. 'Affection!,' responded Elizabeth, 'Affection's false!'[4]

In the summer Essex was given permission to leave his house so long as he did not come to Court. He pleaded to be allowed to see the Queen, not least because he was running short of money. One of his prime sources of income was the monopoly on the tax on sweet wine which Elizabeth had given him, but when the time came for its renewal, the Queen refused to do so, saying 'an unruly beast must be stopped of his provender'. It was when told of this that Essex set about signing his own death warrant. 'The Queen's conditions are as crooked as her carcase,' he screamed for all to hear. She never forgave him.

It is hard not to believe that Essex was actually deranged as he embarked on the plot that was to bring him to the scaffold on Tower Hill, the proposed coup in which he would capture the Queen, force her to dismiss his enemies, summon a new Parliament and take over the running of the country. On 3 September a group of conspirators met with Essex and Southampton at the latter's house to plan their move.

The coup was set to take place on 8 February. So sure were the rebels of their success that they commissioned a special performance of William Shakespeare's *Richard II* at the Globe Theatre to emphasise the point already made in the earlier pamphlet. Presumably quite unaware of the implications, Burbage duly agreed to the request and the play was performed before a large audience. *Richard II* had never been a favourite with the Queen, so much so that the great deposition scene was removed from all three versions published during Elizabeth's lifetime. Giving evidence after the event, Augustine Phillips said: 'Sir Charles Percy, Sir Jocelyn Percy and the Lord Monteagle, with some three more, spoke to some of the players to have the play of the deposing and killing of King Richard II to be played, promising to get them forty shillings more than their ordinary to play it.' Then, trying to extricate himself, he added: 'Where this examinate and his fellows were determined to have played some other play, holding the play of King Richard to be old and so long out of use that they should have small or no company at it. But at their request this examinate and his fellows were content to play it the Saturday.'

Whether it was this that prompted the Privy Council to move, or general intelligence, they summonsed Essex to appear before them at once. Early the next morning Essex marched on Whitehall at the head of 300 swordsmen, despite the attempts of the Lord Chief Justice and others to prevent him. As ever Essex grossly misjudged the situation.

Recalling how the people had once lined the streets to cheer him, he had been sure they would rally to his cause. They did not.

'There was not,' wrote Sir Francis Bacon, 'in so populous a city, where he thought himself held so dear, one man from the chiefest citizen to the meanest artificer or prentice, that armed with him.' What followed was almost farce. He went into the house of a sheriff to change his shirt, whereupon the sheriff promptly left. He decided to return home but by this time messengers from the Queen were proclaiming him a traitor in the streets. A small group of his supporters fought with the Queen's men on Ludgate Hill and, that route being closed to him, he ran down an alley to the river, jumped into a boat and was rowed upstream to his own water gate and into his house, where he found his servants had promptly released the imprisoned Lord Chief Justice and the other dignitaries.

As darkness fell Lord Nottingham and Sir Henry Sydney landed at the water gate and Nottingham called out to Essex and Southampton to surrender, to which Essex replied he would do so only if he could see the Queen. Nottingham's response was to send for ordnance and gunpowder and to give Essex's wife and sister an hour to leave the house with their maids, after which, he told the Earl, he would blow the house up; at which point the two earls came out, knelt before Nottingham and handed him their swords.

Essex and Southampton were tried by their peers and sentenced to death, though Southampton was reprieved and imprisoned in the Tower. There was no mercy for Essex and he and six of his followers were duly executed for treason. As might be expected, one who had never lacked panache went to his death exquisitely dressed and with great dignity and courage. He was just thirty-three years old.

An Elizabethan drama should have an Epilogue. On the morning of his execution the Queen was in her chamber playing the virginals, attended by several courtiers including Raleigh. A messenger entered and, on one knee, informed her that the sentence on Essex had been carried out. Nobody spoke. Then the Queen turned again to her instrument and took up the melody at exactly the point where she had left off.

Shakespeare and the Lord Chamberlain's men now found themselves in a perilous situation for it soon became apparent that reports of their special performance of *Richard II* had reached the Queen. 'I am Richard II, know ye not that?' she had demanded of her courtiers in fury, going on to allege, wrongly, that 'this tragedy was played forty times in open streets and houses'. Essex's partiality to the play had been brought up at his trial when it was said that he was 'often present at the playing thereof . . . and with great applause giving countenance and liking to the same'.

Highly unpleasant consequences now stared the company in the face. Writers and actors had suffered imprisonment and worse, and playhouses been closed down, for far less. That no further action was taken against them is almost certainly because they had such a powerful patron in the Lord Chamberlain who could speak on their behalf and assure the Queen and the Privy Council that they had put on their performance of *Richard II* in all innocence and quite unaware of the implications. They were extremely fortunate.

* * *

Yet there was no halt to the flood of new work. About 145 plays, more than at any other time, were written for the stage in each of the two five-year periods 1594–99 and 1599–1604. In *Playgoing in Shakespeare's London,* Professor Andrew Gurr puts forward the interesting theory that until the end of the century the two major companies which dominated the theatre scene offered very similar repertoires, while after that they went markedly different ways. The plays of the earlier period reflected the taste of the average theatregoer, relying on histories, romances and traditional tales such as that of Robin Hood. 'The values characteristically expressed,' he writes, 'were those of the citizen Simon Eyre in *The Shoemaker's Holiday.* As the Dick Whittington story grew into a legend in prose tales, so the citizen values embodied in such topics as the prodigal son story and the fantasies of apprentice heroics dominated the stage.'

Henslowe's company had favoured military grandeur on the lines of *Tamburlaine,* Burbage the English Kings, but both had in their repertoires plays about Henry V, Owen Tudor, Hieronimo, Jack Straw, King John, Richard III and Troilus and Cressida. Henslowe had *The Shoemaker's Holiday*, Burbage *The Merry Wives of Windsor* – it is possible to draw parallels across the board.

After 1599, however, Gurr senses a change. Henslowe's patron, Lord Howard of Effingham, became more powerful at Court and this might explain 'the distinctive political allegiance which can be seen in the later repertoire of the Henslowe companies'. Looking at the kind of plays written for Henslowe by Rowley, Heywood, Dekker and Webster, they can be seen to uphold not only English Protestant values, but specifically London Protestant values. 'How much these plays were produced under a stimulus from the company's patron and how much they indicate an allegiance to a particular kind of audience and its values is not clear.'

What Gurr does not point out is that from 1597 Edward Alleyn had steadily been distancing himself from acting and by the end of the century was giving only special guest appearances. His greatest achievement had been playing Marlowe's line of over-reachers from Tamburlaine to Faustus. In 1597 he sold his stock in the Lord Admiral's company, though retaining his share, and began buying land in Dulwich. In 1605 he joined Henslowe as joint Master of the Bears (Henslowe had spent years lobbying to become the Queen's Bearmaster) and became a church warden at St Saviour's. From then on he devoted his time to setting up a Foundation in Dulwich and fourteen years later there were almshouses, a Chapel, which was consecrated by the Archbishop of Canterbury in person, and, finally, the college which still exists today.

The consecration of the Chapel prompted Thomas Dekker, during one of his regular periods in prison for debt, to write asking him for assistance:

> It best becomes me to sing anything in praise of charity, because, albeit, I have felt few hands warm through their complexion, yet imprisonment may make me long for them. If anything in my Eulogium

> or praise of you and your noble act be offensive, let it be excused, because I live among Goths and Vandals, where barbarousness is predominant. Accept my will, however, and me ready to do you any service – Thomas Dekker.

It is easy to imagine that what Alleyn would have loved, beyond anything, was a knighthood, something quite impossible at such a date. It would be nearly 300 years before a young man from the village of Halsetown, in Cornwall, born Henry Brodribb, was to become the first theatrical knight under the name Sir Henry Irving.

A final footnote on Alleyn; his marriage to his mouse, Joan, had been happy but childless. When she died in 1623 he cast around for another wife, marrying six months later a girl half his age, Constance Donne, daughter of the famous Dean of St Paul's. Presumably John Donne disliked the match for he would not give Constance a dowry and refused Alleyn's request for a loan, ordering him not to visit the house. Alleyn was then informed that if he insisted on taking Constance, then he could support her sister too. Donne even refused to pass on to Constance her own mother's rings, her favourite horse and the usual gift of childbed linen.

If the Lord Admiral's Men appealed to the conservative, then the Lord Chamberlain's were very popular with the more unconventional and the young and bright, especially the students at the Inns of Court who had flocked to plays about love, romance and doomed passion since the early performances of *Romeo and Juliet.* Burbage continued breaking new ground when dealing with personal relations but the Henslowe playwrights, says Gurr,[5] not only made no attempt to copy this popular taste but, after 1600, actively opposed it and the challenge to citizen views about marriage which it embodied.

It is worth remembering, though, that the playwrights so neatly categorised as Henslowe's or Burbage's usually wrote for both theatre companies and for others as well and no doubt provided what they thought would be appropriate for the company which had commissioned them, much as happens today.

There were still, of course, those who would always loathe the theatre no matter what was put on. Henry Crosse, in *Virtuous Commonwealth* wrote:

> ...a play is like a sink in a town, whereupon all the filth doth run: or a boil in the body, that draweth all the ill humours unto it... is it fit that the infirmities of holy men should be acted on a stage?...there is no passion wherewith the king, the sovereign majesty of the realm was possessed, but is amply and openly sported with, and made a May-game to all the beholders.

* * *

By the winter of 1602/03 Elizabeth was failing physically and mentally. Her memory, which had seemed ageless, began to betray her and at nearly seventy she was very old by the standards of the day. Indeed, whole generations had been born who could not remember a time when Elizabeth had not been their Queen and almost all those who she had known from her youth were dead. Still she refused to name James as her successor although it was unimaginable it could be anyone else.

Early in January she caught a chill and removed from Whitehall to Richmond which was considered the most comfortable palace and the easiest to keep warm. By the end of February it was clear that she was unlikely to recover for she no longer seemed to have the will to live. She told Parliament that she did not wish to live or reign after life and her reign had ceased to do them any good. Her cousin, Robert Carey, said of her 'she grew worse because she would have it so', refusing to respond when he said she was looking better, except to say that she was not. Fever, thirst and sleeplessness added to her breathing problems but she turned all medicines away and when the Archbishop of Canterbury tried to persuade her to take some, she told him tartly that she knew her own constitution better than he did.

She refused to take to her bed and instead sat on a heap of cushions on the floor. Those who thought her tongue might have lost its sharpness were soon disillusioned. When Robert Cecil told her that to please her people she must go to bed, she replied 'little man, little man, the word *must* is not to be used to princes. If your father had lived, you durst not have said so much.' She complained she had 'no one I can trust. My condition is strangely turned upside down.' She continued on this theme when the Lord Admiral tried to persuade her to eat, if only a little broth. 'I am tied with a chain of iron about my neck, I am tied, I am tied and the case is altered with me.'

Constant efforts were made to get her to name her successor, to which she continued to respond in gnomic terms. By 23 March, the Privy Council were desperate and visited her again, insisting that she confirm definitely that James of Scotland was to succeed. By this time she could hardly speak so they asked her to show her intention by signs, which she did. She then signalled that she wanted to see the Archbishop of Canterbury. He came at once and told that she must now prepare herself 'for what she had come to'. He knelt by the bed and began the prayers for the dying, joined by all those present. When, after blessing her, he tried to rise from his knees the Queen motioned him to remain where he was. Although tired and weary he did so until she lapsed into unconsciousness, imploring God to show her mercy. A Catholic priest, imprisoned in the Tower, said that during the days the Queen was dying a strange silence descended over the whole city, 'not a bell rang out or a bugle sounded'.[6] Between two and three on the morning of 24 March 1603 she died peacefully, having reigned, noted a chronicler, 'forty-four years, five months and some odd days'.

William Camden, a Tudor chronicler, noted: 'She was a Queen who hath so long and with so great wisdom governed her kingdoms, as (to use the word of her Successor who in sincerity confessed so much) the like have not been read or heard of, either in our own time or since the days of the Roman Emperor Augustus.' The age of Gloriana had passed and a new era come. It was to be very different.

Part Three

16

The Jacobeans

> Now what shall we say of these rich citizens of London? What shall I say of them? Shall I call them proud men of London, malicious men of London, merciless men of London? No, no. I may not say so: they will be offended of me then. Yet must I speak. For is there not reigning in London as much pride, as much covetousness, as much cruelty, as much oppression and as much superstition as was in Nebo? Yes, I think so and much more too . . . But London was never so ill as it is now. In times past men were full of pity and compassion, but now there is no pity; for in London their brother shall die in the streets for cold, he shall lie sick at the door between stock and stock . . . and perish there for hunger.
>
> In times past, when any rich man died in London, they were wont to help the poor scholars of the Universities with exhibitions. When any man died, they would bequeath great sums of money to the poor . . . but now I hear no good report, and yet inquire of it, and hearken for it; but now charity is waxen cold, none helpeth the scholar, nor yet the poor.

These words, by a sixteenth-century commentator, which seem so appropriate for today, were written at the end of Elizabeth's reign, but were to become even more apposite in the reign of James. While London was not the Great Wen it was to become, slums and tenements were growing fast to the north and increasingly the City and its suburbs acted as a magnet to those believing, like Dick Whittington or the merry apprentices of *The Shoemaker's Holiday*, that they could make their fortune in the City even if the streets were not actually paved with gold.

The biggest single difference between then and now was the proximity of the countryside to inner London. Hampstead and Highgate were far-flung villages, separated from the city by fields and woods. Outside the teeming Bankside of the theatres, playhouses, taverns, brothels and slums lay Kent and Surrey. Women picked lavender, the herb which still gives its name to Lavender Hill and Lavender Sweep, in the fields above Wandsworth for sale in the City, while between Southwark and outlying Greenwich and Deptford were cherry orchards and market gardens. Urban sprawl and modern transport has brought everything nearer. Brentford, now a London suburb, was a popular place of assignation in Jacobean times, as was Brighton in the 1920s, well out of the way of prying eyes.

The accession of James was greeted with general relief, that the years of uncertainty were finally at an end. The hope was that his reign would stop the intrigue and in-fighting among those who still thought they had a claim to the throne. It would also end, finally, the antagonism between Scotland and England since James was now King of both. He had the support of most of the country, prompted by relief that there would be no Civil War. All this ensured James VI of Scotland would be welcomed as James I of England.

The honeymoon period was short-lived. Love her or loathe her Elizabeth had, to the end, offered strong leadership and the people looked to James to provide the same. But instead of a King prepared to set his stamp on the monarchy, take on the various factions and bind men together, they found a weak and incompetent monarch who had married out of duty but who was obviously emotionally, if not physically, homosexual, and who filled his court with pretty young men. Like his mother, Mary Stuart, and his father, the feckless Darnley, he was also wildly extravagant. 'The lowering of standards in the court was immediate,' writes Una Ellis-Fermor in *The Jacobean Drama*, 'slackness of discipline, loss of dignity and increase of expense combined to produce at once dissatisfaction and a feeling of unsteadiness. Plots to depose him broke out again almost at once: Cobham's in 1603 and the Gunpowder Plot in 1605.'

James ruled a Court which was soon rotten with graft and corruption, his young male favourites granted almost unlimited licence, a Court where, to fund his lavish lifestyle, 'honours' were sold. Soon it seemed he presided over a nation where everything was for sale: honours, power, franchises, monopolies – and women. The going price for a knighthood was £30, and he soon created 838 new knights, while for £1,905 you could buy the new rank of knight baronet. Within a comparatively short time James created three dukes, a marquess, thirty-two earls, nineteen viscounts and fifty-six barons strictly for cash down, which brought him in about £120,000 all told. He surrounded himself with sycophants who told him only what he wanted to hear, young hopefuls treading on each other in their haste to claw their way up the ladder of ambition. It is not surprising that what was presented in the theatres soon mirrored the climate of the times.

The number of playhouses continued to grow. North of the river the Curtain, Fortune, Blackfriars and Red Bull (now enlarged) had been joined by the Boar's Head in Whitechapel while on the Bankside Henslowe had built another theatre, the Hope, on the site of the old Bear Garden, close to the Globe and the Swan. The Hope also doubled as a Bear Pit.

A ballad of the time, from 'The Common Cries of London', notes:

> Mark but the waterman attending to his fare,
> Of hot and cold, of wet and dry, he always takes his share,
> He carries bonny lasses over to the plays,
> And here and there he gets a bit and that his stomach stays.

The players on the Bankside, and round the Globe and Swan,
Will teach you idle tricks of love, but the Red Bull plays the man.

Only Shakespeare, now the doyen of playwrights, remained from that earlier golden age of theatre. For the new generation of playgoers, Greene, Kyd, Peele and Marlowe were distant memories, although some of their plays remained popular in the repertoires of the day and odd lines from them were plundered by younger writers. For some reason Tamburlaine's 'Hola, you pampered jades of Asia', a line used by the tyrant to urge on the defeated kings who were pulling his chariot, tickled Elizabethan and Jacobean audiences to death and it turns up again and again, not least in Jonson and Marston's *Eastward Ho!*

The younger writers who had come to prominence in the late 1590s were now well established and Thomas Middleton was a leading light. Possibly because of his upbringing by his tough and independent mother and sisters, he almost alone among his contemporaries found himself an interesting wife. In 1603 he married Mary Morbeck, the well-educated daughter of Edward Morbeck, a Clerk of Chancery, and granddaughter to a famous composer and musician of the day, John Morbeck. Her uncle, Dr Roger Morbeck, an author and physician, was Provost of Oriel College, Oxford. The whole family seems to have been interested in literature and the arts and her brother, Thomas, was an actor.

Dekker, Marston, Chapman and Webster had now been joined by the young Beaumont and Fletcher, certainly sharing a roof if not, as Aubrey gossiped, a bed, girl and each other. There was also Cyril Tourneur, to whom two plays are attributed, *The Revenger's Tragedy* and *The Atheist's Tragedy*. There is some dispute among academics over the first as there are those who think it was written by Middleton but the consensus remains with Tourneur. A very real problem is that we know next to nothing about him.

What little we do know is interesting. Tourneur, like Marlowe, was involved with the secret service. Also like Marlowe, he was arrested and brought before the Privy Council, we do not know on what charge but presumably it did not stick for he was eventually released on Sir Edward Cecil's bond. Eight years later, in 1625, he was appointed Secretary to the Council of War and sailed from Plymouth with the unsuccessful Cadiz expedition under the command of that same Sir Edward Cecil, but in the December of that year he was put ashore in Kinsale, Ireland, with a number of others who had been taken ill at sea and there, in February, he died.

Peter B. Murray in *A Study of Cyril Tourneur* writes:

> The figure emerging from these scant facts is a man whose fine hand as a secretary would never permit time to give full development to a quite correspondingly fine ability as poet and dramatist . . . In what we know of his life there is also evidence that his work as a writer was not of paramount interest to him: he wrote only when he was unemployed and in what he wrote his effort was often directed more to the pursuit of patronage than of what we understand as literary excellence.

For all that, *The Revenger's Tragedy*, rescued for posterity by the young Trevor Nunn in the late 1960s, is a fine piece and the most sophisticated of the canon of revenge plays.

James I may have disappointed those looking for a strong King but he was not without virtues, one of which was an enthusiasm for the theatre. The playhouses had been forced to close during the period of official mourning for the old Queen, prompting much uncertainty within the various companies as they had no way of knowing what the future might hold. In the event, the accession of James was a marked benefit. The King himself became the official patron of the Lord Chamberlain's Men, who were then known as the King's Men. The Lord Admiral's Men were put under the patronage of James's eldest son, Prince Henry, the Worcester's Men under that of the Queen, while the two principal children's companies became the

Children of the Chapel Royal and Children of the Queen's Revels.

The patronage of King and Court produced a flood of new plays and a whole new genre: the 'city comedies' or 'city satires'. These plays were not set in mythical countries such as Illyria or even in Continental Europe but were based firmly in the City of London, and set out to reflect the greed, corruption and mercenary values of the city merchants and minor nobility on the make.

A mixture of the familiar and the new was produced in 1604, including Shakespeare's *Measure for Measure* and *Othello*; Chapman's *Bussy d'Ambois* (a rather dull historical piece) and his *All Fools* and *Monsieur d'Olive*; *The Honest Whore* by Dekker and the emergent Webster, who possibly also wrote *The Play of Thomas Wyatt*; *Westward Ho!*, another Dekker collaboration; Heywood's *If You Know Not Me You Know Nobody* and Marston's *The Wise Woman of Hogsden*, *The Malcontent* and the intriguing *The Dutch Courtesan.*

The latter is of particular interest because of its portrayal of the place of women and their relationship with men. A young and upwardly mobile Londoner, now wanting to make a good marriage, decides to rid himself of his faithful mistress by handing her on to his friend. The friend, however, provides a study in sexual repression well ahead of its time. In this new and merciless commercial world no quarter is given and one of the best speeches in the play is given to the Mistress of the Brothel who points out that in strictly financial terms her trade is the most soundly based of all as there is always a demand for it. 'She sells such divine virtues as virginity, modesty and such rare gems, and those not like a petty chapman, by retail, but like a great merchant, by wholesale.' At the end of the play the Dutch Courtesan, who has first been ruthlessly cast off by her lover and then mauled by his friend (who found he could keep to his sexual principles so long as he was not exposed to temptation), attempts to kill her erring lover for which she goes to prison and he is rewarded with a young wife bringing a large dowry.

Another variation on the theme of women for sale is

The Swan Theatre stage c. 1596 (Johann de Witt's sketch copied by Arend van Burrell)

The Rose Theatre (reconstruction) as built in 1587 (Painting by C. Walter Hodges)

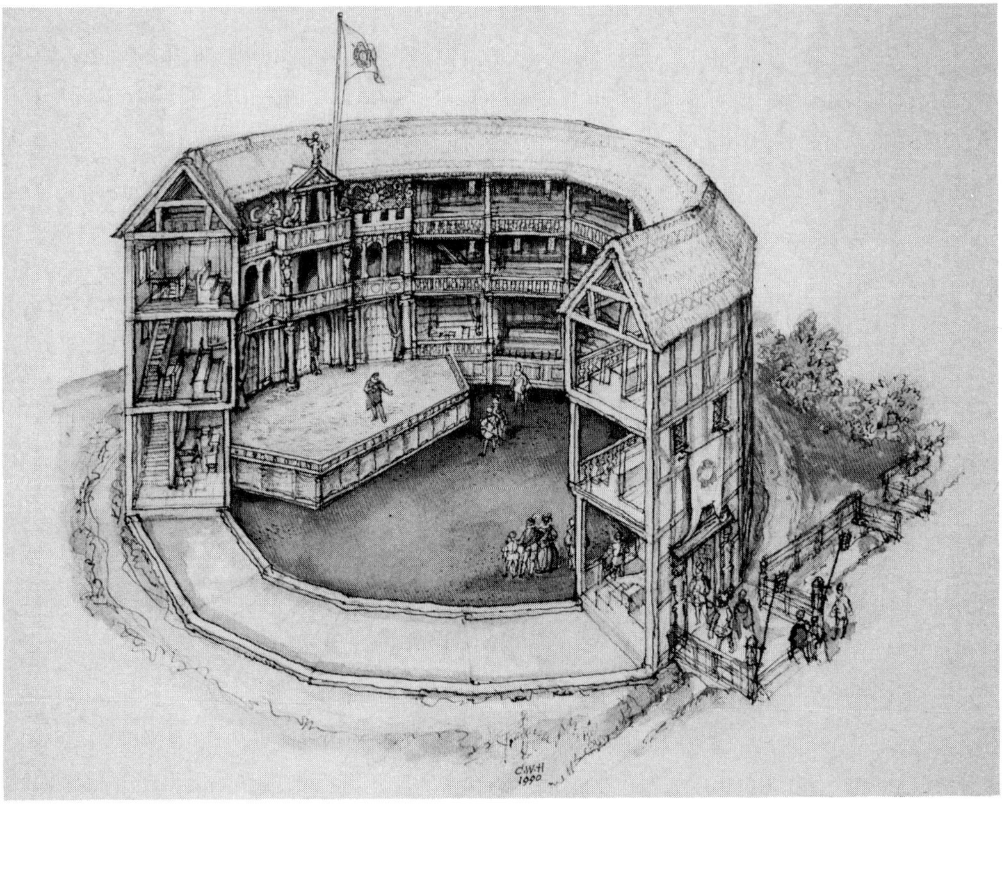

The Spanish Tragedie

OR,

Hieronimo is mad againe.

Containing the lamentable end of *Don Horatio*, and *Belimperia*; with the pittifull death of *Hieronimo*.

Newly corrected, amended, and enlarged with new Additions of the *Painters* part, and others, as it hath of late been diuers times acted.

LONDON,

Printed by W. White, for I. White and T. Langley, and are to be sold at their Shop ouer against the Sarazens head without New-gate. 1615.

The Spanish Tragedy title page

THE LAMENTA-BLE AND TRVE TRA-GEDIE OF M. AR-DEN OF FEVERSHAM IN KENT.

Who was moſt wickedlye murdered, by the meanes of his diſloyall and wanton *wyfe, who for the loue ſhe bare to one* Moſbie, hyred two deſperat ruf-fins Blackwill and Shakbag, *to kill him.*

Wherin is ſhewed the great mal-lice and diſcimulation of a wicked wo-man, the vnſatiable deſire of filthie luſt and the ſhamefull end of all murderers.

Imprinted at London for Edward White, dwelling at the lyttle North dore of Paules Church at the ſigne of the Gun. 1592.

*

Arden of Faversham title page

Putative portrait of Christopher Marlowe (By permission of the Master, Fellows and Scholars of Corpus Christi, Cambridge)

Edward Elleyn (By permission of the Governors of Dulwich Picture Gallery)

Richard Burbage (By permission of the Governors of Dulwich Picture Gallery)

Thomas Middleton

George Chapman

Richard Tarlton (British Library) (above left)

William Kempe, 1600 (British Library) (middle left)

Moll Frith, the 'Roaring Girl' (above)

Caricature of Richard Greene (left)

A Game at Chess title page

The Maids Tragedie.

AS IT HATH BEENE
diuers times Acted at the *Black-Friers* by
the Kings Maiesties Seruants.

Newly perused, augmented, and inlarged, This second Impression.

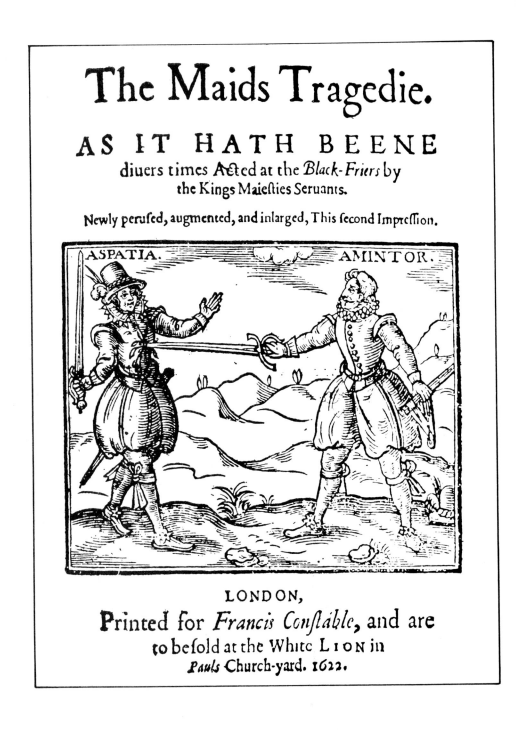

LONDON,
Printed for *Francis Constable*, and are
to be sold at the White LION in
Pauls Church-yard. 1622.

The Maid's Tragedy title page

Middleton's *A Trick to Catch the Old One*, thought to have been written early in 1605. The heroine is referred to throughout only as 'the Courtesan', although that is not strictly true. She has been seduced by her fiancé who then refused to marry her. Ruined in the eyes of her family, she comes to London where she lets it be known that she is a widow with a huge fortune and in no time at all attracts all the fortune hunters. To their surprise she settles on the unpleasant old miser, Walkadine Hoard, who is planning to add her supposed fortune to his immense wealth. By the time he finds out she has nothing it is too late but, as she tells him, she had never actually told him she was rich. Since he is an old man she is likely to find herself a rich young widow.

* * *

The exact dating of almost all Shakespeare's plays remains a matter of academic contention, but the most general consensus is that what are known as the 'great tragedies' were written between 1599/1600 and 1604, beginning with *Hamlet*, then going on to *Othello* and *King Lear*. Students wrestling with the texts of the three plays and the undoubted difficulties surrounding *Measure for Measure*, written during the same period, should know that their author was not spending all his time racked by the creative process, but was also busy consolidating himself as a man of property, culminating on 24 July 1605 with the purchase of thirty-one years of a ninety-two-year lease on part of the Stratford Tithes for the sum of £440.[1] This gave him a claim to one tenth of the annual produce of a number of fields, tithes which could be paid in wool, hemp, flax or wheat, or in money. He was thus assured of a regular income. Also that year he took out a summons against Philip Rogers for a debt of 35s.10d. for 'measures of malt unpaid for'. This was heard in the Court of Record, a sort of Collection Agency and one in which John Shakespeare had figured all too often in the past. Not surprisingly, William does not appear to have travelled to Stratford on such a trivial matter, leaving it to his lawyer to sort out.[2]

Shakespeare might well have found 1605 significant for reasons other than the purchase of the Stratford tithes and the first night of *King Lear.* For many years he had broken his journey to and from Stratford with an overnight stay in Oxford, where he would put up at the Cross Tavern. Now let John Aubrey tell what was common gossip:

> Sir William Davenant, Knight, Poet Laureate, was born in the city of Oxford in the Cross Tavern ... His father was John Davenant, a Vintner there, a very grave and discreet citizen; his mother was a very beautiful woman, of a very good wit and of conversation extremely agreeable.
>
> Mr. William Shakespeare was wont to go into Warwickshire once a year and did commonly in his journey lie at this house in Oxon, where he was exceedingly respected. Now Sir William would sometimes, when he was pleasant over a glass of wine with his most intimate friends, say that it seemed to him that he wrote with the very spirit that did Shakespeare, and seemed contented enough to be thought his son. He would tell them this story as above, in which way his mother had a very light report, whereby she was called a whore.[3]

The suggestion that Sir William Davenant was not only Shakespeare's godson (which he was) but his natural son dates back at least to Aubrey but a recent book on Davenant by Mary Edmond has thrown up fascinating research material.[4] It has generally been assumed that Shakespeare's relationship with the Davenants dates from the later years of his career and, whatever the truth regarding the parentage of young William, was entirely practical: Oxford was the most sensible place to break his journey and the Cross an obvious and comfortable choice.

Evidence now suggests that he knew the Davenants in London from the mid-1590s for they did not move to Oxford until about 1600. Nor is the picture of the honest provincial tavernkeeper and the pretty buxom ale wife anything like an accurate one for the Davenants were substantial city people, merchant venturers, in on the founding of the Muscovy Company. Two cousins, both confusingly called John and one of whom was the father of the Davenant who kept the Cross Inn and Tavern in Oxford, travelled extensively in Russia and Persia and also imported wine from France.

Jennet Davenant was married in 1593. Her maiden name was Shepherd and she came from a family which originated in Durham but had long been official members of the Royal Household. She had three brothers, Thomas and Richard, who were Court embroiderers, glovers and perfumiers, and William who had a responsible post as overseer of the buying of provisions for all the royal palaces. She also had a sister, Phyllis.

Thomas and John Davenant lived first in Maiden Lane, noted for its fine merchants' houses, running a superior tavern on the corner which had once belonged to the Chaucer family. The appalling infant mortality statistics are made evident in Jennet's obstetric history: between Christmas 1593 and Christmas 1597 she gave birth to five infants, all of whom were either stillborn or died shortly after birth. Regular payments of 3s.4d. are noted in the parish book 'for ground and tolling of the bell'. The fifth baby lived long enough to be christened John on 24 October 1597 but was buried on 11 December. A sixth child, and second John, born in 1599, lived only a few months.

Here there is a further reference to Emilia Lanier's doctor Simon Foreman, for Jennet and her sister-in-law, Ursula Shepherd, went to him for advice in 1597. There is no record of Jennet's ailment but Ursula paid several visits to discuss her infertility, finally convincing herself that she was pregnant. 'She hath not been well,' he wrote, 'she supposeth herself with child and is very big but I think it a false conception.'[5] He was right and she died in 1601 and is buried in St Bride's Church off Fleet Street.

So how likely is it that Shakespeare knew the Davenants in London? Mary Edmond suggests there is every possibility. As well as the tavern on Maiden Lane the Davenants had a house on Three Cranes Wharf right opposite the Globe, while John Davenant was described by a contemporary as being 'an admirer and lover of plays and playmakers, especially Shakespeare'.

Sometime in 1600, for whatever reason and possibly to see if a different environment might help them have a live child, the Davenants moved to Oxford. Here again the notion of nothing more than an ordinary tavern is very wide of the mark. The Davenants kept both the Cross Inn and the Cross Tavern, both of which stood on the main route through Oxford. The Inn was indeed primarily an ale house with accommodation for travellers, but the Tavern was extremely grand with more than twenty rooms, with 'twelve hearths and twenty windows', a fine parlour, 'the Sherrif's Chamber', a large panelled dining chamber on the first floor, and a panelled gallery joining the front of the building to the back and the kitchen and stillrooms. Above the gallery were grand bedrooms – the Elm Chamber, the Great Chamber by the Court, the White Chamber and the 'Painted Room', with its splendid murals. Since there were no Common Rooms in the universities of the day, their place was taken by the better taverns, including the Cross, so there would be no shortage of good talk. Ordinary travellers did not lodge at the Tavern, the splendid bedrooms being reserved for special guests or friends, which puts Shakespeare on a footing other than that of an ordinary traveller.

The move proved beneficial to Jennet who went on to have a further seven children all of whom survived, the first of the second set being a daughter, Jane, christened at St Martin's, Carfax, on 11 February 1601.

Is it really possible that William, born in 1605, was Shakespeare's son? Many of his plays contain joking allusions to doubtful paternity but it was a common enough joke of the period. Mary Edmond notes that there have been those who have suggested romantic assignations between William and Jennet in the Painted Room but there is unlikely ever to be any proof. What is certain is that he willingly stood Godfather to young William and the child, who grew up to be the leading playwright of the next generation, was proud to have it thought he might be Shakespeare's son and never denied it when questioned, even though it showed his mother might be 'light'. But then it could hardly hinder an ambitious would-be playwright from the provinces to have it thought he might well be the son of the greatest poet the country had ever known.

* * *

Ben Jonson would also remember 1605 for it was the year of *Eastward Ho!* The 'Ho!' plays, as they are known (*Northward, Westward* and *Eastward*), take their titles from the shouts of the watermen touting for trade. *Eastward Ho!* was written for the Children of Her Majesty's Revels and most probably put on at the Blackfriars Theatre. Children's companies were very popular and Jonson had written for them before both on his own and with others. On this occasion he collaborated with Marston and Chapman. It is hardly surprising that with three ingenious authors there are three intricate plots One concerns Gertrude, the daughter of Touchstone, the goldsmith, an extremely dim girl with a head stuffed full of romances and the latest fashions. She is married off to Sir Petronel Flash, who loves a married woman, but is hard up and seeking a fortune. The second plot follows the progress of a disreputable group of adventurers about to set off to make their fortunes in the New World, while the third deals with Touchstone's two apprentices. The strands of all three plots are drawn together when almost all the characters take part in a wild night of carousel before the ship sails for the New World in the teeth of an enormous gale. It is promptly wrecked and the passengers, convinced they have been washed up on the French shore, address the inhabitants in Franglais, to discover that they have only got as far as the Isle of Dogs. It reads as harmless enough stuff now.

Presumably its authors thought so too but one of them, most probably Jonson, was unable to resist throwing in disparaging comments about 'the King's thirty pound knights' and dim Scotsmen. It was bound to cause offence to a King sensitive to every breath of criticism, especially when put on by a company which had royal approval.

Sir James Murray, a royal favourite, took it particularly badly and rushed to bring it to the attention of the King, who promptly ordered the arrest of the playwrights. This is Jonson's version of what happened next, as told to the poet William Drummond on a visit to Scotland later.

'He was reported,' writes Drummond,

> 'by Sir James Murray to the King for writing something against the Scots in a play, *Eastward Ho!*, and voluntarily imprisoned himself with Chapman and Marston, who had written it amongst them. The report was that they should have then had their ears cut and noses. After their delivery, he banqueted his friends with Camden, Selden and others. At the midst of the feast his old mother drank to him and showed him a paper, which she had (if the sentence had taken execution) to have mixed in the prison among his drink, which was full of lusty poison and that she was no churl, she told him for she minded first to have drunk of it herself.[6]

What a chivalrous picture! Jonson, not even the author of the piece, voluntarily imprisoning himself, rushing to put himself in the firing line with his two friends; his dear old mother prepared to poison herself and him, rather than have him suffer the disgrace of having his ears cut off and his nose slit. Great stuff...

The reality, however, as was often the case with Jonson, was somewhat different. The tale he had told Drummond was believed right up until 1901 when letters from Chapman and Jonson addressed to various members of the nobility, from their prison, turned up in a collection of seventeenth-century manuscripts owned by a Mr T.A. White of New York. First it seems that Marston was never imprisoned at all, secondly there is no confirmation whatsoever that Jonson went to prison of his own free will and, so far from playing the swaggerer while in gaol, he spent his entire time writing obsequious letters pleading with a variety of titled people to get him out.[7]

A typical letter is that addressed to 'The Most-Noble Virtuous and Thrice-Honoured Earl of Salisbury'. After a general preamble, Jonson continues:

> I am here, most honoured Lord, unexamined and unheard, committed to a vile prison, and with me a gentleman (whose name may perhaps have come to your Lordship), one, Mr. George Chapman, a learned and honest man. The cause (would I could name some worthier, though I wish we had known none worthy of imprisonment), is (the word irks me that our fortune have necessitated us to so despised a course) a play, my Lord …

There is much more in the same vein. In conclusion he writes:

> But lest I being too diligent for my excuse I may incur the suspicion of being guilty, I become a most humble suitor to your Lordship that with the honourable Lord Chamberlain (to whom I have in like manner petitioned), you will be pleased to be the grateful means of our coming answer; or if in your wisdom it shall be thought unnecessary, that your Lordship will be the most honoured cause of our liberty. Where freeing us from one prison you shall remove us to another; which is eternally to bind us and our muses, to the thankful honouring of you and yours to posterity; as your own virtues have by many descents of ancestors ennobled you to time.
>
> Your Honour's most devoted in heart and words
>
> Ben Jonson.

Whether it was this, other masterpieces of crawling sycophancy or the more restrained correspondence from Chapman that got them out, we do not know, but the men did not languish in gaol for much longer and by the beginning of October 1605 they had been released.

Whether or not Jonson did throw a party of his own, as

he told Drummond, we have no way of knowing since we only have his word on which to rely, but on 9 October he certainly attended one. It was given by Robert Catesby, one of the conspirators in the Gunpowder Plot which had been timed to take place not quite four weeks later. One feels only Jonson could have gone straight from prison to such an event and in such company.

* * *

The year ended on a deeply unpleasant note. Cecil, even more firmly entrenched now under James, was faced once again with the prospect of a country riddled with intrigue and threatened by plots. There had already been one failed coup. The myth of the unlucky Guy Fawkes and the other conspirators being fortuitously discovered under the Houses of Parliament with their gunpowder is just that, a myth. Maybe Cecil remembered how his predecessor, Walsingham, had finally ended the Catholic plots by placing an *agent provocateur* in the Babington circle.

There seems little doubt now that at the very least he had an informer among the Gunpowder Plotters, even more likely that he did infiltrate an *agent provocateur* to encourage them. So, however delightful the idea, there was never a chance that the conspirators would succeed in blowing up Parliament. Instead they walked straight into a trap and paid a terrible price for it. Guy Fawkes's signed 'confession' ranks alongside that of Thomas Kyd in the chill it arouses. Both signatures are scrawled in the hands of men broken by torture.

17

The Roaring Girl

It is obvious that the role of women in the theatrical scene was very much a subsidiary one. Poor Emma Ball is remembered only for her associations with men – as brother of a highwayman, mistress to Tarleton and lover to Robert Greene, and the mother of his son. We know little or nothing of the playwrights' wives except that Greene left his, yet appealed to her on his death bed; Jonson and his 'honest shrew' also appear to have separated, while Shakespeare of necessity could have spent only limited time with Anne until the last years of his life.

As there was still no question of women becoming actresses their place was firmly in an audience and even there, attitudes had changed little in the previous twenty years, as is shown in a verse attributed to John Lane:

> If he could paint spotless Chastity truly
> The light-tailed housewives which like Sirens sing,
> And like to Circes with their drugs enchant,
> Would not unto the Bankside's round house fling,
> In open sight themselves to show and vaunt,
> Then there, I say, they would not marked go,
> Though unseen, to see those they fain would know.[1]

In 1622 Henry Peacham repeated a version of a story which had circulated earlier:

> A tradesman's wife of the Exchange, one day when her husband was following some business in the city,

> desired him he would give her leave to go and see a play, which she had not done in seven years. He bade her take his apprentice along with her, and go; but especially to have a care of her purse which she warranted she would. Sitting in a box, among some gallants and gallants' wenches, and returning when the play was done, she returned to her husband and told him she had lost her purse. 'Wife,' quoth he, 'did I not give you warning of it? How much money was there in it?' Quoth she, 'Truly, four pieces, six shillings and a silver tooth-picker.' Quoth her husband, 'Where did you put it?' 'Under my petticoat, between that and my smock.' 'What,' quoth he, 'did you feel nobody's hand there?' 'Yes,' quoth she, 'I felt one's hand there but did not think he had come for that.'[2]

As well as lack of equality in education and opportunity, seventeenth-century women had other cards stacked against them. Forty-five per cent of women in the early part of the seventeenth century died before they were fifty, according to Roger Hudson in *The Grand Quarrel*, a book of reminiscences of women of that era. Of that forty-five per cent, at least a quarter died in childbirth or just afterwards, while a substantial proportion of the rest died from causes directly attributable to it.

He quotes instances such as that of Catherine, Lady Danby, who died in childbirth at thirty having had sixteen children, six stillborn, and Anne Fanshawe who had fourteen, of whom only five survived. She also suffered four miscarriages, one of triplets.

It would be foolish to pretend that women during the reign of Elizabeth had had an easy time of it, but the women's roles in Shakespeare's plays do suggest that many of them had a fair amount of independence, as instanced by Maria in *Twelfth Night*, and all the women in *The Merry Wives of Windsor* and were based on reality. Upper-class women and those of the nobility had almost always been brought up to think it their duty to make appropriate marriages but under the new Jacobean regime it was clear that women were now considered marketable commodities either for marriage or sex outside it.

The men who bought themselves honours for cash also bought themselves women. Pimps and procuresses thrived. At the bottom of the heap a young laundress might earn herself sixpence in some dark corner or alleyway, while at the other extreme an expensive courtesan, such as Venetia Stanley, might demand that hundreds of pounds be spent on her by one lover alone. One young sprig, Sir Pexall Brockas, was said to 'own' a young mignon, 'whom he had entertained and abused since she was twelve years old'.

Not surprisingly, double standards were the rule. Husbands who had happily married a neighbouring heiress for her dowry and ran one or two mistresses took it amiss when their wives strayed from a loveless marriage. An aggrieved husband might challenge his rival to a duel or hire some thugs to beat him up; after which he would soundly thrash his wife. *'Nulle fidere'*, was the motto of the Court, 'Trust None'. The Earl of Worcester is quoted as saying of the Queen's ladies: 'Plotting and malice among them is such, that I think envy hath tied an invisible snake about most of their necks to sting one another to death.' The Court, continued the Earl, was a place filled with 'persons betraying and betrayed'.[3]

While the poorest women struggled to feed their families on a husband's labouring wage of seven pence a day, the hangings of the Countess of Salisbury's bedchamber, white satin embroidered with gold and silver thread and real pearls, cost her husband a cool £14,000 in Jacobean money.

The titles of plays such as Beaumont and Fletcher's *The Woman Hater*, and *The Miseries of Enforced Marriage* both written in 1606, reflect the feeling of the times, while in Ben Jonson's magnificent satirical study of greed, *Volpone*, the supposedly innocent and chaste heroine is all too easily tempted almost to the point of seduction by promises of jewels and wealth. The unhappy young woman in Middleton's *The Spanish Gypsy* is left ruined and friendless after being raped by the man she trusted.

An oddity of the period is *A Yorkshire Tragedy*, another

example of a drama based on a true murder story. It is of interest because it shows that those tragic cases where a husband or wife takes the lives not only of themselves but of their children is not a twentieth-century phenomenon, although there were two well-publicised examples of it in January 1994 alone. The play was once attributed to Shakespeare, though it is hard to see why as it is written in little more than doggerel. It is also short and bleak: a young man who has run through the fortunes of both himself and his wife, and thus faces ruin and imprisonment for debt, kills two of his children, attempts to murder his wife and a third, then turns his knife on himself rather than have them all shamed and his wife and children turned onto the road as paupers. But where we would now look for unbearable pressures and stress or mental breakdown, the Jacobeans sought explanations in demonic possession or inherent evil.

Women fared little better in the solo works of George Chapman (which he dedicated to Thomas and Audrey Walsingham), while Ben Jonson in *Epicene or The Silent Woman,* anticipated by some 400 years the film comedy *Some Like It Hot* in which the bride destined to bring her husband much wealth turns out to be a man.

Beaumont and Fletcher almost alone returned to that jolly world of merchants' wives with *The Knight of the Burning Pestle.* Indeed the main female character in the play is the type of person we have all sat next to in the theatre or cinema, the one who talks loudly throughout the show and tells her friend the plot. In this instance she also tells everyone that her apprentice is a better actor than any on the stage, finally persuading him to join in with the actors and take part in the romance she has come to see.

The difference between all these women and those in the plays of Shakespeare during the same period is marked, for his female characters range from Cleopatra and the chillingly dominant Volumnia *(Coriolanus),* to the enchanting and apparently orphaned Marina who, in *Pericles,* even survives incarceration in a brothel, and the chaste and faithful Imogen in *Cymbeline.* It is, however, difficult to imagine even the most talented boy actor tackling the role of Cleopatra and there is no record of the play actually having been performed in Shakespeare's lifetime, though equally there is no proof that it was not. But it must be safe to assume that the Jacobean dramatists realised that eventually England would follow the Continent in allowing women onto the stage and wrote accordingly. Both A.L. Rowse and the critic Ivor Brown, among others, see in Cleopatra the last appearance of the Dark Lady in Shakespeare's work.[4]

There is one play, however, which really does differ from all the rest in that its heroine is a real person who lived among the players on the Bankside and who, in spite of its being illegal, played herself on stage several times. The woman was Mary Frith and the play is *The Roaring Girl*, written by Middleton and Dekker.

Mary, or Moll as she was usually known, was born in 1584 into the same kind of background as the dramatists among whom she lived and socialised. Like Marlowe, her father was a shoemaker: 'a fair and square conditioned man, that loved a good fellow next to himself, which made his issue so sociable', according to a pamphlet written shortly after her death: *The Life and Death of Mrs. Mary Frith, commonly called Mal Cutpurse exactly collected and now published for the delights and recreations of all merry disposed persons – 1662.*

Although there could not be any grammar school education for a girl,

> particular care was expended on her education, for her boisterous and masculine spirit caused her parents much solicitude. A very Tomrigg and Rumpscuttle she was and delighted and sported in boys' play and pastimes, not minding the company of girls; many a blow and bang this hoyting procured her, but she was not so to be tamed or taken off from her rude inclinations. She could not endure the sedentary life of sewing and stitching, a sampler was as grievous as a winding sheet, her needle, bodkin and thimble, she could not think on quietly, wishing them changed into a sword, dagger

and cudgels.

'She would fight the boys and courageously beat them, run, jump, leap or hop with any of them or any other play whatsoever,' continues the unknown biographer.

Came the day when Moll was expected to repay the family efforts to educate her, first by bringing in money from 'good service', then by marrying a suitable young man. Neither appealed to Moll, nor did housework for 'household work of any kind was distasteful to her and above all she had an abhorrence to the tending of children, to whom she ever had an aversion in her mind equal to the sterility of her womb, never being made a mother to the best of our information.'

So at sixteen Moll ran away from home and embarked on a lifestyle which would have raised eyebrows well into the twentieth century. She wore men's clothes when she felt like it and smoked a pipe. Determined to be able to look after herself, she learned to fence and handle a pistol, becoming a brilliant swordswoman and an excellent shot. She consorted with thieves, vagabonds, cutpurses and other low life, as well as the players and playwrights of the Bankside where she set up home and was roundly condemned by her critics for being 'a bully, whore, bawd, pickpurse, fortune-teller, receiver and forger'.

It was easy for any woman who stepped out of line to be labelled a 'whore', yet although Moll readily admitted to forging, stealing (in an upmarket way) and a variety of confidence tricks, she was always adamant that not only had she never been a whore but would never procure any other girl to be one. There have been suggestions that she was a lesbian; maybe she was bisexual. In any event she had two long-term, male lovers, first 'the notorious Captain Hind, highwayman', and second 'one, Richard Hannam, a worthy who constantly wore a watchmaker and jeweller's shop in his pocket and could at any time command £1,000'. Most interesting of all is that she was also charged with appearing on stage in a play.

Middleton and Decker had written their affectionate

portrait of Moll about 1608 and it is known that from time to time she would sit on a stool on stage while the play was performed, for it is noted in the epilogue that 'Venus, being a woman, passes through the play in doublet and breeches, a brave disguise and a safe one if the statute untie not her codpiece point.' It ends with the lines:

> The Roaring Girl herself, some few days hence,
> Shall on this stage give larger recompense,
> Which mirth that you may share in, herself doth woo
> you,
> And craves this sign, your hand, to beckon her to you.

This had been thought to mean that Moll might sometimes have got up from her stageside stool and sang a song, perhaps even have performed the 'jig', which still ended a play, but later reading of the Court Indictment suggests she had on some occasions actually taken part in a performance. It would have been quite in character for her to do something so outrageously against the law.

The Indictment states that she had appeared on the stage of the Fortune Theatre nine months earlier and there is no explanation as to why the case took so long to come to court. A man called John Chamberlain writes in a letter to his friend, dated 12 February:

> this Sunday Moll Cutpurse, a notorious baggage that was used to go in men's apparel, was brought to St Paul's Cross, where she wept bitterly and seemed very penitent, but it is since doubted this was so but that she was maudlin drunk, being discovered to have tippled some three quarts of sack before she came to her penance.
>
> She had the daintiest preacher, or ghostly father, that ever I saw in a pulpit, one Ratcliffe of Brazen Nose of Oxford, a likelier man to have led the revels in some Masque at court than to be where he was, but the best is he did so extremely badly and so wearied his audience that the best part went away and the rest tarried to hear Moll Cutpurse rather than himself.

After this starring role at St Paul's Cross, Moll was removed from circulation, spending six months in Bridewell Prison beating hemp while being urged to ponder on her sins. On her release, she immediately returned to the players, continuing to eat with them in the ordinaries and drink with them in the taverns. She was, and would remain, their friend.

The underlying theme of *The Roaring Girl* is, again, sex and money but its main purpose is to provide a vehicle for the character of Moll. The adjective 'roaring', usually used in the context of 'a roaring boy', meant literally a noisy, lively, boisterous person. Three plots are twisted into a single strand: Laxton, a womaniser, seduces every woman he comes across and brags about it; a young man wants to marry his sweetheart but is forbidden to do so by his father who has planned a wealthy match for him; an unfortunate prodigal, Jack Dapper, is attempting to stay out of a debtor's prison. Dekker, who spent a considerable amount of time in one, would have been able to provide plenty of in-depth research for the last.

Much use is made of the Three Pigeons at Brentford as a place of assignation, the additional in-joke being that the tavern in question was actually kept by an actor, John Lowin, a member of the cast. Lowin was also famed for playing Falstaff and Mohammed. The Three Pigeons long outlasted its Jacobean topicality and was still being portrayed as a place of assignation well into the eighteenth century. Indeed in Oliver Goldsmith's *She Stoops to Conquer* the whole trail of comic misunderstandings arises out of the fact that the hero mistakes the Hardcastles' home for the Three Pigeons, and thus triggers off the events of the play's sub-title, *The Mistakes of a Night.*

By the end of the play Moll has solved everyone's problems, but the high spot is her trouncing of the libidinous Laxton who, having met her in women's clothes, makes an assignation with her only to find, when he turns up ready to enjoy himself, that the object of his desire is now dressed as a man and is insisting on fighting a duel. When he finally agrees, he finds he is not only hopelessly outclassed but his antagonist insists on telling him exactly what she thinks of men like him, on behalf of all women:

...thou art one of those,
That thinks each woman thy fond flexible whore;
If she but cast a liberal eye upon thee,
Turn back her head, she's thine: or amongst company
By chance drink first to thee, then she's quite gone.
There is no means to help her; nay, for a need,
Will swear unto thy credulous fellow lechers
That thou art more in favour with the lady
At first sight, than her monkey all her lifetime.
How many of our sex, by such as thou,
Have had their good thoughts paid with a blasted name,
That never deserved so lowly? Or did trip
In path of whoredom beyond cup and lip,
But for the stain of conscience and of soul?

Moll outlasted most of her contemporaries, for long after both Middleton and Dekker were dead, and she in her fifties, she acted as a courier and spy for the Royalist cause during the Civil War. She is authentically reported to have harried and set upon parties of Parliamentarians, and once actually robbed General Fairfax on Hounslow Heath, shooting him in the arm and killing the two horses on which his servants were riding. She was then hotly pursued by some officers, finally apprehended at Turnham Green and promptly sent to Newgate. The obvious end for such highway robbery would have been the scaffold, but not in her case. Her sheer nerve and spirit so appealed to Fairfax that he allowed her to be ransomed for £2,000 – a truly enormous sum for those days.

She lived to a ripe old age, dying at her small home in Fleet Street at the age of seventy-four on 26 July 1659, and was buried in St Bride's churchyard, appropriately now the journalists' church. As her last act she willed £20 'so that the conduits might run with wine on the restoration of the King'. T.S. Eliot said of her play persona: 'She is always real. She may rant, she may behave preposterously, but she remains a type of the sort of woman who has renounced all happiness for herself and who lives only for a principle . . . a real and unique human being.'

Even theatre historian Una Ellis-Fermor, who did not much like the play, says of Middleton and Moll: 'He can see simultaneously the fierce, active virginity in a character like Moll and can draw it clearly without scoffing at it as a pretence or fantasy.'[5] From start to finish of the play Moll remains absolutely true to herself and, presumably, to the life. There is nothing else like her in the whole canon of Jacobean drama.

* * *

On 5 June 1607 Shakespeare's elder daughter, Susannah, married the distinguished physician Dr John Hall; the couple's fine house, Hall's Croft, still stands in Stratford. It was an excellent match for Hall, also an Oxford MA, had patients among the very best families in Warwickshire. On 21 February 1608, just seven weeks after that bitterly cold burial of Edmund Shakespeare on the Bankside, Susannah gave birth to a daughter, Elizabeth, Shakespeare's first grandchild. There were to be no more children. Whether she ever became pregnant again but was unable to carry a child to term we do not know. There would have been little or nothing that could be done about it then even when, as in this instance, the father was himself a doctor.

18

William Shakespeare, Resident Dramatist

In 1609 Thomas Thorpe published 'Shakes-speares Sonnets – Never before imprinted. At London'. There are still those who do not believe that Shakespeare wrote his own works preferring, among others, Sir Francis Bacon, the Earl of Oxford and, like Calvin Hoffman, Christopher Marlowe from exile. Indeed, one theory put forward during the events to mark the quatercentenary of Marlowe's death was that Marlowe wrote the first part of the Shakespeare canon and Jonson the second, a variation on this theme having Jonson kill Marlowe in a duel...

Yet what such romantics refuse to accept is that Shakespeare's work is credited to him by those who knew and worked with him. To pass off other people's work as your own for twenty-five years demands deception on a scale unknown in any other artistic endeavour. What his contemporary Frances Meres described as the 'sugr'd sonnets' had been widely read by the poet's friends before being finally collected together for publication.

If you argue that the William Shakespeare who bought and leased property in Stratford and London did not necessarily have anything to do with the theatre, then why is he listed as a Sharer in the companies first of the Lord Chamberlain's, and then the King's Men? Why were plays in his name registered at Stationer's Hall, or payments to him listed in Court records where he was paid after performances along with Burbage? Who is William Shakespeare the actor whose name appears opposite that of Mr Knowell in the first performance of Jonson's *Every Man in his Humour?* Contrary to popular repute, it is not difficult to find documentary evidence of Shakespeare's activities.[1]

Not least, of course, would have been the difficulty of carrying on such a deception among the actors with whom he worked for so long. The Elizabethan and Jacobean stage may not have had directors as we understand them today but they most certainly had rehearsals at which someone told them what they had to do. Most often this would have been Burbage himself but there is little doubt that this task must also have fallen to the author of the piece, especially as he was also an actor himself. The process of putting on a play from first draft through script changes to performance has not changed so drastically that Shakespeare would not then, as now, have discussed his new play with those who were going to appear in it.

That Shakespeare was a working dramatist, indeed the first 'house' dramatist, is important for in the enormous body of work devoted to Shakespeare criticism and commentary, where the meaning and nuance of everything from an entire play to the smallest phrase is examined in minute detail, discussions over timescales and exits and entrances worried over, consideration is rarely given to the fact that he must have had to concern himself with the practicalities of acting and the technicalities of staging.

An average playing company of fifteen, plus apprentices, would have meant the doubling and trebling of roles in such large cast plays and, simply in order to get actors on and offstage, adjustments must have had to be made to the text. Lines, even whole scenes, might be judged not to work even late into rehearsal and have to be written at speed while the dramatist was actually sitting there in the playhouse with the actors on stage. How could anyone pass off another's work as his own in such circumstances?

Rather than always seeking an academic reason for supposedly flawed scenes, it would be useful to imagine that resident playwright at work and with no time, frantically making script changes while leaving it to the Bookkeeper to come up with a clean, fair copy. It is accepted that pirating, bad copying and poor memories have contributed to some of the problems we have with Shakespeare's texts, but little consideration has been given to the circumstances in which he must have had to work.

What is also clear is that in a literary world given to gossip and backbiting, he continued to be referred to as a most pleasant man and a witty man. He is called 'friendly Shakespeare' and 'good Will', while John Davies of Hereford said of him:

> And though the stage doth stain pure gentle blood,
> Yet generous ye are in mind and mood.[2]

Towards the end of the seventeenth century and into the next there were numerous anecdotal stories about Shakespeare still in circulation and Thomas Fuller in his *Worthies of England* wrote:

> Many were the wit combats betwixt him and Ben Jonson, which two I behold like a Spanish great galleon, and an English man-of-war; Master Jonson, like the former, was built far higher in learning: solid, but slow in his performances. Shakespeare, with the English man-of-war, lesser in bulk, but lighter still in sailing, could turn with all tides, tack about and take advantage of all winds, by the quickness of his wit and invention.

Another, a meeting of Shakespeare and Jonson in a tavern, has Jonson writing down his own epitaph, beginning 'Here lies Ben Jonson that was once one', whereupon Shakespeare takes the pen from him and adds:

> Who while he lived was a slow thing,
> And now being dead is no thing.

The handful of portraits of actors and dramatists of the day, almost all painted by unknown artists, are touching in that no attempt is made to flatter the subject, as would have been the case with a wealthy commission. The face of

Christopher Marlowe would be arresting even if we knew nothing of his history while that of Burbage ('Master Burbig – his head' is scrawled on the back of the panel) is one that would pass unnoticed in the street: like many great actors he became what he played. Ben Jonson looks as one might expect, fleshy, round-faced and florid, while Shakespeare's surviving likeness could, with its high domed forehead, be that of an academic. What are known as the 'Flower' portrait and the Droeshout engraving, possibly one having been taken from the other, present an oval-faced man of about forty with strong features and large dark eyes whose remaining hair falls to his shoulders.

He was still buying property at the time of the publication of the sonnets and had acquired cottages in Chapel Street, around the corner from New Place, and land a few miles away near the village of Rowington. There is nothing to say when he gave up acting though presumably he must have been competent enough to keep his place in the company for a number of years. It is likely he was a reliable, but not outstanding actor, capable of playing modest roles well. Apart from Master Knowell in *Every Man in his Humour*, we have only hearsay evidence as to what parts he did play. His brother Gilbert, the haberdasher, who visited London to see Will's plays and watch him act (and possibly Edmund too) is said to have told a neighbour that he had seen Will play Adam in *As You Like It*, and that he was 'brought on to the stage on another man's back', presumably that of the actor playing Orlando. Theatre tradition also gives him the Ghost in *Hamlet* and far more showy and unlikely roles, Mercutio in *Romeo and Juliet* and Berowne in *Love's Labour's Lost*.

Actor Ian Richardson, however, who played a splendid Berowne in the Royal Shakespeare Company's 1975 production of the play, feels that it might be possible:

> It stands out above all the Shakespeare roles I've ever played, as being the one I loved most and curiously enough, it does seem to me that my growing awareness of what Shakespeare is about, my coincidental knowl-

> edge of what he himself must have been about, all that had gone before in learning about the man and his works was in some strange way a preparation for one role – playing the man himself. I know there is some scholarly dispute about that but I think Dr Rowse would agree. Here is Shakespeare talking, here he is with all his verbal quips . . . it is the only Shakespeare role I have played where, on the last performance, I wept.[3]

Another actor, Richard Huggett, has an even more unusual suggestion regarding *Macbeth*, the play specifically written to flatter the new King James, by praising his ancestry (through Banquo) and his interest in witchcraft. Huggett believes that immediately before the first performance before the King in 1606 the boy actor playing Lady Macbeth fell ill with a fever, and that the only possible substitute at such short notice was the author himself. He writes: 'Since he had written the play himself and had directed rehearsals, it could hopefully be assumed that he had more than a passing acquaintance with the text and with its four brief scenes. Lady Macbeth is the shortest leading part he ever wrote.'[4]

Huggett attributes the information to John Aubrey and gives the name of the boy player as Hal Berridge. It has not been possible to confirm Aubrey as the source, even with the diligent assistance of the staff of the Shakespeare Centre in Stratford. Mr Huggett, when referred to, suggests it may have been seen in unpublished fragments of Aubrey and also that there is a reference to it in a letter written by King Christian of Denmark which is in the Danish Royal Archives.[5] It remains therefore only a tantalising possibility.

By the end of the first decade of the seventeenth century, Shakespeare's great tragedies were behind him and only a handful of plays remained to be written, though that his early plays remained popular is shown by Frances Meres who writes of seeing *The Comedy of Errors*, one of 'his six excellent comedies', adding that 'the sweet witty soul of Ovid lives in mellifluous and honey-tongued Shakespeare'.[6]

Dr Simon Foreman also noted visits to Shakespeare plays. He saw *Macbeth* at the Globe on 20 April 1611: 'First came "Macbeth and Banquo, two noblemen of Scotland, riding through a wood and there stood before them three women fairies or nymphs. And saluted Macbeth saying three times unto him, "Hail, Macbeth, king of Cawdor; for thou shalt be a king but beget not kings, etc . . ."' He follows this with a detailed resumé of the plot in which he notes that Lady Macbeth cannot wash the blood off her hands: 'Observe also how Macbeth's Queen did rise in the night in her sleep, and walked and talked and confessed all. And the doctor noted her words.'

A few days later, on an unspecified date, he saw *Cymbeline*, and on 20 April 1611 *Richard II*, obviously back in repertoire. On 15 May of the same year he went to *The Winter's Tale* and gives us our first picture of Autolycus, that snapper-up of unconsidered trifles. 'Remember how also the rogue that came in all tattered like Coll Pixie; how he feigned him sick and to have been robbed of all he had. How he cozened the poor man of all his money. And, after, came to the sheep-shearing with a pedlar's pack and there cozened them again of all their money. How he changed apparel with the King of Bohemia's son, and then how he turned courtier, etc.' He ends with a memo to self: 'beware of trusting feigned beggars or fawning fellows'.

* * *

Foreman's practice continued to be highly successful, his *Casebook* providing interesting links both with theatre people such as Henslowe and Mistress Burbage and those indirectly involved with them. For instance, among his patients was a Mrs Webb who at the time of her visit was the mistress of Marlowe's old patron and lover, Thomas Walsingham. She had wanted to know if he would be true to her. Soon, however, the lady transferred her affections to her doctor who described her as 'very fair, of good stature, plump face, little mouth; desired to go gay [in its original meaning], and to have many jewels, fare well and keep good company'. Her husband, he noted, was a 'tall, slender, honest man' who had given her 'eight or nine children'. Foreman notes: 'Haleked Martha Webb 15 March at ten past two p.m. plene and volenter [fully and freely].' How exact! Was there a clock in the bedchamber? If so, did he look at it after the lady had removed much of her clothing, for making love in a seventeenth-century corset would have been crippling. Or did he note the time in his consulting room, before rushing her up the stairs?

Shakespeare's landlady also consulted Foreman. Her name was Mistress Mountjoy and her husband, Christopher, was a wig and head-dress maker, possibly also supplying both for the theatres. Mountjoy was of Huguenot stock and his shop is shown on Ralph Agas's pictorial map of London as being on the corner of Silver Street and Mugle Street.

Mistress Mountjoy had first consulted Foreman back in 1597 when she lost out of her purse 'a gold hoop ring and a French crown'. She wanted him to divine where they might be. Ten days later she returned, this time for a medical consultation, saying she was suffering from pains in her head, side and stomach, along with weakness of the legs. Foreman diagnosed: 'She seems to be pregnant for eleven weeks – seven weeks more and it will come from her, or stay hardly [with difficulty].' If she was, then she never carried the pregnancy through, as there was no child. Over the years she consulted him about both her own and her husband's health; if a would-be lover was serious about her, and if that was the case, whether she should grant him her favours; and later, whether she should join forces with a female friend to set up a shop of their own. If Dr Foreman haleked her, he made no note of it.

* * *

Shakespeare lodged with the Mountjoys for a number of years and in 1604 he had been a witness to the 'handfast betrothal' of their daughter, Mary, and to the subsequent negotiations over the girl's dowry. Mary was engaged to Stephen Bellott, her father's apprentice, also from a Huguenot family. Mountjoy was described as a 'stranger', i.e. foreigner and not a 'denizen' of the Bankside, while Shakespeare, who had encouraged the match, gave his status as 'gentleman of Stratford-upon-Avon'.[7]

The marriage was not happy and soon Stephen and Mountjoy were quarrelling over Mary's dowry of £60, which Stephen claimed had never been paid to him; he also alleged that Mountjoy had not kept his promise to change his will to leave his son-in-law £200. All the couple had received was £10 and 'some household stuffe'. By 1612 the matter had still not been resolved and so Stephen took his father-in-law to court.

Shakespeare's role in the matter was described by the Mountjoys' servant, Joan, who 'remembreth the defendant did send and persuade one Mr. Shakespeare that lay in the house to persuade the plaintiff to the same marriage'. This was backed up by friends of the family and among the sheaf of documents referring to the case, there is Shakespeare's own deposition in the form of written answers to a series of questions. In it he states that he had known the Mountjoys for ten years or thereabouts, and that during that time Stephen Bellott 'did well and honestly behave himself'. Mountjoy, says Shakespeare, often spoke well of his apprentice and had encouraged the marriage and he, Shakespeare, had supported Mountjoy in pressing for it. He deposed that Mountjoy had promised a proportion of money and goods but could not remember the amount. He did not know anything about a promise in the will to pay Bellott £200 or what the household goods were that were given to the young couple on their marriage. He signed himself 'Willm Shakp.'

As is often the case with such litigation nobody seems to have come out of it well. The court adjudged Mountjoy should pay Bellott only twenty nobles (£6.13s.4d.).

These documents, unearthed by Professor Charles Wallace in 1909 among the records of the Courts of Requests, provide proof that Shakespeare lived on the Bankside for at least ten years but tells us little more about him even though his name appears twenty-six times. The discovery led to suggestions that Shakespeare named his herald in *Henry V* 'Mountjoy' after his landlord but the dates are wrong for Shakespeare was still living north of the river when he wrote the play.

The Shakespeare of the Globe and Blackfriars was also the William Shakespeare, gentleman of Stratford-upon-Avon. John Shakespeare had died in 1601. His mother followed in 1608 and if William was not there when she died, as the eldest son it would be unthinkable that he would not have returned home for the funeral and to see to the disposition of her goods. In the October of that year he stood Godfather to the infant son of Alderman Henry Walker, the child being called William after him.

In *William Shakespeare* Rowse puts a good case for his having written *Coriolanus* in Stratford at New Place, not only because it contains much country detail but also because, unusually, he gives elaborate stage directions with notes for positions, movements and even gestures. Rowse suggests that as he could not be present at its rehearsal, he was giving detailed instructions to someone else, presumably Burbage.

During the next few years there were other melancholy pilgrimages to the Waterside and Holy Trinity Church. Shakespeare's surviving brothers both died young. The Burial Register for Stratford notes that Gilbert died in 1612 at the age of forty-five and was followed in 1613 by Richard, who was thirty-nine. Gilbert is described as 'adolescens', which meant bachelor. With the exception of Joan, the children of John and Mary Shakespeare were not blessed with long life.

In 1613 Shakespeare made his last major purchase, a smart house in Blackfriars. This big property, conveyed to him on 10 March of that year, was bought for £140, of which he put £80 down as a deposit, the balance of £60 to be paid off as a mortgage. The Conveyance Deed says: 'The dwelling house, shops, cellars, sollars, plot of ground and all and singular other the premises above, by the presents mentioned, to be bargained and sold and every part and parcel thereof with the appurtenances, unto the said William Shakespeare and William Johnson, John Jackson and John Hemings', the three men providing the sureties for the mortgage. Hemings, as we know, was an actor and fellow Sharer in the King's Men, John Jackson a city merchant, and William Johnson landlord of that favourite tavern of the actors and writers, the Mermaid. They were never called upon to honour their guarantees for Shakespeare paid off his mortgage in full and on time. Shakespeare created a trusteeship for his London property and it has been suggested that by so doing he must have deliberately set out to prevent Anne inheriting it as of right, but this cannot have been the case as, on his death, the trustees sold the property on behalf of his family with the profit going to them.[8]

19

Revenge Plays and City Satires

...in this warm shine
I lie and dream of your full Mermaid wine.
O, we have water mixed with claret lees,
Drink apt to bring in drier heresies
Than beer, good only for the Sonnet's strain,
With fustian metaphors to stuff the brain.

What things have we seen,
Done at the Mermaid! heard words that have been
So nimble, and so full of subtle flame,
As if that every one from whence they came,
Had meant to put his whole wit in a jest . . .

wrote Francis Beaumont to Ben Jonson from the country, where he and Fletcher were busily working on two plays 'then not finished, which deferred their merry meetings at the Mermaid'.

It is easy to romanticise life in Jacobean London. In reality it was a dangerous, noisy place, it stank and through its streets stalked Nashe's King Pest. Yet to be alive and well and writing for the theatre at that time must have been, in its excitement, its exchange of new ideas and sheer joy of creativity, akin to being part of the arts scene in Paris at the turn of the nineteenth century; the nights at the Mermaid, under the benevolent eye of landlord William Johnson, something to be remembered years later. Jonson, puffing as always on his pipe, leaning over the table to exchange witty insults with Francis Beaumont, his voice booming around the bar like a drum in what had become a kind of theatre club with members such as Dekker, Middleton, Webster, Drayton, Fletcher and, presumably, Shakespeare too, since its landlord knew him well enough to stand surety for him.

The Mermaid had its own watersteps and among the boatmen who plied for hire was one, John Taylor, who became known, because of his trade, as 'the water poet'. Born in Gloucester of artisan parents, he had been sent to grammar school but had proved a poor scholar. On leaving, he had been apprenticed to a Thames waterman, a career cut short when he was impressed into the navy for Essex's abortive venture to Cadiz. Having survived that, when many of his comrades did not, he returned to the Thames and soon became infatuated with the world of the playhouses to the point where he decided he, too, would be a poet. His is a very minor talent, but we are indebted to him for his first-hand accounts of the writers and players of the time, often written in the form of doggerel. So certain was he of his own talent that he had most of his work published in his lifetime.[1]

We know therefore that on many occasions he joined in the sessions at the Mermaid continuing whatever argument in which he had become embroiled (for he was very argumentative) as he rowed the Mermaid clientele over the river to the Globe, Swan or Hope.[2]

The decade 1603 to 1613 was remarkable not only for the sheer number of new plays but also for the quality of the work. Throughout that time Beaumont and Fletcher continued to live and work together and it was not only Aubrey who commented on how inseparable they were and 'the wonderful consimility of fancy' between the two. Jonson brought them into his *Bartholomew Fair* as 'two faithful friends o' the Bankside who have but one drab [woman] between them and enter together carrying a gammon of bacon under a shared cloak'. Aubrey also throws light on their working relationship: 'I have heard Dr. John Earles, since Bishop of Sarum, who knew them, say that Mr. Beaumont's main business was to lop the overflowings of Mr. Fletcher's luxuriant and flowing wit.'[3]

Whatever the reality, it was a fruitful and creative partnership from which flowed pastorals, romances, comedies and tragedies. On the whole the women in Beaumont and Fletcher plays are either charming girls or epitomise suffering womanhood, and Euphrasia in *Philaster* is just such a one. Euphrasia disguises herself as a boy to follow the man she loves and is so besotted by him that even after she has helped him to a successful conclusion of his adventures, only to see him marry someone else, she is quite content to live with them both as a kind of superior servant just to be near him.

But different from all the rest is *The Maids Tragedy*, in which the dramatists created, some three centuries early, a plot worthy of a television megaseries and in its villainess, Evadne, the Joan Collins role. The plot concerns a King who decides his mistress should marry for practical reasons, choosing a husband who has to jilt his fiancé in order to marry Evadne, only to be told on his wedding night by his new bride that there is to be no sex. The bridegroom, Amintor, is plainly disappointed even though it is hinted that he has enjoyed a sexual relationship with Evadne's brother. The King begs Evadne to promise that she will never make love either with her husband or anyone else, insisting that she swore she never would. Evadne replies pragmatically:

> I never did swear so; you do me wrong . . .
> I swore indeed that I would never love,
> A man of lower place, but if your fortune
> Should throw you from this height, I bade you trust
> I would forsake you and would bend to him that won
> your throne.

She then sums up her philosophy: 'I love with my ambition – not my eyes.'

The 'tragedy' comes about when Evadne's family finally find out the true situation and her brothers tell her the only way she can save the family honour is by murdering the King or submitting to instant death. Faced with such a choice, she agrees and what follows throws light on what must have gone on in the bedrooms of some of the more sophisticated circles of the day for when Evadne ties the King to the bed he happily anticipates another of the sex games the two are obviously used to playing.

In 1613 Frances Beaumont married and the productive and creative working relationship immediately ceased. His bride was Ursula, heiress to a Henry Sly of Hundridge in Kent and there were two daughters of the marriage, the younger, Frances, being born posthumously as Beaumont died on 6 March 1616. He was only thirty-two and we do not know what caused his death. He was buried in Westminster Abbey and lies near to Chapman and Spenser. Born into money, he married wealth, yet he seems to have lost it, for his eldest daughter, Elizabeth, fell on hard times and married a Scots' colonel, while Frances was so poor she had to go into service.

Although we know a great deal about Fletcher's work after Beaumont's death, we know virtually nothing of the rest of his life. He may have married in 1613, shortly after Beaumont, for someone of that name was married in the actors' church, St Saviour's in Southwark.

* * *

John Webster is a dramatist unlike any other of his time, his two great plays, *The White Devil* and *The Duchess of Malfi* being stately processions of corruption, passion and death, woven around with dense, glittering language and haunting imagery. In the words of T.S. Eliot:

> Webster was much possessed by death
> And saw the skull beneath the skin,
> And breastless creatures underground
> Leaned backward with a lipless grin[4]

while his contemporary, Henry Fitzjeffrey jibed:

> But h'st! with him Crabbed Websterio,
> The playwright, cartwright: whether? either? ho!
> No further. Look as ye'd be look't into:

Sit as ye would read: Lord! who know of him?
Was ever man so mangled with a poem?
See how he draws his mouth awry of late,
How he scrubs; wrings his wrists; scratches his pate.
A midwife! Help! By his Brain's coitus,
Some centaur strange: some huge Bucephalus,
Or Pallas (sure) engendered in his brain,
Strike Vulcan with thy hammer once again.[5]

He concludes this unpleasant attack on Webster and his latest play with the words:

But what care I, it will be so obscure
That none will understand him (I am sure).

The White Devil had its first performance in 1611 at the Red Bull and was not a notable success, but then the Bull, with its rough and ready audience, was hardly a good choice of venue although it employed some talented actors. Webster rated the young Richard Perkins so highly that he mentions him in his postcript to the play. 'In particular I must remember the well-approved industry of my friend, Master Perkins, and confess the worth of his action did crown both the beginning and end.' This was the first time any actor had been given such an honour in print. Perkins went on to be a principal actor in Queen Anne's Company where it is noted he was popular as Goodlack in Heywood's *Fair Maid of the West.* His portrait, in Dulwich Picture Gallery, is that of a dour middle-aged man quite unlike an actor.

The plots of *The White Devil* and *The Duchess of Malfi*, brimful of intrigue and madness as they are, are both based on fact.[6] While there was no foreign news service in the sixteenth and early seventeenth centuries as we know it, many merchant and venturing houses had offices and representatives all over Europe from which reports of interesting happenings were regularly sent back to London.

One of these was the banking house of Fugger and in 1586 its Venetian office reported the recent grim happenings in the city of Padua over Christmas. Padua, a university city, had a reputation for student unrest but on this occasion a band of armed men, led by Ludovico Orsini, a member of the great Orsini family, invaded the palace of a young widow, Vittoria, Duchess of Accoramboni. Her husband, Bracciano, had died the previous November in mysterious circumstances after taking the waters at Lake Garda for his health. Orsini's men broke into the palace at two in the morning and slaughtered Vittoria and her brother while they were kneeling at Mass.

News of the outrage soon spread and students took to the streets demanding justice. The government in Venice reacted by sending in troops armed with cannons and, after heavy fighting, the palace was taken from Orsini. Three of his men were torn to pieces by the mob outside, the rest were hanged. Orsini, who claimed to have committed the crime at the command 'of great personages', was sentenced to death by garotte; as he was a nobleman he was granted the right to death in private and to be allowed to pay the executioner fifty crowns to make it quick.

But when the full facts came out a somewhat different complexion was put on the matter. Bracciano and Vittoria had been lovers since she was twenty-three and both were married to other people. Indeed, Bracciano was suspected of being responsible for the deaths of both his own first wife and of Vittoria's husband, although her brother had also been fingered for undertaking this task. The two had made powerful enemies, for Bracciano's first wife had been Isabella de Medici, the daughter of yet another powerful mediaeval Italian house. As Vittoria's first husband had not only been a nobleman, but also nephew to the Pope, the stage was set for a plot worthy of any seventeenth-century Revenge play. Before his death, Orsini implied that the mysterious great personage who had put him up to the murder was none other than the Duke of Florence, head of the Medici clan. It reads like a modern day Mafia feud with the Duke of Florence as the Godfather.

From this true story Webster wove a compelling pageant of adultery and intrigue in which murder becomes an exotic art. Isabella, for instance, is shown in dumbshow being poisoned after kissing a poisoned picture. The plot roughly follows the course of the real history, though with a great deal of poetic licence as to the characters of those involved, ending with a spate of deaths. As Vittoria and her brother lie dying after the assault she speaks of her soul being 'like a ship in a black storm, is driven, I know not where', to which he responds: 'I recover like a spent taper, for a flash, and instantly go out.'

The story behind the tragic Duchess of Malfi is shorter and less complicated and was first reported in England as early as 1554. The real Duchess of Amalfi was born in 1477, her father, the son of Ferrante I of Naples, dying young of mushroom poisoning – or so it was said. Her brother could well be termed a precocious high-flyer for by the time he was twenty he had inherited his father's title and wealth, married the granddaughter of Pope Innocent VIII, made his name as a famous soldier, been left a widower and become the Cardinal of Arragon.

The Duchess had been married off at the age of twelve to the elderly Amalfi, who died of gout not long afterwards, leaving her to run a substantial estate. To assist her she employed a steward, Antonio Bologna, who had run the household of the late King of Arragon. The two fell in love and were secretly married. When her brother discovered this misalliance he had them both put to death.

Webster took the bare bones of the story and constructed out of them a catalogue of horrors. The Duchess has another brother, Ferdinand, who harbours an incestuous passion for her. She has three children by Bologna before the relationship is discovered, whereupon the brothers determine to avenge the insult to the family honour, and the Duchess, after being imprisoned with lunatics, then tortured, is finally garotted in an underground dungeon after Webster has given her one of the most extraordinary speeches in any play in the English language:

> What would it pleasure me to have my throat cut with
> Diamonds? Or to be smothered with cassia?
> Or to be shot to death with pearls?

I know death hath ten thousand several doors
For men to take their exits; and 'tis found
They go on such strange, geometric hinges,
You may open them both ways . . .

Yet also at the last, Webster gives her ordinary and touching concerns as she begs her murderers to make sure her little girl says her prayers and to 'give my little boy some syrup for his cough'. The play ends with Ferdinand suffering from lycanthropy (believing he has become a wolf) and the Cardinal, who had seen in his fishpond 'a thing armed with a rake which seemed to strike at me', stabbed by his mistress.

The Duchess of Malfi was given its first performance by Shakespeare's company at the Blackfriars Theatre, with an actor called William Osler in the role of Antonio. What role Burbage played we do not know but the son of John Hemings, who had also been in it, wrote later in a satirical elegy for the amputation of his duelling finger:

It had been drawn and we in state approach,
But Webster's brother would not lend a coach,
He swore that all were hired to convey
The Malfi Duchess, sadly on her way.[7]

Webster's life indirectly touched a character in another murder story which might also have furnished him with a plot had it not been too near home for he was asked to take over the task of completing the sixth edition of 'the late Sir Thomas Overbury's collection of *Characters Drawn to the Life from Several Persons of Quality*, a plot which also includes Dr Simon Foreman.

About the time of the first performance of *The White Devil*, Simon Foreman was consulted by a very distinguished client, Lady Frances Howard, daughter of the Earl of Suffolk, who, egged on by a wife who might have modelled for Lady Macbeth, had ended up in the Tower on a charge of embezzling state funds.

In 1606 at the age of fifteen, Frances was married to the fourteen-year-old son of the executed Earl of Essex. The young husband was promptly sent abroad to grow up, returning three years later keen to consummate the marriage. His young wife, however, was not and the resultant fumblings left the lady informing her friends that he was totally unskilled and that coitus with him turned her stomach. Beautiful, wilful and very spoiled, Frances soon looked elsewhere and promptly became infatuated with one of King James's favourites, and his possible lover, Robert Carr.

Frances made a confidante of a Mrs Anne Turner, wife of the successful physician, George Turner, a Fellow of the Royal College of Physicians. Here the story begins to sound like a Middleton satire for Anne Turner was also the mistress of Sir Arthur Mainwaring, a courtier and one of the King's £30 knights. Like Master Allwit in Middleton's *A Chaste Maid in Cheapside*, her husband was complacent so long as the money rolled in. Frances asked Anne Turner, who was famous for making a special brand of fashionable yellow starch for ruffs, if she could suggest someone who might be able to assist her in her intrigue and Anne duly sent the Countess along to Dr Foreman.[8]

Frances wept prettily, telling Foreman that she had been forced into marriage with her husband and that she would rather die 'a thousand times over' than lie with him for if she did, it might well cost her Carr's love. Foreman provided her with love philtres and she soon became so emotionally dependent on him that she signed herself his 'daughter'. 'Keep the Lord Carr still to me,' she wrote, 'for that I desire and be careful you name me not to anyone, for we have so many spies that you must use all your wits.' Whether it was indeed the love potions or Frances' single-minded pursuit, she finally got Carr into her bed. The deed being done, Carr, sure of his place in the King's affections, suggested they appeal to him for help and Frances duly pleaded with the King that her marriage be annulled claiming her husband was impotent and she still a virgin, both of which the young Essex hotly denied. It was during the subsequent protracted court case that Foreman died, of natural causes, but his death did not prevent his name from becoming notorious.

Sir Thomas Overbury, who was painstakingly writing his *Book of Characters*, was a close friend of Carr and did his best to persuade him against marrying Frances even if she succeeded in getting an annulment, warning him that she would destroy him. When Frances learned of Overbury's intervention, she had him put in the Tower on a trumped-up charge. She then organised his poisoning using as her instrument Anne Turner. At the subsequent trial blame was heaped on the late Dr Foreman who was said not only to have provided the Countess with love philtres, erotic figurines and various charms, but also the poison used in the murder although this is considered highly unlikely.

There was no equality before the law and while all parties were found guilty, the Countess and Carr were merely sent to kick their heels in the Tower, while Anne Turner and some lesser associates were hanged and it is possible that Foreman would have joined them had he lived for the Judge at the trial, Lord Chief Justice Coke, actually described Anne Turner as 'the daughter of the Devil Forman'. In his editor's notes to *The Casebook of Simon Foreman*, A.L. Rowse writes:

> A tell-tale note by Foreman was exhibited 'signifying what ladies loved what lords in the Court'. Lord Chief Justice Coke opened it, and then refused to have it read: he had seen that the first name was that of his own wife, Lady Hatton, whom he had married for her money and who was, herself, no better than she should be, a termagant and a scandal.

So it was that the task of completing the murder victim's book fell, appropriately in the circumstances, to John Webster.

* * *

Meanwhile that other Foreman client, Emilia Lanier, had become a poet in her own right. In 1611, only a few weeks after the publication of Shakespeare's *Sonnets*, a volume of her own verse appeared 'published by Richard Bowen to be sold at his shop in St Paul's Churchyard', printed by the printer of a number of Shakespeare's plays, Valentine Simms.

Emilia, her children grown up, had turned to God after undergoing a religious conversion and there were those who were quick to point out that she had much from which to be converted. However, just as the male poets, including Shakespeare, had acquired patrons, so did Emilia and her poems are dedicated to, among others, the Queen; Arabella Stewart; Susan, Dowager Countess of Kent; Lady Margaret, Countess of Cumberland; Katherine, Countess of Suffolk and Ann, Countess of Dorset

Born-again Christian or not, Emilia had lost none of her spark for the longest poem in the book contains a stout defence of the role played by Eve in the scheme of things. Eve, she writes, was deceived by cunning and intended no harm when she handed Adam the apple to eat. Indeed, it was more fool him for taking it:

But surely Adam cannot be excused
Her fault, though great, yet he was most to blame;
What weakness offered, strength might have refused,
Being Lord of All, the greater was his shame:
Although the serpent's craft had her abused,
God's Holy Word ought all his actions frame,
For he was Lord and King of all the earth,
Before poor Eve had either life or breath.

and

If any Evil did in her remain
Being made of him, he was the ground of all.
Her weakness did the serpent's words obey,
But you, in malice, God's dear son betray.

There is much more in the same vein, along with stirring stories of heroines of the past, such as Sisera, who killed Jael and Judith, who did the same for Holofernes.

Most remarkable of all, however, is her preface to the 'Virtuous Reader', surely one of the earliest pieces of feminist writing that we have. It is a passionate plea on behalf of women, so often misunderstood and blamed throughout history for all the world's ills, so rarely given an opportunity to answer the charges laid against them. After lining up impressive argument for a recognition of the status of women, she writes:

> As also in respect it pleased our Lord and Saviour Jesus Christ, without the assistance of man, being free from original and other sins, from the time of his conception, till the hour of his death, to be begotten of a woman, born of a woman, nourished of a woman, obedient to a woman; and that he healed women, pardoned women, comforted women; yea, even when he was in his greatest agony and bloody sweat, going to be crucified, and also in the last hour of his death, took care to dispose of a woman: after his resurrection, appeared first to a woman, then sent a woman to declare his most glorious resurrection to the rest of his Disciples.

A most remarkable lady, Emilia. We know little else about her except that some years later she was involved in a court case. She was renting a house as a sub-tenant, when the real tenant, who was an army officer, returned from Europe and wanted it back. For three years she refused to move out even though she was taken to court by the tenant and the owner. She finally left in August 1619, without paying her last quarter's rent and after deliberately leaving the house 'in great decay and a nasty filthy state'.

She lived to become a grandmother and great-grandmother, living, like her contemporary, Moll Frith, to a good age. She died in 1645 at the age of seventy-six.

20

Embarrassment of a Water Poet

On 3 July 1613 Sir Henry Wotton wrote a letter to his nephew, Sir Edmund Bacon, detailing a dramatic event which had taken place four days earlier, on 29 June:

> Now to let matters of state sleep, I will entertain you at present with what hath happened this week at the Bank's side. The King's Players had a new play called *All is True,* representing some principal pieces of the reign of Henry VIII which was set forth with many extraordinary circumstances of pomp and majesty, even to the matting of the stage; the Knights of the Order with their Georges and Garters, the Guards with their embroidered coats, and the like: sufficient in truth, within a while, to make greatness very familiar if not ridiculous.
>
> Now, King Henry, making a masque at Cardinal Wolsey's house, and certain chambers [cannon] being shot off at his entry, some of the paper, or other stuff, wherewith one of them was stopped, did light on the thatch, where being thought at first but an idle smoke, and their eyes more attentive to the show, it kindled inwardly, and ran round like a train, consuming within less than an hour the whole house to the very grounds.
>
> This was the fatal period of that virtuous fabric, wherein nothing did perish but wood and straw, and a few forsaken cloaks; only one man had his breeches set on fire, that would perhaps have broiled him if he

had not by the benefit of a provident wit, put it out with bottle ale.

The play being performed at the time was Shakespeare, possibly Shakespeare and Fletcher's *Henry VIII.*

Immediately the sharers made plans for a new theatre and the new building rose from the ashes of the old within a year at a cost of £1,400. It was described by John Chamberlain in a letter dated 30 June 1614 as 'the fayrest that ever was in England'.

The King's Men were fortunate in that they could transfer their entire operation to the Blackfriars Theatre while the Globe was being rebuilt. As the popularity of enclosed theatres grew, they could almost certainly have written off the Globe site and concentrated on their more upmarket audience at the Blackfriars, but it was decided that there was still a demand for the open theatres which could cater for very large, popular audiences and so the Globe was rebuilt. Presumably each production was rehearsed in two ways, one for the smaller and more intimate private theatre, and the other for the open one with its massive thrust stage; indeed the new Globe could hold up to 3,000 people, according to a report concerning a later scandal. The sum spent on the rebuilding was enormous by any of the standards of the day, far more than that spent either on the first Fortune Theatre built in 1600, its replacement in 1622 or, according to Professor Gurr, than that spent on the new Hope.[1]

Few details have come down to us as to the appearance of either the Globe 1 or Globe 2. Gurr estimates that both theatres offer about 2,500 feet of space, built on a circular or polygonal frame with an outside diameter of a hundred feet and a yard with a diameter of seventy feet. He draws attention to the fact that while the yard area may not have been packed very often, when it was those standing would have been anything but comfortable. Playwright John Marston refers to visiting a theatre where he was 'pasted to the barmy jacket of a Beer-brewer'.

The basic design was still that of an open space surrounded on three sides by three tiers of galleries but the entrance to them was now likely to be more sophisticated with an outside staircase giving access to the yard and separate access to each gallery. The shape of the stage remained the same, with its 'heavens' to shelter the actors, its gallery for use in the play or by musicians, and its discovery space, but Globe 2, as pictured in Wenceslas Hollar's 'Long View of London', has two timber-framed gable ends above the stage rather than the roof of a four-sided thatched construction as in de Witt's sketch of the earlier Swan.

Between 1613 and 1616 the unfortunate Dekker was languishing in the Clink Prison for debt and Shakespeare was spending more and more time back in Stratford, John Fletcher having finally taken over from him as the principal dramatist of the King's Men. As well as most likely co-operating on *Henry VIII*, Shakespeare and Fletcher almost certainly worked together on *The Two Noble Kinsmen.* Shakespeare however did not sever his connection with the London theatre scene for in 1613 a household account of the Earl of Rutland notes: 'Item 31 March, to Mr. Shakespeare in gold and to R. Burbage, symbolic design on shield ('impresa'), R. Burbage for painting design, Shakespeare for motto'.[2] Presumably Richard Burbage could turn his hand to graphics, while Shakespeare was quite happy to provide a patron with a 'motto'. As late as 1615 he was still listed as a sharer in both the Globe and Blackfriars Theatres.

1614 saw the first production of Ben Jonson's picaresque drama *Bartholomew Fair* and also a hilarious event concerning John Taylor. Taylor, considering he had been grossly maligned by William Fennor, who described himself as 'King James's Rhyming Poet', challenged Fennor to an insult competition at the Hope Theatre. Fennor agreed and Taylor hired the theatre and paid for 1,000 handbills advertising the event which he assiduously distributed throughout the City and Bankside. 'I divulged my name in some 1,000 ways and more, giving my Friends and diverse of my acquaintance notice of this Bear-garden of dainty conceits.' Nor was that all: he gave Fennor ten shillings 'in earnest of his coming to meet me.'[3]

His aim was to attract the largest possible crowd to the Hope and he certainly succeeded, for when the big day came the theatre was packed from the top gallery to the back of the pit. Taylor, in his best suit, could look out from backstage on to a vast and noisy audience waiting below. They waited and waited and it was then that the awful realisation began to dawn on him that Fennor was not going to appear. The audience grew more and more restive and it was then Taylor made his big mistake. He decided to announce that as the contest could not take place, he would read them some of his poems instead. Even had he been a better poet it is unlikely in the circumstances that he would, in theatrical parlance, have held the house.

The inevitable result was described by a furious Taylor in a poem he sent to Fennor.[4] He had wronged the audience, he wrote, caused them great offence and many of them had come a long way at considerable expense. Their mirth had swiftly turned to madness, the liking to loathing. As for Fennor:

In no Church book thy name recorded is,
But that thou wert begotten in some ditch,
Betwixt a Tinker and a Maundering Witch!

He then describes what happened:

. . . some laughed, some swore, some stared and stamped and cursed,
And in confused humours all out burst.
I (as I could) did stand the desperate shock,
And bid the brunt of many a dangerous knock.
For now the stinkards in their ireful wrath,
Bepelted me with loam, with stones and laths,
One madly sits like bottle-Ale and hisses,
Another throws a stone and 'cause he misses,
He yawns and bawls and cries Away, away . . .
One swears and storms another laughs and smiles,
Another madly would pluck off the tiles,

Some run to the door to get again their coin
And some do shift and some again purloin,
One valiantly stept up upon the stage,
And would tear down the hangings in his rage
(God grant, he may have hanging at his end),
That with me for the hangings did contend.
Such clapping, hissing, swearing, stamping, smiling,
Applauding, scorning, liking and reriting,
Did more torment me than a Purgatory.

In the end the Hope's players took matters into their own hands and offered the audience a show. Taylor refused to leave the stage and for some time attempted to continue reading his verse while the action of the play took place around him until he finally admitted defeat and gave up.

During that year Taylor had been somewhat at odds with the players for the growing number of private theatres on the 'London' side of the Thames had led to a decrease in the amount of work for the watermen and they had signed a petition asking that no more licences be granted for playhouses 'in London' or 'Middlesex within four miles of the City on that side of the Thames'. Ever a self-publicist, Taylor volunteered to deliver the petition to Court which he did 'with care and integrity'. As the King was on a progress at the time Taylor had to catch up with him in Theobalds, Newmarket and Royston, thus running up expenses of £7.2s. for 'horse-hire, horse-meat and man's meat, brought to a consumption'. Granted a hearing before the relevant Court authorities, Taylor treated his hearers to a ramble through history, from the services he had personally performed at Cadiz to those of the watermen who had fought against the Armada and in other famous engagements. Indeed, so many watermen had either fought in the Low Countries or served with Drake, Frobisher and the rest, that 'every summer 1,500 or 2,000 of them were employed to the places aforesaid, for then there were so few watermen and the one half of them being at sea, those that stayed at home had as much work as they would do'.

This had resulted in extra apprentices being taken on to

cope with all the new business, 'which boys are since grown to men and keepers of houses, many of them being overcharged with families of wife and children. So that the number of watermen, and those that live and are maintained by them, and by the only labour of the oar and scull, betwixt the bridge of Windsor and Gravesend, cannot be fewer than forty thousand; the cause of the greater half of which multitude, hath been the players playing on the Bankside, for I have known three companies, beside bear-baiting, at once there; to wit, the Globe, the Rose and the Swan.' Now, though, 'it hath pleased God in this peaceful time, that there is no employment at sea, and the players, all except the Kings Men, left their usual residency on the Bankside and do play in Middlesex far remote from the Thames, so that every day in the week they do draw unto them three or four thousand people, that were used to spend their monies by water.'

In 1614 Taylor noted that the players 'did exhibit a petition against us, in which they said that our suit was unreasonable, and that we might as justly remove the Exchange and the walks in St Paul's and Moorfields to the Bankside for our profits, as to confine them.'[5]

The dispute dragged on until finally the Commissioners appointed Taylor, on behalf of the watermen, and the players to come before them for arbitration but before this could happen its chairman, Sir Walter Cope, died 'and Sir Julius Caesar was made Master of the Rolls, by which means the Commission was dissolved and we had no further hearing'. Sir Julius Caesar is not a figment of Taylor's lively imagination but was the son of an Italian immigrant, Cesare Adelmare, a court physician. The young Julius changed his name from Cesare to Caesar, trained for the law, was called to the Bar in 1580 and became a Judge in 1584. He was noted for his fairness and generosity.

Finding that all their efforts and expense had come to nothing, the watermen turned and rent Taylor who noted, huffily:

Some of my Company, through malice or ignorance,

> reported that I took bribe of players to let the suit fall, and to that purpose I had supper with them at the Cardinal's Hat on the Bankside. These and more the like such petty aspersions, the out-cast rubbish of the Company hath very liberally, unmannerly and ungratefully bestowed upon me.

Presumably by the end of 1614 with both the new Hope and the new Globe busy, Taylor and his watermen had little to grumble about, not even the opening of another new theatre on the Middlesex side, the Cockpit in Drury Lane.

* * *

In 1615 the last of the great clowns for whom Shakespeare had specifically written, Robert Armin, died. It was Armin who had moved his role in the plays on from the stand-up comedy of Tarleton, and the ad-libbing of Kempe and his 'jigges', to the ambivalent humour, laced with melancholy, of Feste in *Twelfth Night.*

If 1593 had marked the end of the first great era of English drama, then 1616 marked the second. It was the year when in the world outside the playhouses, Raleigh mounted his expedition to Guiana; when Hakluyt, of *Hakluyt's Voyages* died; and when the physician, William Harvey, discovered the circulation of the blood.

It was the year when Ben Jonson, who alone of his contemporaries saw his work as something for posterity, collected together his best poetry and existing play texts and had them published in a Folio edition and when his own status was recognised by King James, who gave him a pension for life. It was the year which saw the deaths of Francis Beaumont and of Shakespeare's exact contemporary, Cervantes. It was also the year that William Shakespeare died.

Part Four

21

'He was not of an age but for all time . . .'

> . . . But this rough magic
> I do here abjure; and, when I have requir'd
> Some heavenly music – which even now I do –
> To work mine end upon their senses, that this
> Airy charm is for, I'll break my staff,
> Bury it several fathoms in the earth,
> And deeper than did ever plummet sound
> I'll drown my book.
>
> *The Tempest*

As Prospero, his time on his magic island drawing to its close, prepares to leave it and, with it, the enchantment he has woven for so long, so Shakespeare bade farewell to the stage with his last great play.

Death, as well as taking its toll on his own family, was fast cutting down his friends. Judith and Hamnet Sadler, after whom he had named his twins, had moved to Sheep Street where, in 1614, Judith died and another friend, the rich bachelor John Combe, also died the same year leaving Shakespeare £5 in his will. Combe's memorial is next to that of Shakespeare in Holy Trinity Church. Combe's death provides further information on Shakespeare as landowner and collector of tithes, for his heir, William Combe, promptly began the enclosure of what he alleged was common land. Some of it, however, actually belonged to Shakespeare who got the town clerk, Thomas Green, to draw up a note of all the interests involved, at the top of which is: 'Master Shakespeare, four yardland, no common nor ground beyond Gospel Busy, nor ground in Sandfield, nor none in Sloe Hill Field beyond Bishopton, nor one in the enclosure of Bishopston.' Combe then had to agree to compensate Shakespeare for any loss of tithes consequent upon his wrongly enclosing land.[1]

On 17 November 1614 Green wrote:

> My cousin Shakespeare, coming to town, I went to see him how he did. He told me that they had assured him they meant to enclose no further than to the Field, to the gate in Clopton hedge and take in Salisbury's piece; and that they mean in April to survey the land and then give satisfaction and not before. And he and Master Hall say they think will be nothing done at all.

No compensation or consideration was offered to the ordinary folk who had used the common as of right for centuries and as Combe continued with his illegal enclosing, hedging and ditching, they rose in a body, filling in his ditches and uprooting his hedges. Combe set his men on them 'to throw them to the ground' and 'sat laughing on his horseback and said they were good football players'. He referred to the town council, who tried to prevent the mayhem as 'Puritan knaves and underlings in their colour'.

The tenants returned with reinforcements from neighbouring villages and Green noted in his diary: 'September. Master Shakespeare's telling Green that he was not able to bear the enclosure of Welcombe.' The row was to rumble on for years, eventually reaching Lord Chief Justice Coke himself, before William Combe finally gave up. As a coincidental link with the world of the playhouses, Thomas Green's sponsors for admission to the Middle Temple in 1595 had been John Marston and his father.

In 1616 Judith Shakespeare, now aged thirty-one and considered an elderly spinster, finally married. From the little we know of her she seems to have been quite unlike Susanna, more wild in her ways, illiterate and difficult. She married Thomas Quiney, second son of the Richard Quiney, Shakespeare's old friend, who had written asking him for a loan all those years ago.

It should have been a suitable match, but trouble attended the couple right from their wedding, as it would their lives thereafter. They were married at Holy Trinity church on 10 February and then almost immediately summoned to appear before the consistory court in Worcester Cathedral for marrying without a licence. Quiney refused to attend the hearing and was promptly excommunicated. No mention is made of whether or not Judith shared the same fate. The reason for the summons was probably because a special licence was needed for Lent Weddings and although the banns for Richard and Judith had been properly called for three Sundays, no special licence had been applied for.

The marriage was immediately followed by a much greater local scandal. While supposedly courting Judith, Thomas had also been involved in an affair with a girl called Margaret Wheeler who was now expecting his child. The proper and expected thing for him to do in the circumstances would have been for him to marry her, not Judith. Margaret suffered a difficult pregnancy and barely a month after Quiney married Judith, the unfortunate girl died in childbirth and her baby with her. They were buried on 15 March.

Quiney was duly summonsed before an ecclesiastical court of a kind especially set up to deal with cases of 'whoredom and uncleanness'. They were popularly known as 'bawdy courts'. Thomas appeared before it on 26 March and confessed to *'fassus est se carnalem copulacionem habuisse cum dicta Wheeler'* (having had carnal copulation with the said Wheeler). The 'judge', vicar John Rogers, sentenced Quiney to the usual punishment which was to perform open penance dressed in a white sheet before the church congregation for three Sundays in a row.

Somewhat unusually and possibly due to Shakespeare's influence, this was commuted to paying a fine of five shillings to the poor of the parish and acknowledging his crime, in his ordinary clothes, before the minister of Bishopton Chapel.[2]

The excommunication must also have been a token one, for the first child born to the Quineys, christened 'Shakespeare', was baptised at Holy Trinity the following November. He lived only six months, dying on 8 May 1617. The couple had two other sons, Richard, born in 1618 and Thomas, in 1620, both of whom died in 1639, Thomas on 28 January, twenty-nine days before Richard who died on 26 February at the age of twenty-two. The closeness of their deaths and their ages suggest they were the victims of an epidemic of some kind

Judith's marriage was not a happy one. Thomas Quiney was a vintner and before his marriage kept a tavern in the High Street next to his mother's house. After it he and Judith took another tavern the Cage, at the corner of High Street and Bridge Street. Apparently he had a drink problem and was also in trouble on more than one occasion for selling poor and adulterated wine. He got into debt. His later life is something of a mystery for some sources say that in 1625 he went to London and was never seen again, but this does not tally with local records in which he continues to appear, generally accused of various petty offences. There is, however, no record of his being buried in Stratford which would be expected.

During the winter of 1615/16 Shakespeare called in his old friend the lawyer, Francis Collins, and drafted his will, the likely date being some time in January. In March it was substantially altered by the addition of a new first page, possibly due to Judith's marriage. The rest of it was allowed to stand, but with a number of alterations and corrections, each validated by Shakespeare with his signature on the foot of each page. On the last page he added the words 'By me William'.[3]

Did he know he had only weeks to live? He signed his will as being 'in perfect health and memory' but this was a phrase most often used to denote that the person signing the will was of sound mind. Although aged only fifty-two, Shakespeare had already outlived most of his siblings. Had he retired to Stratford, exhausted and drained from his vast output of work, feeling he had no more to say?

A cull through mountains of surmise has him dying variously of alcoholism, Bright's disease, exposure after sleeping a night under a crab apple tree, typhus, typhoid, paralysis, epilepsy, apoplexy, arterio-sclerosis, excessive smoking (!), gluttony, angina pectoris, pulmonary congestion and locomotor ataxia (syphilis). There is not a shred of evidence for any of it and no suggestion from his friends or his own writings that he regularly drank too much, smoked heavily or suffered from the pox.[4]

The most famous suggested cause, and one that has something of the ring of truth, is that put forward by a later vicar of Stratford, the Reverend John Ward, in 1662: 'Shakespeare, Drayton and Ben Jonson had a merry meeting and it seemed drank too hard for Shakespeare died of a fever there contracted.' It is not impossible to believe that the three met up in such a fashion in Warwickshire that spring. Drayton, now established as a poet, came from nearby Nuneaton and was often at home there. Ben Jonson took every opportunity to call on friends out of town. It has been suggested that the occasion was the celebration of Judith's marriage. Local tradition in Warwickshire has the Bell Inn at Welford (which still exists) as the venue for the fatal meeting and Shakespeare either walking back to Stratford along the river bank or riding on horseback along the Evesham Road. Either way he was said to have got soaked with rain. If this was the case and he was already suffering from a weakened constitution, then he might well have died of 'pulmonary congestion' or pneumonia; we simply do not know.

Shakespeare died on 23 April 1616, possibly the fifty-second anniversary of his birth. The Burial register reads: '1616 April 25. Will Shakespeare, gent.' His standing as a landowner and owner of tithes entitled him to be buried inside the parish church within the chancel rail and it is for that rather than his reputation as a playwright and poet which ensured he lies where he does. It was the second funeral his family had attended within a fortnight, for his brother-in-law, David Hart, husband to his sister Joan, had died only nine days previously at the old house in Henley Street. Local repute gave him a grave seventeen feet deep, hardly possible so close to the River Avon, and also credits him with having written his own epitaph, but if this is indeed the case it seems he fell back on the kind of sentiment which could have been written by anyone:

Good frend for Jesus sake forebeare,
To digg the dust encloased heare:
ET
Blest Be Y Man Y spares thes stones,
T
And curst be he Y moves my bones.

A whole industry has grown up around the epitaph and its meaning. Some of those who will not have it that Shakespeare wrote Shakespeare assume the proof lies inside the grave and that he was ensuring nobody would discover the deception. Others see it as a curse. The most likely and prosaic explanation is that all too often those buried inside the church were later dug up to make room for other worthy citizens. His bust, above it, was sculpted by Gheerart Jansser, a Dutch immigrant, later known as Gerard Johnson. He and his four sons ran a stonemason's business close to the Globe on the Bankside and would have known Shakespeare.

His face stares foresquare out of the monument below the Shakespeare coat of arms. Underneath are the words:

Judicio pylium, genio socratem, arte maronem:
Terra Tegit. Populus Maeret, Olympus habet.
Stay, passenger, why goest thou by so fast?
Read, if thou canst, whom envious death hath plast,
Within this monument Shakespeare: With Whom
Quick nature dide; whose name doth deck ys tomb,
Far more then cost: sieh all yt he hath writt,
Leaves living art, but page, to serve his witt.
Obiit ANO DOi. 1616
Aetatis. 53 DIE 23 Apr.

We know it was recorded as being there by 1634 but it is

likely to have been installed much earlier.

So to the detail of the will. The excellent commentary in *Shakespeare in the Public Record Office* notes that the will was finally dated March and that the writing on the bottom of the first page was squeezed in when the second draft was made to save the clerk having to copy out two other pages as well. The final alterations, says Jane Cox, who edited the section on the will, were possibly made following not only Judith's marriage but the scandal regarding Quiney's abandonment of Margaret Wheeler that followed it.

Many commentators have found the wording of the will lacking. So great a poet, they say, should have left for posterity something far more impressive. 'Its austerity,' writes Jane Cox 'is a disappointment.'

It begins with the conventional Protestant opening, that he commends his soul into the hands 'of God my creator, hoping and assuredly believing through the only merits of Jesus Christ, my Saviour, to be made partaker of life everlasting and my body to the earth where of it was made.' The first bequest is: 'Item I give and bequeath to my son-in-law. . .' but it is then crossed out. Was that Quiney? £150 is then left to Judith, £100 for a marriage portion and the rest so long as she gives up any claim to a cottage in Chapel Lane. She is left a further £150 in the event she has a living child at the end of the next three years. If she does not, then £100 goes to his granddaughter, Elizabeth Hall and the rest to his sister Joan and her children. If Judith and any child or children are still living then the £150 is to be invested and the proceeds paid to her 'so long as she is married'. Quiney and his behaviour had obviously left Shakespeare concerned as to Judith's future. He also left her a large 'silver-gilt bowl'.

To his sister, Joan, he leaves wearing apparel, £20, and permission to stay on in Henley Street at a nominal rent. Each of her sons is left £5. Apart from Judith's bowl, the rest of his silver plate goes to Elizabeth Hall. He left £10 for the poor of Stratford, a substantial sum, and various bequests to Stratford friends, including his closest, Hamnet Sadler.

Yet more proof of Shakespeare's close association with the London theatre is in the bequests, with affectionate remembrance, to 'my fellows' John Hemings, Richard Burbage and Henry Condell 'a peece to buy them rings'.

The bulk of his estate went to Susannah and her husband. This included the big house of New Place and its gardens, barns, stables, orchards, along with other lands, tenements in the towns, fields and villages, and grounds of Stratford-upon-Avon, Oldstratford, Bishopton, Welcombe, or any other in Warwickshire, and also 'the messuage or tenement with the appurtenances wherein of one John Robinson dwelleth, situate . . . in the Blackfriers in London, near the Wardrobe; and all other my lands, tenements and hereditaments whatsoever'. A fine bequest indeed. Only in the default of living issue were these riches to go to Judith and any male heirs. There is no mention as to manuscripts or books.

As is well known, his wife, Anne, receives only the briefest of mentions with the bequest, interlined as if as an afterthought: 'Item. I give unto my wife my second best bed with the furniture' (i.e. curtains and bedding). That is all. Scholars have argued about it ever since. One view is that the best bed was always the most prized, used for visitors, and passed on to the eldest child as a family heirloom, while the second-best bed was the family bed, the marriage bed. Another is that it was accepted at the time that a widow was automatically entitled to a third of the value of the estate and that even a common-law wife had rights. Even so, in many wills of the time this entitlement was spelled out. Did he assume Susannah would look after Anne and that she would continue living at New Place? Jane Cox asks was she such a loyal, domestic and simple a soul that she expected no more, was it even that she might be mentally incapacitated in some way?

Whatever the reason, the greatest poet of the age chose not to refer to Anne in any of the terms used by many lesser men of their wives, such as 'sweet wife', 'dearest bedfellow', 'loving companion'. A trawl by Jane Cox through 150 sample wills of the period shows wives as executrixes and residuary legatees. 'None,' writes Jane Cox, 'left his wife anything as paltry as the second-best bed.'

The will was witnessed by Julius Shaw, John Robinson, Hamnet Sadler and Robert Whatcott. Shakespeare's death was as unlike those of that earlier generations of poets and playwrights as could possibly be imagined, surrounded as it was by evidence of substantial wealth. William Shakespeare, man of property, died in his bed at home.

* * *

There has never been his like again and it was the misfortune of his contemporaries, so many of whom were most exceptionally talented, that they wrote at the same time and in the same field as a man whose genius has since reached out to the whole world.

'He was not of an age but for all time', wrote Ben Jonson. In his long biographical poem 'To the Memory of my beloved Master, William Shakespeare, and what he hath left us', he offers praise indeed:

> . . . Soul of the age!
> The applause! Delight! the wonder of our stage!
> My Shakespeare, rise! I will not lodge thee by
> Chaucer or Spencer, or bid Beaumont lie,
> A little further off, to make thee room:
> Thou art a monument without a tomb.
> And art alive still while thy book doth live,
> And we have wits to read, and praise to give.
> That I not mix thee so, my brain excuses,
> I mean with great, but disproportion'd Muses:
> For if I thought my judgement were of years,
> I should commit thee surely with thy peers
> And tell how far thou didst our Lily outshine,
> Or sporting Kyd or Marlowe's mighty line.

Though he could not resist adding:

> And though thou hadst small Latin and less Greek,
> From thence to honour thee, I will not seek

For names . . .

After much more in the same vein, he concludes:

Sweet Swan of Avon! What a sight it were
To see thee in our water yet appear,
And make those flights upon the banks of Thames,
That so did take Eliza, and our James.
But stay, I see thee in the hemisphere
Advanced, and made a constellation there!
Shine forth, thou Star of Poets, and with rage,
Or influence, chide, or cheer the drooping stage,
Which, since thy flight from hence, hath mourned like
night,
And despairs day, but for thy volume's light.

Twentieth-century lover of Shakespeare, A.L. Rowse, writes of his plays:

Their themes reach below the rational into the realm of the sub-conscious, into the primitive experiences which exist in the recesses of every human mind, although we are unwilling to acknowledge them.

Whether it is the son's suspicion of his mother's falseness, the mental torture of being in love with a girl suspected of betraying him to his enemies, an ageing man's jealousy of an old friend over his wife and his final realisation of the wreck he has made of life and happiness, the soul sleep-walking in agony for a crime committed, or the realisation that all men kill the thing they love, all these things reach down to such depths in us that sometimes we can hardly bear to look at what is being portrayed on stage.

Merely on an intellectual level, we now know that the successive stages of Leontes' jealousy exactly parallel Freud's analysis of the stages of psychotic jealousy, from the obsessional to the delusional. Hamlet's suspicions of his mother offer virtually a text-book case of the working of the Oedipus complex; Macbeth, the sleeplessness, the retribution of guilt. When Coriolanus' obsessive love for Rome is denied and himself rejected, he wants to set fire to it – a reaction well known in pathological psychology. Shakespeare knew, or intuited, it all; the miracle is that, by trusting his intuition, he found the appropriate images to express it: his genius found a language.[5]

22

Master Jonson visits Scotland

In the summer of 1618 a large, portly gentleman in his mid-forties set off on a walking tour to Scotland. He had no reason to travel on foot as he was not at that time short of money, so presumably he did it by choice. Ben Jonson arrived in Edinburgh towards the end of the summer, where he was received with honour by civil dignitaries, which was only right for a man who, two years earlier, had had his major works published in Folio form, and who was about to receive an honorary Oxford degree.

As he stomped steadily northward he had plenty of time to look back on his life so far and his present situation. It is very likely that it was Shakespeare's death that had prompted him to publish his own works while he was there to oversee and edit them, rather than leaving them at best to the mercies of posthumous editors and at worst to those who did not think them worthy of being put into print at all. Their publication had led to widespread accusations of arrogance but Ben had had no problem dismissing these, especially as the Spanish playwright, Lope de Vega, had soon followed suit.

Jonson was feeling somewhat disillusioned with the theatre because of the growing passion for Masques. He was perfectly prepared to write these when commissioned to do so but he felt as many writers for the stage do today that what was now paramount was 'designers' theatre', rather than that of writers'. As time went on he grew to feel even more sour. Paired most usually with the foremost designer of the day, Inigo Jones, his words increasingly took a back seat to Jones's exotic sets and magnificent costumes. His exasperation had led him to confide to the young Prince Charles (later Charles I) that 'when he wanted a word to express the greatest villain in the world, he called him "an Inigo"!'

He was still annoyed that he had never been recognised as he would have wished, as a leading tragedian. It was the great comedies *Volpone, The Alchemist* and *Bartholomew Fair* that audiences flocked to see and he had recently added another witty play to these, a play which has strong contemporary resonances today.

The apprentice demon in *The Devil's An Ass* has to fulfil a qualifying task in order to graduate. Full of confidence and bored with souring cream and causing minor mischief, the demon, Pug, asks Satan to give him the Big One: corrupting the City of London merchants and financiers. Satan's response is that he is not ready for it. Lancashire, maybe, Northumberland, yes, but the City? However, he gets his way and assiduously sets about duping and corrupting the City professionals, only to find himself totally outclassed. So dishonest, so corrupt, so fraudulent are those with whom he comes into contact, that in the end he cannot cope and has to beg Satan to step in and rescue him:

Oh put me to yoking foxes, milking he goats,
Pounding water in a mortar, laving
The sea dry with a nutshell, gathering all
The leaves are fallen this autumn, drawing farts
Out of dead bodies, making ropes with sand,
Catching the winds together in a net,
Mustering ants and numbering atoms; all
That hell and you thought exquisite torments rather
Than stay me here a thought more …

Being set for a term in the eternal fire would be 'refreshing' compared with the City. In a rage, Satan appears in a clap of thunder to take the failed demon home to Hell, pointing out as he does so that he is only saving him so that

Hell is not shamed by the human beings finding out that they are more than a match for the worst of devils. It cries out to be put on in modern dress with computer screens and personal phones.

There is a sub plot taken from the *Decameron* in which the young wife of a possessive husband is seduced by a clever man who has permission to talk to her so long as she says nothing. The new twist is that the man in question falls deeply in love with the woman, who, rarely for Jonson, is intelligent and sympathetic; he no longer merely wants to bed her as just another conquest.

We know what Jonson looked like at this period in his life from Thomas Dekker, who described him as having a 'face like a bruised, rotten russet-apple, or a badly pock-marked brass warming pan'.

Certainly his wilder years now lay behind him: his fatal duel with Gabriel Spencer, his terms of imprisonment, the plays that worried the authorities. He had lost his eldest son at the age of seven in the major visitation of the plague in 1601. When he reached his main destination in Scotland, the castle of Sir William Drummond of Hawthornden, he was to tell him, among many other things, that at the time of the boy's death he, Jonson, was staying with a Sir Robert Cotten out in the country.[1] One night he woke suddenly to see a vision of 'his eldest son appear unto him with a mark of a bloody cross on his forehead as if he had been cut with a sword, at which he prayed to God, and in the morning he came to Mr. Cotten's Chamber to tell him, who persuaded him it was but an apprehension of his fantasy at which he could not be dejected. In the meantime came letters from his wife of the death of the boy in the plague.'

As on the death of his baby daughter, Mary, he wrote a moving epitaph for his little boy which ends:

Rest in soft peace and asked, say here doth lie
Ben Jonson, his best piece of poetry.

A rare glimpse of the man behind the bombast. There would be no more children for by 1618 Ben and Anne had drifted apart. Jonson told Drummond that he had not bedded with her for some five years.

Whether as a direct result of Jonson telling everyone he was going off on a visit to Scotland, or by a strange coincidence (depending on who you choose to believe),[2] John Taylor the Water Poet, recovered from his nasty experience at the Hope Theatre, decided to walk to Scotland as well. He called his trip his 'Penniless Pilgrimage' and before setting off tried to get as many people as possible to agree to pay him a small sum on his completion of the round trip, thus inventing, so far as we know, the first ever sponsored walk, even if the charity concerned was himself.

He caught up with Jonson in Edinburgh. Jonson was impressed with the fact that Taylor, who had not left London until 14 July, had reached Edinburgh by 13 August. Taylor left an account of his journey, in rather terrible verse, of how he conned and begged his way into taverns and inns, beds and board, often limping from blisters, sometimes spurned, sometimes welcomed – an old woman in Prestwich washed his clothes, while an importunate serving wench, who he did not fancy, had to be heaved out of his bed.[3]

When he presented himself before Jonson, Jonson's first reaction was that Taylor 'had been sent thither to scorn him'. Taylor's response was that had he decided to do so he would have got to Edinburgh first. He then set down his version couched in his usual terms of justification. 'Many shallow-brained critics do lay an aspersion on me, that I was set on by others, or that I did undergo this project either in malice or mockage of Master Ben Jonson. I vow by the faith of a Christian, that their imaginations are all wide ...' Taylor alleges he and Jonson parted friends, indeed that Jonson contributed to his funds.

But for an account of Jonson's sojourn at the castle of Hawthornden we have to rely on William Drummond, for Jonson's own perished in the fire which destroyed his library in 1629.[4] Just what Drummond had in mind when he invited Jonson to Hawthornden is not clear; what is apparent is that he had not expected his guest to stay several months, make heavy inroads into his ale and wine and consider himself entitled to throw parties and entertain at his host's expense. Jonson's view of Drummond was that 'he was too good and simple and that often a man's modesty made a fool of his wit', which could never have been said of Jonson.

Jonson, it seems, talked and talked – to Drummond, informing him of his life and times, regaling those of Drummond's friends invited to meet the sophisticated writer from London with court gossip and tales of the famous and/or notorious. He bragged that in his youth he was 'given to venery', that he thought 'going to bed with a maid nothing to the enjoyment of the wantonness of a wife' (someone else's wife, that is), and that at one time a man 'made his own wife to court him', so that he enjoyed her for two years before he knew of it, and that while married he had lain with another woman diverse times who allowed him all privileges 'except that last act that she would not agree unto'. Whether Drummond, who seems to have been a studious and quiet kind of a man appreciated such confidences, he does not say, but he appears to have felt the need to note it down.

Jonson gave freely of his opinions of his contemporaries:

> Spencer's stanzas pleased him not, nor his matter. Samuel Daniel was an honest man, had not children, but was no poet. That Mr. Drayton's *Polybon*, if he had performed what he promised to write had been excellent. His long verse pleased him not; that Chapman's translations of Homer and Virgil in Alexandrines were but prose; that John Harington's *Ariosto*, under all translations, was the worst; that Donne, for not keeping of accent [beat] deserved hanging; that Sharpham, Day and Dekker were all rogues and that Minshaw was one.

We learn that 'Daniel was at jealousies with him', that 'Drayton feared him and esteemed not him', that 'Francis Beaumont loved too much himself and his own verses.' Once, he told his audience, 'he beat Marston and took his pistol from him'. Nathan Field, the boy actor who played women, became a leading adult actor and also a playwright, was 'his scholar', and Markham, 'a book-seller's hack [was] a plagiarist and was but a base fellow, that such also were Day and Middleton'. Chapman and Fletcher were 'loved of him', Sir John Overbury was first his friend, then turned mortal enemy, and that when Beaumont died 'in the arms of the Pest', he, Jonson, had written 'How I do love thee, Beaumont, and thy muse'. Marston, he said, wrote his father-in-law's preachings, and his father-in-law his (Marston's) comedies and Shakespeare, in a play, 'brought in a number of men saying they had suffered shipwreck in Bohemia where there is no sea nearer than some hundred miles'.

After such a catalogue it is surprising to find that he rated his host's poems as highly as he did. Jonson told Drummond that 'they were all good, especially my Epitaph on the Prince, save they smelled too much of the Schools and were not after the fancy of the times'.

Obviously a man with such an access to the Court was asked for gossip: 'Queen Elizabeth never saw herself in a mirror after she became old' and 'they painted her'; that 'she had a membrane on her which made her incapable of a man, tho' for her delight she tried many'. Leicester's wife, he affirmed, 'poisoned him with a potion he had given to her to cure faintness', while the noble Sir Philip Sydney 'was no pleasant man in countenance, his face being spoiled with pimples'. Then there was Sir Henry Wotton, caught in the act of seducing one of his maids who 'before his Majesty's going into England, being disguised at Leith on a Sunday when all the rest were at church, being interrupted of his occupation by another wench who came in at the door, cried out "Pox on thee for thou hast hindered the procreation of a child" and thus betrayed himself.'

He made much of his friendship with Sir Walter Raleigh who 'was esteemed more of fame than conscience. The best wits in England were employed for making his history.' Indeed, Ben had written 'a piece for him of the Punic Wars, which he altered and set in his book'. Raleigh had however sufficient faith in Jonson's learning to send him to France in 1613 with his own son to act as 'governor'. The trip proved a disaster:

> This Youth being knavishly inclined, among other pastimes (as getting of the favours of Damsels on a codpiece) caused him (Jonson) to be drunken and dead drunk so that he knew not where he was, thereafter laid him on a cart which he made to be drawn by Pioneers through the streets, at every corner showing his governor stretched out and telling them that there was a more lively image of the Crucifix than any they had, at which sport young Raleigh's mother delighted much (saying his father young was so inclined), though his father abhorred (it).

Jonson, as he drank his way steadily through Drummond's cellar, explained how 'after he had stopped being a Recusant' (a rare reference to his possibly having become a Catholic convert during his imprisonment for the death of Gabriel Harvey) and 'that at his first communion, in true token of reconciliation he drank out all the full cup of wine'. In view of this it will come as no surprise to learn that sometimes, after a heavy session, 'he hath consumed a whole night in lying looking to his Great Toe, about which he has seen Tartars and Turks, Romans and Carthaginians fight in his imagination ...'

When finally Jonson marched off into the mist and back to England, it is easy to picture Drummond standing watching him, almost entirely surrounded by his own empty bottles and filled with an immense sense of relief:

> He is a great lover and praiser of himself, a contemner and scorner of others, given rather to lose a friend than a jest, jealous of every word and action of those about him (especially after a drink which is one of the elements in which he liveth), a dissembler of ill parts which reign in him, a bragger of some good that he wanteth, thinketh nothing well but what either he himself or some of his friends and countrymen hath

> said and done. He is passionately kind and angry, careless either to gain or keep, vindictive but if he be well answered, at himself ... Interpreteth best sayings and deeds often to the worst, oppressed with fantasy, which hath ever mastered his reason, a general disease in many poets.

Presumably Jonson did not feel he had outstayed his welcome in any way, for on 10 May 1619 he wrote to Drummond asking if he would do a little research for him on a project on which he was engaged, and sending his regards to a formidable list of people he had met while staying with him. We do not know what Drummond replied, but looking at it nearly four centuries later, we can only be grateful that he recorded the meeting in such detail, for it gives us not only a most lively first-hand account of what it was like to be in Ben's company but also how the fame of the London poets and playwrights had spread far enough for his listeners to want news of them.

* * *

Before Jonson's walk to Scotland a major theatrical light had gone out, for on 13 March 1618 Richard Burbage died. He had risen, alongside Edward Alleyn, in the late 1580s, had matched him for ten years then, as Alleyn gradually withdrew from the stage in the late 1590s, he had gone on to become the greatest actor of his day over a span of over twenty years. In an age of gossip, it is impossible to find anyone with a bad word to say of Richard Burbage, a happily married family man, who remained, to the end, enormously popular with audiences.

Those who saw him vied with each other to describe his performances, always a difficult matter with so ephemeral a craft. There are five versions of a 'Funerall Elegy on the death of the famous Actor Richard Burbage: who died Saturday in Lent, the 13 March 1618':

> The Play now ended, think his grave to be

The retiring house of his sad Tragedie.
Where to give his fame this, be not afraid,
Here lies the best Tragedian ever played.
No more young Hamlet though but scant of breath
Shall cry revenge for his dear father's death:
Poor Romeo never more shall tears beget
For Juliet's love and cruel Capulet:
Harry shall not be seen as king or Prince,
They died with thee, dear Dick
Not to revive again. Jeronimo
Shall cease to mourn his son, Horatio…
Edward shall lack a representative,
And Crookback, as befits, shall cease to live.
Tyrant Macbeth with unwash'd bloody hand
We vainly now may hope to understand.
Brutus and Marcius henceforth must be dumb
For ne'er thy like upon our stage shall come
To charm the faculty of eyes and ears,
Unless we could command the dead to rise…
Heartbroke Philaster and Amintas too
Are left forever; with the red-haired Jew,
Which sought the bankrupt merchant's pound of flesh,
By woman lawyer, caught in his own mesh.

Richard Corbet wrote:

Mine host was full of ale and history…
Besides what of his knowledge he could say,
He had authentic notice from the Play;
Which, I might guess, by mustering up the ghosts,
And policies, not incident to hosts;
But chiefly by that one perspicuous thing,
Where he mistook a player for a King.
For when he would have said, King Richard died,
And called – A horse! a horse! he, Burbidge, cry'de.

It ends:
What a wide world, the Globe thy fittest place!
Thy stature small, but every thought and mood
Might thoroughly from thy face be understood

And his whole action he could change with ease
From Ancient Lear to youthful Pericles.
But let me not forget one chiefest part
Wherein beyond the rest, he moved the heart,
The grieved Moor, made jealous by a slave
Who sent his wife to fill a timeless grave,
Then slew himself upon the bloody bed.
All these and many more with him are dead,
Thereafter must our poets leave to write.
Since thou art gone, dear Dick, a tragic night
Will wrap our black-hung stage. He made a Poet.
And those who yet remain full surely know it;
For having Burbadge [sic] to give forth each line
It filled their brain with fury more divine.

Another anonymous admirer wrote:

Oft have I seen him leap into the Grave
Suiting the person, which he seemed to have
Of a sad lover, with so true an Eye,
That there I would have sworn he meant to die ...

It is clear from the touching obituaries in verse that Burbage had been successful in many major roles outside those of Shakespeare such as Hieronimo (or Jeronimo) in Kyd's still-popular *The Spanish Tragedy*, Philaster in Beaumont and Fletcher's play of that name and Amintas in their *Maid's Tragedy*, Jonson's Volpone and 'subtil Alchemist' and no doubt many more. But overshadowing them all is his playing of Shakespeare.

He is remembered as a young actor for his Antipholus in *The Comedy of Errors*, though we are not told which one: maybe he doubled as the twins. Also, from the same period, for Romeo and Benedict, possibly Petruchio too and we know from Thomas Nashe that when he played the chivalrous Talbot in *Henry VI*, it had seemed to him that England's great military hero lived again. 'Crookback Richard' came early, though it was a role he played throughout his life, and played so convincingly that a simple innkeeper 'mistook a player for a King', not least when

Burbage cried real tears on Bosworth Field. Then came the great line of Kings – Richard II and his poetry, Prince Hal growing into Henry V, that mighty procession leading towards the major tragedies of 'tyrant Macbeth', and a Hamlet remembered not least for the passion with which he leapt into Ophelia's grave. The unknown elegist says he was matchless as the 'grieved Moor' and 'ancient Lear', that he played Brutus, Shylock in a red wig, a tradition which lasted for centuries, and, in common with a number of serious actors today, that he also played Malvolio in *Twelfth Night.* Prospero is not listed but he must almost certainly have played Shakespeare's last great role too.

No actor in the world ever had written for him such a line of parts. Truly Shakespeare and Burbage found each other. 'He made a Poet', says the anonymous elegist of Burbage and certainly Shakespeare was magnificently served by his great friend, leading actor and fellow shareholder of the Globe. But 'made a Poet'? At the very least the Poet also made the actor.

23

End of Act Two

From 1616 onwards not only did the sheer quantity of new work begin to fall off but also its quality. And while the playhouses remained popular with the general public, they were now rivalled in more rarefied circles by the form of entertainment which so annoyed Jonson, the Masque. The appetite for Masques at Court and among the aristocracy was insatiable and here, at least, women – even the Queen and princesses – could take part in them and appear on a public stage without scandal.

After Henslowe, the most energetic theatrical innovator was Christopher Beeston who had begun his professional life as an actor with the old Lord Chamberlain's company. He went over to Henslowe and the Lord Admiral's men in 1602, after which he first joined, then ran, the Queen's Men who were based at the Red Bull. Finally, in 1616, he took a lease on a piece of ground in Drury Lane which had been the site of an old cock pit, on which he built a new covered theatre called unsurprisingly, the Cockpit Theatre.

In 1616 the office of the Master of the Revels licensed just four major companies to work in London, the King's and Queen's Men, Palsgrave's company and that of Prince Charles. The King's Men played at the Globe and Blackfriars, being wealthy enough to have both a covered winter theatre and an open summer one, the Queen's at the Cockpit, Palsgrave's were at the Fortune, while Prince Charles' Men took over the Red Bull. Audiences were also becoming more disparate as it cost six times as much to see a play at the Cockpit, Blackfriars or Fortune than in the open theatres of the Globe and Red Bull.

When Beeston moved his company from the Red Bull to the Cockpit he took his repertoire of plays with him and the hard-up apprentices who had made up the Red Bull's faithful audience found that their choice was now between paying more to see the plays they most enjoyed or remaining at the Red Bull with its new repertoire.

They became increasingly annoyed at their enforced lack of choice and John Chamberlain, writing in 1617, describes how, on Shrove Tuesday of that year, an ugly mob of apprentices decided to take the law into their own hands and punish Beeston.[1] They broke into the Cockpit, wrecked its new interior and went on to demolish Beeston's own house which was next door.

The players fought back with some spirit, firing on the mob and hitting some of them 'yet they entered and defaced it, cutting the players' apparell alle to pieces, and all other they're furniture, and burnt theyre playbooks and did what other mischief they could'. The following year the apprentices planned a return match but this time the authorities got wind of it and took steps to prevent it.

With regard to Plays versus Masques, Professor Gurr rightly points out that in English we have no word that entirely describes the experience of those who go to see a play. 'Audience' really means those who hear, while 'spectators' go to football matches. Playgoing combines both. The Elizabethan and Jacobean playwrights, who usually described themselves as 'poets', intended the words to be the most important part of the show and wrote to be listened to.[2] Masques offered words as well but they took second place to the spectacle, often magnificent, at which Inigo Jones excelled, and it was because Ben Jonson so often found himself working with Jones, that he took so much against him, feeling that the artist's extraordinary designs wrecked his own poetry.

However, while women at the highest level in society could paint their faces, dye their hair and exhibit themselves in outrageous costumes at Court performances, ordinary women were still legally prevented from taking up acting as a profession, while even after thirty years of public theatre-going, those who continued to venture into the playhouses were still considered little better than harlots by the anti-playhouse zealots such as Robert Anton:

> Oh why are women rather growne so mad,
> That their immodest feete like planets gad
> With such irregular motion to base playes,
> Where all the deadly sinnes keep holidays,
> There shall they see the vices of the times,
> Orestes incest, Cleopatra's crimes.[3]

Foreign visitors often remarked on the freedom afforded English women to go out without male protection. A certain Thomas Platter of 'Basel', Switzerland, writing at the end of the previous century had noted: 'The women count it a great honour to be taken there [to a tavern or beer-garden] and given wine with sugar to drink. If one woman only is invited she often brings three or four other women and they gaily toast each other.'

Father Orazio Busino, who was appointed to the Venetian Embassy at the Court of St James and who lived in England between 1617 and 1619, left a graphic account of a lady he came across at the Fortune Theatre.

> These theatres are frequented by a number of respectable and handsome ladies, who come freely and seat themselves among the men without the slightest hesitation. On the evening in question his Excellency and the Secretary were pleased to play me a trick by placing me amongst a bevy of young women. Scarcely was I seated ere a very elegant dame, but in a mask, came and placed herself besides me . . . she determined to honour me showing me some fine diamonds on her fingers, repeatedly taking off no fewer than three gloves which were worn one over the other. This lady's bodice was of yellow satin richly embroidered, her petticoat of gold tissue with stripes, her robe of red velvet with a raised pile, lined with yellow

> muslin with broad stripes of pure gold. She wore an apron of point lace of various patterns: her head-tire was highly perfumed, and the collar of white satin beneath the delicately-wrought ruff struck me as extremely pretty.[4]

Father Busino could, one feels, have earned his living covering the equivalent of the spring collections had there been such things as women's magazines, his calling giving an added frisson to what he to say.

* * *

On the same day as the Lord Mayor's Show in 1618, Sir Walter Raleigh, the last link with Christopher Marlowe, finally went to the block for treason. While back in the 1590s Cecil had been unable to rake up sufficient proof to move against Raleigh over the School of the Night, he did not give up trying to destroy him.

In the hotbed of rumour and intrigue which was London in the summer the old Queen died, he had Raleigh arrested on charges of treason, although there has never been any proof that he was ever disloyal. Raleigh conducted his own defence brilliantly but he was condemned to death, a reprieve being granted literally at the last moment when he was already on the scaffold.

Condemned to life imprisonment, Raleigh spent the next ten years writing books, including his *History of the World*, of which only one volume, that referred to by Jonson in his discussions with Drummond, survives.

In 1616 Raleigh was released to lead an expedition up the Orinoco River in search of a mythical goldmine – yet another El Dorado. He did not find it, his son died on the journey and possibly as a result of both misfortunes, he turned with savagery on a Spanish town, razing it to the ground and behaving with the ruthlessness he had shown to the Irish in Ulster years earlier. But Spain was no longer at war with England and when he returned home, the Spanish Ambassador complained bitterly to the King. As a result, Raleigh's suspended death sentence was invoked and he died on the scaffold in Whitehall.

While it no doubt gave Cecil great satisfaction to have his last great rival under lock and key from 1603 onwards, he did not live to see Raleigh's final downfall. Cecil, still the King's Chief Minister and now an Earl, had died four years earlier in 1612. He was only forty-nine.

* * *

New names were appearing alongside those of Dekker, Rowley, Heywood and the rest. Two such were John Ford and Philip Massinger who shared a common experience with many that have come after them, that neither was able to make much of a living out of writing for the theatre. John Ford was admitted to the Middle Temple at sixteen but his early career was disrupted and stormy and he was rusticated for two years for failing to pay off his Buttery bill. He was never called to the Bar but practised as a lawyer at least until 1620. Ford was one of the many Jacobean playwrights who lost a number of their play scripts at the hands of 'Warburton's Cook'. Again and again, when trying to track down plays recorded as having been performed, there is a note to the effect that a certain play has disappeared because the 'script was burned by Warburton's cook', or a play title is mentioned as 'one of the manuscripts destroyed by Warburton's cook'.[5]

Betsy Baker, for it is she, was the cook/servant of John Warburton who lived from 1682 to 1759 and was an indefatigable collector of almost everything, but especially of old manuscripts. He managed to acquire the original 'books' of a large number of old plays by famous Elizabethan, Jacobean and Carolinian playwrights, from early Jonson, through Middleton, to Shirley and Brome. Many were very rare editions indeed and, thanks to Betsy Baker, have now become 'lost plays'.

Unfortunately Warburton's passion was almost entirely for *acquiring* objects and manuscripts; it did not extend to looking after anything once he had achieved his aim. He lived riotously, drank hard and continually ran out of money. In July 1720 he sold one batch of valuable manuscripts to the Earl of Oxford in order to bring in some money for drink, but at a later date most of his rare collection of plays were, through his carelessness and the ignorance of Betsy Baker, 'unluckily burned or put under pye bottoms'. A list of some fifty-five lost plays exists in his own handwriting. Many were unique, their loss irreplaceable, and among these are plays by Tourneur and four written by John Ford.

It is as well John Ford did not know what fate had in store for his scripts since he had a reputation for being a dismal fellow, according to an anonymous contemporary:

Deep in the dumps John Ford was got,
With folded arms and melancholy hat.

Philip Massinger was born in relatively comfortable circumstances as his father was the manager of the Earl of Pembroke's business affairs. It is possible that it was the Earl being patron to a company of players that encouraged young Philip's interest. Massinger senior then went on to become a Member of Parliament and Examiner to the Council of the Welsh Marches, but he died when Philip was about nineteen and, surprisingly in view of his career, left his family destitute. It is interesting that Marlowe, Shakespeare, Middleton and even Jonson (whose money always ran fast through his fingers), all playwrights from artisan backgrounds, made a better hand at getting a living out of writing plays than did some of their contemporaries who were born into comparative wealth.

Like so many before him, Massinger gravitated first to Henslowe, spending his early years writing plays in collaboration with others. Early on in his career he approached the Earl of Pembroke, pleading for patronage and inviting him:

. . . to cast an eye
Of favour on my downtrod poverty.

He told the Earl that if he received such patronage it would enable him to write much better than if he was having to struggle all the time to make ends meet, which sounds like an applicant for a publisher's commission or Arts Council grant today. He does not seem to have had much of a response for by 1613 he was in prison for debt.

In 1616 he joined the King's Men, leaving them briefly in 1623, to return two years later after John Fletcher's death. Possibly the two men did not get on. It would seem that Massinger's views, as did those of John Marston (who had been a close friend of John Pym at university), inclined towards political reform and, like Middleton and Jonson, he wrote some plays which offended the Court. In *Think What You List* and *The Emperor of the East,* he only thinly conceals criticism of James I's favourites and other political figures. Later, as Arthur Symons notes in his introduction to the nineteenth-century Mermaid edition of Massinger's plays, while Queen Henrietta Maria paid the dramatist the compliment of attending a performance of one of his plays, *Cleander* (since lost), Charles I insisted on various cuts being made to another lost play, *The King and the Subject,* saying: 'This is too insolent, and to be changed!'

His most popular play by far was *A New Way to Pay Old Debts,* possibly written about 1624. Nowadays it seems far more akin to a Victorian melodrama than to its own age, particularly in the character of Sir Giles Overreach. This rumbustious villain is described as 'a cruel extortioner', his nastiness extending even to his trying to make his daughter snare a lord by seducing him into making her pregnant and thus enforce marriage. However, while the plot may seem Victorian, the language does not and it is unlikely that any Victorian heroine would have had her 'ruin' explained to her in such forthright terms. The part of Overreach has given a host of actors ever since a chance to go over the top in performance, including Edmund Kean in 1816 (of which there is a painting) and the late Emrys James.

Hazlitt says of Massinger that 'his impassioned characters are like drunkards or madmen, their conduct is extreme and outrageous, their motives unaccountable and weak'. Massinger, he continues, 'shows a peculiarly corrupt tone of thought even in his heroines when they are intended as models of virtue. Their morality lies entirely in their obedience to outward observance, not to inner principle. Purity is not to be found in his world and his obscenity seems purposeless'. Massinger might have foreshadowed melodramatic Victorian characters but he saw human nature with more honest eyes.

The play *The Second Maid's Tragedy* is sometimes attributed to Massinger, in collaboration with Ford, and has also been attributed to Tourneur. In July 1993 an American, Charles Hamilton, rushed into print in the media with the declaration that he had found in the British Library a 'new' play by William Shakespeare in his own handwriting which he identified as one known as *The History of Cardenio.* Needless to say he was soon shot down, the play in question being *The Second Maid's Tragedy.*

The plot begins conventionally enough with a usurping King who desires his predecessor's mistress, the 'Lady'. Pushed by her family to accept his advances (shades of Tourneur) she declines, is abducted, raped and commits suicide. So far so good for a Jacobean play. But her would-be lover, determined to have his way, has her dug up and brought back to him at Court to indulge in some necrophilia. A sub-plot has a jealous husband persuade his friend to attempt to seduce his wife to see if she is faithful (overtones of *Cymbeline*). The text is quite unlike anything Shakespeare ever wrote and most strongly suggests Middleton in the vein of *Women Beware Women* and *The Changeling.* While anonymous plays can never be attributed with total certainty, it does seem that recent scholarship comes down in favour of Middleton and the play has been included in a recent collection of his works published by Oxford University Press.

Women Beware Women, one of Middleton's great plays, was given its first performance in 1621. It is a remarkable study of several women, their passions and jealousies and their reactions to the extreme situations in which they find themselves. It is a play which still has the power to grip modern audiences and which offers marvellous roles for actresses.

Another play given its first production in 1621 is the 'drama-documentary', *The Witch of Edmonton*, credited to Dekker, Rowley and Ford. On 16 April 1621 an old woman, Elizabeth Sawyer from Edmonton, was hanged as a witch at Tyburn. Eleven days later, on 27 April, a pamphlet was published about her alleged witchcraft and the crimes she was supposed to have committed: *The Wonderful Discovery of Elizabeth Sawyer Witch, late of Edmonton*, written by 'Henry Goodcole, Minister of the Word of God, and her continual visitor in the Gaol of Newgate'. On 29 December, the Prince's Company acted a play on the subject before the King and Court, secure in the knowledge that King James would always be sympathetic to such a subject.

In a period when any eccentric old woman could all too easily be deemed a witch and made a scapegoat for all local ills, Elizabeth Sawyer fitted the bill all too well as she was an unprepossessing-looking woman, stunted in growth and with only one eye. During her interrogation she was asked why this was and how she had been blinded, to which she replied: 'With a stick which one of my children had in the hand: that night my mother did die it was done, for I was stooping by the bedside and by chance did hit my eye on the sharp end of the stick' – believable in view of the dark hovel in which the family had lived.

What means were used to make a lonely, poverty-stricken, terrified old woman confess to witchcraft hardly bear thinking about, but 'confess' she did, down in the depths of Newgate Gaol, as the report of her interrogation testifies:

Question: In what shape would the Devil come to you?
Answer: Always in the shape of a dog and of two colours, sometimes black and sometimes white.
Question: And from where did the Devil suck your

blood?

Answer: The place where the Devil did suck my blood was a little above the fundament and that place chosen by himself and in that place by continual drawing, there is a thing in the form of a teat at which the Devil would suck me and I asked the Devil why he would suck my blood and he said it was to nourish him.

The Devil, Elizabeth Sawyer told her interrogators, had asked for her 'body and soul or he would tear me to pieces'. He had taught her three Latin words as a spell: *'Sanctibetur nomen tuum'.*

There were numerous ludicrous 'tests' of witchcraft and as a local JP called Arthur Robinson had a long-standing dispute with Mother Sawyer, he had ordered one to be carried out under his supervision. It was '. . . to pluck the thatch of her house, burn it and it being so burned, the author of such mischief should presently then come; it was observed and affirmed to the court that Elizabeth Sawyer would presently frequent the house of them that burned the thatch which they had plucked off her house, without any sending.'

On such evidence was the poor old woman convicted. Asked before her death why she had confessed, she replied, 'I do it to clear my conscience and now having done, I am the more quiet and better prepared and willing thereby to suffer death, for I have no hope at all of my life, although I must confess I would live longer if I might.'

The Witch of Edmonton is interesting not only because it is based on a true story but because it is quite clear that the sympathies of at least one of its three authors, Thomas Dekker (for he is generally credited with the witchcraft strand of the play) are so clearly with the Mother Sawyer. From the first we are shown how she is continually persecuted to the point where she finally decides that since she is unable to convince people that she is not a witch, she might just as well claim to be one and see if she can gain something from it. Dekker also draws an extremely unflattering portrait of the real life Arthur Robinson, thinly disguised as Sir Arthur Clarington. In the play Clarington is credited with starting the whole thing off by palming his pregnant mistress off on an unsuspecting young man with whom she has also slept but who is already committed to marrying a neighbouring heiress. The young man thus marries twice within a week after which he decides his only recourse is to murder one of the brides, the motivation for his crime being blamed on the witch. Dekker gives Mother Sawyer knowledge of Clarington's prior involvement with the first bride, along with other of his unsavoury secrets, making it imperative that he get rid of her.

Clarington/Robinson gets off scot free at the end of the play, leaving one onlooker to comment: 'If luck had served Sir Arthur and every man had his due, somebody might have tottered ere this without paying fines, like as you list . . .' How much truth there is in the portrayal of Robinson as Clarington (and he is shown carrying out the 'thatch' test as Robinson had testified in court), we do not know, but it would keep the libel lawyers busy and in funds today.

* * *

In 1623, Shakespeare's old friends and fellow-actors, John Heming and Henry Condell, published thirty-six of his plays in what is now known as the First Folio. Sixteen of them had been published during his lifetime in 'Quarto' editions but it is not known if he had any hand in their publication or supervised how they were printed. It is even possible they were published without his authority.

Heming and Condell took the plays in the existing sixteen Quartos and added to them twenty more, putting them into a single volume 'in order to keep the memory of so worthy a friend and fellow alive'. A thirty-seventh play, *Pericles*, was added in 1664 when the Third Folio was published. Heming and Condell had authenticated the thirty-six plays in the First Folio but presumably had some doubts as to the authorship both of *Pericles* and *The Two Noble Kinsmen*, now credited to Shakespeare and Fletcher.

* * *

Two further plays from the early 1620s, *The Changeling* and *A Game at Chess* deserve special note, the first because it is the most extraordinary psychological study of an amoral woman, and the second because it caused a major political scandal which almost led to war between England and Spain.

The Changeling was written by Middleton and Rowley, the main plot being Middleton's. A wealthy young woman, affianced to a suitable young man, falls in love with someone else. The family steward, who has long lusted after her, offers to kill her fiancé for her. Delighted, she promises him a reward for doing so, imagining he will want money:

> . . . belike his wants are greedy, and to such
> Gold tastes like angels' food.

Having killed her fiancé, and hacked off a finger bearing the engagement ring as proof, the steward, de Flores, returns to claim his reward but it is not money he wants but the lady. Thus Beatrice–Joanna embarks on a course of deception and murder during which she constantly deceives herself as to her motives for so doing and only at the end of the play does she finally see herself as she really is. The scenes between Beatrice–Joanna and de Flores are riveting and beautifully written, a recent production by the Royal Shakespeare Company holding a theatre full of secondary school pupils in total silence.

Middleton wrote *A Game at Chess* on his own. Towards the end of the first week in August 1624, a gentleman called John Chamberlain wrote to a friend about the play which everyone who was anyone just had to see.

> I doubt not but you have heard of our famous play of

> Gondomar, which hath been followed with extraordinarie concourse, and frequented by all sorts of people – old and young, rich and poor, masters and servants, papists and puritans, wise men, etc., churchmen and statesman as Sir Henry Wotton, Sir Albert Morton, Sir Benjamin Ruddier, Sir Thomas Lake and a world besides; the Lady Smith would have gone if she could have persuaded me to go with her. I am not so sour or severe but that I would willingly have attended her, but I could not sit for so long, for we must have been there before one o'clock at farthest to find any roome …

Such was the play's notoriety that it brought about one of the earliest recorded traffic jams, as carriages blocked the narrow streets around the Globe and people fought each other in their attempts to get in to the theatre to see it. It was so popular that it was put on for an unprecedented nine performances in succession, the first 'long run', and grossed the truly huge sum of £1,500. It also made Middleton a wanted man.

The play came at a sensitive time. The young Prince Charles and his bosom friend, the Duke of Buckingham, had recently returned from their abortive adventure to Spain in search of 'the Spanish Bride', a Spanish princess for the young prince. The venture failed dismally, the two young men returning without the bride and with King James's amateurish attempts at political intrigue revealed for all to see. This embarrassing incident, coupled with the sending of 6,000 English troops to Flanders on what turned out to be an abortive mission, had brought about a surge of jingoism of the kind which periodically afflicts the country.

Middleton set the continuing rivalry between Spain and England in the context of a game of chess, in which all the moves become part of the plot. The white pieces, naturally, are the English, the black pieces from the mythical country of 'Gondomar', the Spanish. The characters on both sides are only thinly disguised. The forces of good led by the White Knight (Prince Charles) and the White Duke (Buckingham) are presented in a highly ambivalent manner and the history of James's inept political intrigue treated with biting satire.

On the other hand there was little doubt as to the identity of the black pieces either, especially the representation of the Spanish Ambassador, an astute politician. Just to make quite sure everyone recognised him, the players had actually managed to acquire one of his cast-off suits for the actor playing the part, who was also carried around on a litter as the poor Ambassador was suffering from a fistula at the time. Middleton appears to have updated his play throughout the time he was writing it as current events were added as they took place; he based the treacherous White King's Pawn on Lionel Cranfield, Earl of Middlesex and Lord Treasurer, who was impeached in the April of 1624.

News of jammed streets, queues and people turned away from trying to get into the Globe soon reached the Court even though the production had been carefully timed for when King and Court were out of London for the summer. The dramatic equivalent today would have to be one which not only portrayed all the recent royal scandals but threw in major government corruption for good measure, the whole being set against the background of the Falklands campaign.

King James was told about it by the enraged Spanish Ambassador who complained of 'this very scandalous comedy, acted publicly by the King's own players', in which he himself was represented on stage 'in a rude and dishonourable fashion'. He added that 'there was such merriment, hub-bub and applause that had I been many leagues away it would not have been possible for me not to take notice of it. There were,' he concluded bitterly, 'more than *3,000* people there on the day the audience was smallest'. On 12 August James wrote to the Privy Council asking whatever the Master of the Revels had been about to sanction such a play, and requiring the Council to summon the King's Men before them immediately to demand an explanation, along with the author, Middleton, who must be severely punished.

On 21 August the Council replied to the King by letter that they had indeed summoned the players who had 'produced a book, being an original and perfect copy thereof (or so they affirmed) as seen and allowed by Sir Henry Herbert, Knight, Master of the Revels, under his own hand and subscribed by him in the last page of the said book.' The players were discharged with a 'round and sharp reproof', on the grounds that they had portrayed the monarchy on stage, and were then forbidden to act in anything at all until the King's pleasure was known. To ensure they complied with this, they were bound over in the sum of £300. It was also made clear to the unfortunate Sir Henry Herbert that he was scarcely fit to hold his office. The simple explanation is likely to be that the script had passed through on the nod among a number of others.

As for Middleton, his arrest ordered by Royal Decree, at first he simply refused to obey the summons to appear before the Council. As they duly reported to King James, the author of the piece was indeed, 'one Middleton, who, shifting out of the way and not attending the Board as was expected, we have given warrant for the apprehending of him'. Finally, after scouring London for him without success, on 27 August the Council ordered the arrest of his son, Edward, on the assumption that this would bring Middleton in. It did. Three days later he gave himself up, and his indemnity was formally accepted. A tradition, preserved in a note by a contemporary hand in a manuscript of the play belonging to a man called Dyson, says 'Middleton was committed to prison where he lay for some time and at last got out upon a Petition to the King'.

In the end the furore died down. The players returned to the Globe and Middleton to his joint employment as playwright and City Chronologer. He had been appointed to the latter position in 1620 at salary of £6.13s.4d a year, later raised to £10. The post was no sinecure if undertaken properly as the incumbent had a number of duties from keeping a journal of events in the City and writing speeches for the Lord Mayor and leading Alderman, to devising entertainments for civic banquets when requested to do so.

Middleton appears to have worked conscientiously in the post, unlike his successor, Ben Jonson, who found it useful for the money it brought in but did as little as possible.

24

'O Rare Ben Jonson . . .'

Death was cutting a swathe through the actors and dramatists who had been part of the great days of the early professional theatre: Burbage, Pope, Nathaniel Field, Edward Alleyn. Alleyn left £10,000 to endow his college; Constance Alleyn's unsatisfactory marriage had lasted only a short time.

The *Oxford Companion to the Theatre* gives the date of William Rowley's death as 1637 but all other sources put it either at the end of 1624 or in February 1625, depending on which calendar is used. Plague had raged again in London during the winter of 1624/25 and we are told John Fletcher was one of its victims. Rowley may well have been another for 35,000 people died in London and its surrounding suburbs in less than a twelvemonth.

Of Fletcher's death, Aubrey writes:

> John Fletcher, invited to go with a Knight of Norfolk or Suffolk in the Plague time of 1625, stayed to make himself a suit of clothes, and while it was making fell sick of the Plague and died. This I had from his tailor, who is now a very old man, and the clerk of St Mary Overy's in Southwark. Mr. Fletcher had an issue in his arm. The clerk (who was wont to bring him leaves to dress it), when he came, found the spots upon him. Death stopped his journey and laid him low here.[1]

Fletcher was buried in St Mary Overy's, the church in

which the John Fletcher, who may well have been him, was married in 1613 and where a number of his contemporaries already lay, including Edmund Shakespeare.

King James also died in 1625, not of the plague, but from what is vaguely described as a lingering fever. As a mark of respect the theatres were closed immediately but the closure then continued until the end of November as a precaution against the plague.

James' death was to herald great change, the consequences of which would lead eventually to the Civil War. He had never succeeded in becoming a popular King but he had become generally accepted, even considered with affection by some, as he grew older. He had remained interested in theatre. It was his good fortune to inherit an extraordinary flowering of theatrical talent but he deserves the credit for recognising it and so giving the major companies the royal seal of approval. He went out on an expensive and truly theatrical high note, his funeral ceremony 'designed' by Inigo Jones.

While James had been content to surround himself with his '£30 knights', he had also been accessible to those writers, like Jonson, whom he personally favoured and he had happily tolerated his Falstaffian person about the Court. More, in recognition of Jonson's undoubted talent, he had given him a state pension of a hundred marks a year making him in effect our first Poet Laureate. So many ambitious, sycophantic and place-seeking men rose and fell under both Elizabeth and James that it might be a cause for wonder that someone of Jonson's temperament should have avoided disaster, but Marchette Chute in *Jonson in Westminster*[2] rightly emphasises that unlike so many hangers-on at Court, Jonson wanted neither power nor riches, only the honour due to him as a writer and poet. He felt, therefore, that the gift of a state pension was a public recognition of his worth, giving him the 'bays' he felt his considerable body of work deserved.

The accession of Charles I was to change all that. He was the classic example of a man placed in a position of great authority who is both weak and stubborn. He suffered from what today would be described as 'mind set' and he believed he could never be wrong. Within four years of coming to the throne, he rejected the Petition of Rights, disbanded Parliament, and embarked on the collision course which was to lead to war.

It became immediately apparent that the court of King Charles would be quite unlike that of his father. James had been content for it to be almost slovenly, thinking nothing of being seen in public in an old dressing gown and slippers. Charles made it apparent from the very beginning that he would not tolerate slovenliness in dress or rude or drunken behaviour from anyone. His was to be a time, and his Court a place, of elegant sobriety and to this end his own Coronation was a downbeat occasion, of which his nobles said that they had never seen any solemnity performed with so little noise and so great order.

Those who, in spite of this being known, presented themselves to Charles the worse for drink received short shrift. A nobleman who bragged how well he could hold his drink was told by Charles that he deserved to be hanged, nor, the King informed those around him, would he tolerate 'any sordid words'. It can, therefore, easily be imagined how well the hard-drinking, hard-swearing Jonson went down under the new regime, even if he was supposed to be the official Court poet.

His kind of writing was also going out of fashion. Elegant and amusing comedies were the popular order of the day and, of course, the Masques. While Jonson had heavily criticised Masques as a form of entertainment he had been quite prepared to write them so long as he was paid to do so. Now he was no longer in demand either for plays or Masques. The Court, following the lead given by the new King, made it clear that it now had very different tastes.

At first it had looked as if Jonson might find similar favour with Charles as he had with James, for the first play performed before the new King after the coronation was *The Staple of News*, given by the King's Men, now run by Condell and Heming. Jonson's account of its first night rings all too true to anyone who has had a play performed;

his hanging helplessly around backstage before the performance, his trundling in and out of the 'tiring house' or dressing room (which would not be permitted now) to give his final advice to the actors, before going off to drown his nerves in drink.[3] Jonson's interference in productions was legendary, actors complaining that he prompted them loudly if they lost their words, railed at the bookholder, cursed the wardrobe master, shouted at the musicians and made them sweat for every last mistake they made.

The Staple of News took as its subject matter the new fashion for publishing 'newspapers', an innovation the authorities were greeting with an increasingly jaundiced eye. Only in Holland were newspapers legally allowed to print uncensored and unbiased news and when English newspapers attempted to follow suit some six years after Jonson's play, Charles promptly ordered the Star Chamber to suppress them, but that was all in the future and Jonson's play was received if not with any great enthusiasm, then at least without any trouble.

After the play, Jonson dutifully continued to write the verses he thought expected of him and to begin with these were accepted, but it soon became apparent that he was unable to tailor his work to suit the new regime. Nor did his person suit which, as he said himself was now 'fat, olden and laden with belly', musing that when visiting friends he had a tendency 'to crack' the coach in which he travelled to see them and break their chairs after his arrival. He told a portrait painter that he looked like 'one great blot'.

Snubbed by the new regime at Court, Jonson's response was to found a milieu of his own. The evenings at the Mermaid, remembered with such nostalgia by Francis Beaumont from his exile in the country, were a thing of the past. What had been described in 1616 as 'a club of right worshipful, sirenical gentlemen', had been decimated by the deaths of so many of its unofficial membership that in 1624 Jonson had founded what he called the Apollo Club. It was here that he now proceeded to make himself the centre of his small world. Not surprisingly, he had chosen for its headquarters a meeting room in a Fleet Street tavern, the

Devil and St Dunstan. The sign showed the saint tweaking Satan's nose with a pair of pincers. It was generally known simply as 'the Devil' and was kept by a popular landlord called Simon Wadloe. Jonson had drawn up a set of club rules in Latin, which were put up on the wall while over the door he placed the following verse:

Welcome all who lead or follow,
To the Oracle of Apollo –
Here he speaks out of his pottle,
Or the tripos, his tower bottle:
All his answers are divine,
Truth itself doth flow in wine.
Hang up all the poor hop-drinkers,
Cries old SIM, the king of skinkers,
He the half of life abuses,
That sits watering with the Muses.
Those dull girls no good can mean us;
Wine it is the milk of Venus,
And the poet's horse accounted:
Ply it, and you all are mounted.
'Tis the true Phoebian liquor,
Cheers the brains, makes wits the quicker,
Pays all debts, cures all diseases,
And at once three senses pleases.
Welcome all who lead or follow,
To the Oracle of Apollo.

At least one of Jonson's rules would appeal to those who still prefer to drink without their ears constantly being assaulted by loud music: 'Let no saucy fiddler presume to intrude unless he is sent for . . .', while another, which specifically allowed women to take part in the activities, is well ahead of those who run today's Garrick Club, who as late as 1993 refused female membership once again.

It was taken as read that all members enjoyed eating and drinking well, but they were also expected to offer plenty of good talk and witty conversation. Jonson, as founder and unofficial President, presided over its meetings from a specially raised seat at the end of the room, a seat provided with a robust handrail to enable him to get in and out of it. Wild or unruly behaviour was not allowed, nor drunkenness to the point of stupor or worse:

> . . . mong'st offenced unpardoned will rank,
> of breaking of windows or glasses for spite,
> and spoiling the goods for a rankhelly prank.

However, this did not mean there should be abstinence:

> Let the freedom we take be perverted by none,
> To make any guilty by drinking good wine.[4]

The Apollo Club survived until well into the next century and was used by another Johnson, when Dr Samuel Johnson held a party there to celebrate the publication of a friend's book.

By virtually withdrawing from the Court, Jonson must have thought there was no longer any possibility of getting into any political trouble. His spells in prison for upsetting the authorities with *The Isle of Dogs* and *Eastward Ho!* were twenty years behind him, let alone his branding at Tyburn. It was sheer bad luck, therefore, that was caught up in the aftermath of the murder of George Villiers, Duke of Buckingham.

Jonson had known the Duke quite well in the old days when Villiers had been King James' prime favourite, for he had been a keen participant in Court Masques. James had been besotted with him, heaping honours on him and raising him from a mere indigent gentleman hanger-on at Court to a Duke and one of the wealthiest men in the country. At first Prince Charles had deeply disliked Villiers and his influence on his father but eventually the Duke had married and taken to calling James his 'dear old Dad' as he set about ensuring a place with the next King. Soon Charles and Villiers were so inseparable that Charles had readily agreed to the Duke's mad notion of the venture for the Spanish bride. Indeed, immediately before leaving for Spain, the two had danced in Jonson's Masque *Time Vindicated.* If anything the failure of the Spanish escapade had cemented the relationship between the two young men even more firmly.

In one respect James, whatever his faults might have been, showed great sense. He was prepared to go to almost any lengths to ensure the country did not become embroiled in any unnecessary wars. He had done his best to ensure peace with the old enemy, Spain, from agreeing to the execution of Raleigh to smoothing down the injured feelings of the Ambassador over *A Game at Chess.* James looked across at the Continent, riven by internal disputes and civil war, and announced that such wars solved nothing and that it should not be beyond the wit of man to consider 'other expedients'. On his deathbed, fearing what his son might do, he warned his government that soon 'they should have more war than they knew how to manage', a prophecy which came all too true.

On his death, the strongest influence on his son was now Buckingham. He leaned on him for advice and for emotional support. He said openly that he could not enjoy anything unless Villiers was with him and he allowed the Duke to select a princess for him and negotiate his marriage. Not surprisingly the chosen French princess, the very young Henrietta Maria, intensely disliked Buckingham's influence over her husband. So also did Parliament.

Egged on by the Duke, Charles found himself in rapid succession involved first in a war with Spain, then with France. English troops were humiliated first by the Spaniards at Cadiz, then by the French at La Rochelle, after Buckingham had tried to force a landing on the Ile de Rhé. To cap it all the Duke had also embarked on an affair with the French Queen, a romance which was to provide a later writer with a plot for a best seller, *The Three Musketeers.*

Buckingham returned from France not in the least cowed by his defeat and welcomed by Charles as if he were a great war hero. Buckingham then organised a great naval show off Plymouth, to which he invited the King but his troops, let loose after weeks at sea and smarting from their defeat, set about Plymouth as if it were an enemy port. They also unleashed disease on the town. The people of Plymouth never forgot and the city endured a long siege as they held out for Parliament during the Civil War.[5] Parliament, already outraged, could scarcely believe it when Charles compounded the disaster by encouraging Buckingham to mount a second attack on La Rochelle. Fate, however, intervened.

The lone assassin who believes he is carrying out God's will is no new phenomenon and such a one was the disaffected subaltern and 'loner', John Felton. One morning, as the Duke was having breakfast in his Portsmouth lodgings, Felton made his way in and stabbed him to death; so devastated was the Duke's young pregnant wife, who was upstairs at the time, that she tried to kill herself and her child by throwing herself out of a window.

Charles was never to recover from the death of his friend. Felton was duly executed but was treated by the people not as a murderer or felon but as a national hero. Admiring verses poured off the presses, including one by a young divinity student, Zouch Townley, one of the group of young men who had now attached themselves to Jonson. He not only admired Jonson as a man, but also his style of poetry, so that the verse he wrote, praising Felton's action to the skies, might well have been taken for run-of-the-mill Jonson.

It was assumed that the offending poem *was* by Jonson and he was promptly brought before the Attorney General who demanded to know if he was the author of it. He said he was not. When pressed further Jonson, knowing that Townley had prudently left the country and gone into hiding in the Hague, said he understood it had been written by his young admirer. Townley's lodgings were searched and a dagger found belonging to Jonson, who then underwent a second interrogation. The record of it notes Jonson's response on being told of the discovery:

> On a Sunday after this examinant had heard the said Mr Townley preach at St Margaret's Church in Westminster, Mr Townley, taking a liking to the dagger with a white haft which the examinant ordinarily wore at his girdle, this examinant gave it to him two nights

after, being invited by Mr Townley to sup.

Already considered an unfashionable writer, this final brush with the authorities, who remained deeply suspicious of Jonson's part in the affair, ensured he could never again hope to find favour at Court. There were no more commissions and although he retained his pension of a hundred marks a year until his death, he lived out the rest of his life in real poverty. Worse, whether as a result of the strain of his recent experiences or because he was overweight and drank too much, or possibly through a combination of both, he suffered a paralytic stroke which left him virtually bedridden for the rest of his life. He described himself as being 'blocked up and straitened, narrowed in, fixed to the bed and boards, unlike to win, health or scarce breath.'

Sinking his pride he appealed to the King for an increase in his pension, writing:

That whereas your royal father,
James the blessed, pleased the rather,
Of his special grace to letters,
To make all the Muses debtors,
To his bounty; by extension
Of a free poetic pension,
A large marks annuity,
To be given me in gratuity,
For done service, and to come

He continues in witty vain, explaining how the pension has enabled him to write better verse than would otherwise be the case as it has enabled him to keep body and soul together, ending with the hope that it might:

Please your majesty to make
Of your grace, for goodness sake,
Those your father's marks, your pounds . . .

The King did not respond and Jonson's pension remained at a hundred marks.

In his latter years Jonson had gathered around him a

coterie of young men, known as 'the Tribe of Ben', who were primarily interested in him as a poet rather than a dramatist. Those from comparatively wealthy backgrounds assisted Ben when they could and among these was Sir Lucius Cary, son of a formidable mother. As a girl she had been so mad about reading that her family forbade candles to be put in her room. The result of this edict was that by the time she was twelve she owed her maids for some 800 candles they had smuggled in. She taught herself modern and classical languages and, after her marriage, opened schools in Dublin to enable Irish children to become literate (they failed eventually for lack of funds). Finally she was received into the Catholic church, after which she left her husband who, she said, she had always considered dull and boring.

Sir Kenelm Digby, another 'Tribe' member, was the son of one of the Gunpowder Plot conspirators, who had been at the party thrown by the conspirators which Ben had attended after coming out of gaol in 1605. Sir Kenelm had married the notorious, but beautiful, courtesan Venetia Stanley. In his *Private Memoirs*, he argues that the odds were weighed unfairly against women who had affairs before marriage, since a man actually added to his reputation by so doing. 'There are,' he wrote, 'innumerable vices, incident to them as well as to men, that are far more to be condemned than the breach of this frozen virtue.' It was in the interests of men, not women, that women should be chaste. Other members of the Tribe included Edward Hyde, the future Earl of Clarendon, Thomas Randolph and the young and talented Robert Herrick.

There was also Richard Brome, not a member of the Tribe but variously described as Jonson's servant, secretary or a member of his household. Secretary seems the most likely for Brome went on to become a successful dramatist in his own right, his career cut short only by the Civil War. He has recently received something of a revival.

That Jonson's mind and skill did not suffer from the stroke that had crippled him is shown by the fact that a year later he wrote his last play, *The New Inn*, which was given its first performance at the Blackfriars Theatre by the King's Men.

But gregarious as he remained to the end, he must have felt increasingly lonely, aware that he was rapidly becoming the only survivor of the great days. The actors who he had known and exasperated for so long were gone. Condell and Heming, the last known close intimates of Shakespeare, had died in 1627 and 1630 respectively. Condell described himself in his will as 'citizen and grocer', which suggests he prudently gave himself a second income against the vagaries of being an actor by investing in a grocery business which could also be run by his wife.

Thomas Middleton's burial is recorded as having taken place on 4 July 1627 at the parish church of Newington Butts. He died, as he had lived, in straitened circumstances and the following year his widow, Magdalen, had to apply to the civic authorities for financial assistance. She was granted twenty nobles.

We do not know when John Webster died, but by 1634 he was bracketed with Fletcher as a 'dead poet'. Chapman proved one of the longest-lived, dying in 1634 at the age of seventy-five and was buried in the churchyard of St Giles in the Fields in a tomb designed by his friend, Inigo Jones. The deaths of Thomas Dekker and Philip Massinger are harder to trace.

Dekker continued writing into the 1630s, in spite of his constant battle with debt and, as well as his plays and the amusing *Gull's Hornbook*, wrote a number of hard hitting journalistic pamphlets on the poor and oppressed people among whom he lived and worked. They include *The Wonderful Year*; the story of the Plague of 1602, *News from Hell*, and *The Seven Deadly Sins of London*. A Thomas Dekker died in Clerkenwell in 1632 and it might well be our Dekker for he died in debt and his widow refused to administer his estate. Yet a pamphlet by Dekker was published in 1638 in which he refers to his 'more than three score years'. It could, of course, have been published posthumously. Did he live to see the Civil War? We simply do not know. He disappears into the dark from which he came, having illuminated for us so wittily the life of his fellow actors and dramatists.

Massinger's burial is registered as having taken place on 18 March 1638 and some mystery also surrounds his death. He lived at the Bankside, near the Globe Theatre, and was apparently in good health up to the day before his death. It is said 'he went to bed well and was dead before morning', whereupon his body 'being accompanied by comedians [actors] was buried about the middle of the churchyard belonging to St Saviour's church'. His burial entry reads: '1638 March 18. Philip Massinger, stranger in the church – 21'. Once again the word 'stranger' means only that he was not a parishioner and possibly this was why the large burial fee of £2 was charged. Tradition has it that he was put in the same grave as his friend and collaborator, John Fletcher.

If Fletcher truly had been the victim of an earlier epidemic of the plague, then he was fortunate to have received separate burial and in a church, rather than being promptly thrown into a plague pit with other victims. The years 1637 and 1638 were also plague years but while its effects were not as severe as the earlier scourges of the early 1590s and mid-1620s it lasted for longer and the theatres were closed for fifteen months. Possibly Massinger was one of its victims as he sickened and died so quickly. If so, then like Fletcher, it was kept quiet so that he could be properly buried, accompanied to his grave by his friends, 'the comedians'.

* * *

In spite of being what he described as a 'mere bed-ridden wit', Jonson kept that wit to the very end. His greatest sorrow was that poverty forced him to sell the library of books which were so dear to him. He died on 6 August 1637 leaving behind numerous unfinished manuscripts, an old wicker chair ('such as old women use') and goods to the value of only £8.8s.10d., a puny amount compared to Shakespeare and Alleyn. His estranged wife was long dead and there were no surviving children.

He was buried in Westminster Abbey as befitted our first, if unofficial, Poet Laureate, but in the North Aisle, not in Poet's Corner with Chaucer and Beaumont. There was a tradition that Jonson had joked with the Dean of Westminster that he could not afford to be buried alongside the other poets as he was too large and so the plot would cost too much. He suggested therefore that he should be buried standing up which would require only some two feet.

The story had been considered to be apocryphal until, in the nineteenth century, a Lady Wilson was also buried in the North Aisle. The burial disturbed Jonson's grave and, lo and behold, there was Jonson's cheap coffin standing upright instead of horizontal.[6]

His epitaph reads, simply, 'O rare Ben Jonson' and he was, indeed, a rare spirit. Poets vied with each other to say farewell to him in verse. The most touching is Herrick:

When I a verse shall make,
Know I have prayed thee
For old religion's sake,
Saint Ben to aid me.

Make the way smooth for me
When I, thy Herrick,
Honouring thee, on my knee,
Offer my lyric.

Candles I'll give to thee
And a new altar;
And thou, Saint Ben, shalt be
Writ in my psalter.

25

Restoration

The death of Ben Jonson finally drew a line under that extraordinary era that had begun with the accession of the young Queen Elizabeth and the birth of the English Renaissance and had witnessed not only the very beginnings of professional theatre but also its greatest flowering. It had produced, in William Shakespeare, one towering genius of world proportions and a school of great dramatists whose misfortune was to be overshadowed only because of his unique and blazing talent.

The theatrical world on the eve of the Civil War was very different. Elaborate Masques had accustomed the Court and aristocracy to highly artificial performances and the use of elaborate scenery and costumes, entertainments in which the design was more important than either the text or the acting. The old courtyard theatres were now out of fashion. Playgoers expected comfort while they were entertained and courtiers, accustomed to the kind of scenery and special effects used in Masques, expected similar sophistication in the playhouse. The wooden O' of Shakespeare, where members of the audience were able to fill in what could not physically be shown on stage by the use of their imaginations, was a thing of the past. This, naturally, set bounds to what a playwright could do.

Adrian Noble, now artistic director of the Royal Shakespeare Company, in a discussion shortly before the opening of the Swan Theatre in 1986[1] suggested that Shakespeare:

existed as much at the end of the Dark Ages as at the beginning of the Age of Enlightenment. He took into himself a huge amount of mysticism, paganism, the different attitude towards where man stands in nature. It shifted during the Jacobean period and further during the Caroline. When you go right back to the Greeks you have man in the open air. The audience sees man and nature at the same time because of the way their theatres were built. They saw everything – sky, man, earth, in a natural setting. In the Elizabethan period it shifted, it was still man but not man in nature, although he was still seen under an open sky: he was man on a bare stage. By that time the nature was filled in by the poetry, the landscape of verse.

They created whole universes which can actually change and transform before the audience because what they see with their eyes they are also hearing about with their ears. Then came the next stage, which was moving indoors, and this was the beginning of the move towards bourgeois theatre and that frightful man, Brumante, who invented perspective theatre. So you end up with one seat which has the perfect view and that is the King's seat, and eventually the popular theatre becomes elitist theatre, as we move first indoors, and then into perspective, then scenery and this is the death of popular theatre and simultaneously, the death of a certain relationship between men and society which ceases to be the preoccupation of the playwright. What became the preoccupation after the Restoration was not man and nature but just a few men in a bourgeois society, and the slice of life became ever narrower with less and less interest in man and nature until it virtually disappeared.

By the end of the 1630s there was no longer a demand for satires such as *Chaste Maid in Cheapside* and *A Trick to Catch the Old One* with their robust attitude to sex nor, in such uncertain times, would any writer have taken the risk of offering the equivalent of *Eastward Ho!* or *A Game at Chess.*

This is not to say, however, that there were no more accomplished playwrights; there were a number including James Shirley, Richard Brome and the young William Davenant. Shirley wrote tragedies, comedies and Masques, always designing his work to stay within the bounds of what was fashionable. He was a shameless plagiarist, stealing plots, characters and speeches from former playwrights. He wrote his version of *The Duchess of Malfi*, under the title *The Cardinal*, but the characters are pale shadows of their originals; the fascinating villain Bosola and the incestuously inclined Ferdinand disappear, while the Duchess is reduced to a good woman making a choice between two fairly acceptable suitors, neither of whom has a physical relationship with her. While the play still ends with a heap of corpses, it is a curiously sanitised affair.

Shirley's most serious work is *The Traitor*, which more closely harks back to the old Revenge Plays with its gothic ending of a Masque of the Lusts and Furies, but his popularity came from his comedies of manners such as *Hyde Park* and *The Gamester*, plays which foreshadow those of the Restoration. Amusing and reassuring, they are set in the world the Royalist audiences knew and loved.

Brome is more interesting, bringing with him a whiff of that older world and of his master, Jonson. *The Jovial Crew* with its band of beggars, many of whom have been thrown on to the roads because of the Enclosure Acts, has remarkable resonances to the problems of the homeless and the New Age Travellers of today. In 1992/93 it was given an extremely successful revival by the Royal Shakespeare Company in a stunning production by Max Stafford Clarke. Another Brome play, also successful in its day, might well be similarly due for revival. In *The Antipodes*, its protagonist, a miserly autocratic man, is persuaded that he has been transported to the Antipodes where everything is stood on its head and the poor rule the rich and women have the upper hand on men.

Neither writer would go on to work after the Restoration. Shirley, who fought for the King during the Civil War, became a schoolmaster after it, dying of exposure following the Great Fire of London in 1666. Brome died in 1653 at the age of sixty-three at a time when theatre was banned.

The third of the trio, William Davenant, later knighted for his gallantry during the civil War, had had his first play, *The Cruel Brother*, performed by the King's Men at the Blackfriars in 1627. His plays were popular at the time but cannot be said to be of tremendous literary importance. He was, however, to play a crucial role in the rebirth of English theatre.

* * *

In 1642 the curtain came down completely on professional theatre with the passing of an Edict which said all stage performances must cease. As we know, there had always been a powerful anti-theatre lobby which had hitherto been held in check. Now, with the uncertainty of the times, it was in the ascendant. The assumption that the Royalists were in favour of theatre while the Parliamentarians of the Commonwealth were not is incorrect, as the closure of the theatres took place early in the Civil War and before its resolution. Indeed, there were factions supporting the King who were opposed to theatres, while there were some for the Commonwealth who believed there was a place for plays so long as they carried a strong moral message.

The closure was catastrophic for the players who, for sixty years, had had a licence to perform. Whole generations of players had at least had that amount of security in their insecure world. Theatre might have been continually threatened by its critics, playhouses closed because of plague, individuals sent to prison for offending authority, but plays and players had overcome all obstacles and flourished. Now the ban was total. Pathetic pamphlets were circulated telling of the plight of those whose living had been in theatrical entertainment and now found themselves without any means of earning a livelihood.

But theatre always fights back and in spite of the ban, underground performances of plays began to take place until 9 February 1648 a new and Draconian ordinance was enacted. This ordered the demolition of all playhouses, the arrest of any actors found performing and substantial fines for each and every person attending a dramatic presentation of any kind. Nor did the authorities stop there: virtually all forms of entertainment were banned, even simple country festivals and dancing round maypoles.

The anti-theatre faction set to work with a will and most of the theatres were torn down and destroyed. Only the Phoenix survived virtually intact, along with part of the Red Bull. We have this legislation to thank for the fact that no open courtyard theatre survived long enough for a careful drawing to have come down to us. It is known that the Red Bull still existed during the earliest years of the Commonwealth and that the management actually risked putting on a few performances, because there are accounts of a number of raids on it followed by arrests. There was also a small amount of reading aloud of underground pamphlets by out-of-work actors and possibly the odd illicit performance given in some remote place, its venue and timing passed on by word of mouth, rather like illegal 'raves' today. It was not an atmosphere in which new writing could flourish for while a writer might secretly write plays in the privacy of his own home, it was unlikely he could have his work read to know how it sounded, let alone see it performed; for not only were the professional actors now scattered far and wide, any who might have been tempted to take part in an illicit performance would have to be very dedicated indeed to risk a long period of imprisonment.

One lone survivor from those old Mermaid days was John Taylor, the Water Poet. He had spent the war years in Oxford writing propaganda pamphlets for the Royalist cause, returning to London when the young King went into exile. There was little work for an ageing waterman, so he took a pub, the Crown Tavern, subjecting his clientele to regular readings of his verse. After the execution of Charles I he changed its name to The Mourning Bush, but having had it made clear that this was politically incorrect he settled on The Poet's Head, with a portrait of his own painted on a board as a sign. As he said:

There is many a head hangs for a sign;
Then, gentle reader, why not mine?

He died in 1653.

* * *

For eighteen years theatre went dark in England. It was only towards the very end of the Commonwealth that anyone was brave enough to put his head above the parapet and that person was Sir William Davenant. At first he had followed the King into exile in France but after a few years returned to London, determined one way or another to bring back theatre.

In the mid-1650s he wrote a number of what he described as 'entertainments in the manner of the ancients'. They consisted of programmes of songs and poetry enacted in his own home. In 1656 he got a little braver and actually advertised his newest entertainment with the unwieldy title *The Siege of Rhodes Made by a Representative of the Art of Prospective* [perspective] *in Scenes and the Story Sung in Recitative Musick*, a kind of opera, in fact, which he described as an evening of music with instruction. Next, having managed to ingratiate himself with Oliver Cromwell, he suggested a little entertainment on the marriage of Cromwell's daughter, which he kindly offered to supply, following this with a patriotic piece in the same genre, geared to promote the government line on its deteriorating relationship with Spain: *The Cruelty of the Spaniards in Peru* (the rest of the title is taken up with explaining that it is not exactly a *play*!)

The latter proved a major breakthrough for the government, which for its own political reasons allowed it to be put on in a building in Drury Lane, with all that street's associations with the theatres of the past. It may not have been a play as we understand the term, but it was a public show and the audience had to pay to see it and some old professional actors were used rather than the amateurs who had taken part in Davenant's home theatricals.

Gradually, as it became evident that the restoration of

the monarchy was in sight, the actors returned to London and quietly started to rehearse and in 1660 the Phoenix Theatre opened its doors to celebrate the return of King Charles II. Theatre was back in business.

The new King not only authorised the performance of plays, he directly encouraged them and immediately after his coronation, Davenant and Thomas Killigrew, a fellow-playwright and up-and-coming theatrical entrepreneur, obtained patents giving them a monopoly on acting performances in London. Killigrew took on most of the remaining old professional actors, while Davenant recruited new blood, including the young Thomas Betterton.

But it was theatre of a very different kind. The King and those of his entourage exiled with him were now accustomed to the continental way of doing things, especially that of the French. They demanded playhouses with the new 'picture frame' stage, or proscenium arch, along with what Davenant called 'prospective', distancing the actors from the audience and altering the style of acting. Another major change, however, was for the better: women were allowed to become professional actresses. These early pioneers deserve more than the kind of prurient stuff written about them even today. The acting profession was still not accepted as respectable, but the implication that all the women who took to the stage were whores using performance as an eye to a wealthy bed is grossly insulting. The first two women to appear on the English stage, Mrs Hughes and Mrs Rutter, did so in *Othello* and played Desdemona and Emilia respectively in a production put on by Thomas Killigrew in 1660.

How true this production was to Shakespeare's original we do not know. The old plays which had ceased to appeal to the pre-Civil War audience were considered positively archaic by that of the Restoration. Style was everything and Shakespeare, when performed, bowdlerised or rewritten. Until the time of Edmund Kean it was Colley Cibber's version of *Richard III* that audiences flocked to see, and Davenant himself was not above 'improving' Shakespeare by rewriting parts of plays and altering the plots. Dislike of the Jacobean style did not stop Restoration playwrights from plundering the earlier plays for material but the results make dull reading today, the most successful in the genre probably being Dryden's *Love for Love*, based on *Antony and Cleopatra*. The loss of such a large body of work, coupled with the new type of theatres, meant that the tradition of Elizabethan and Jacobean acting was lost too.

The new theatre bred new writers – John Dryden, William Wycherley, William Congreve, Thomas Otway, George Farquhar, Sir John Vanbrugh and Sir George Etheridge and that remarkable woman dramatist and ex-spy, Aphra Behn. Of their work, it is the comedies that remain popular today. What is known as Restoration Comedy is certainly amusing but it is limited, lacking the bite of a Jonson or Middleton. Seduction and cuckoldry (also standbys of that earlier time) provide the theme time after time, though put over with much style and wit and only in Aphra Behn do we see the role of the sexes reverse.

* * *

No other age has produced anything to match that which produced Shakespeare and went on to offer a Marlowe, a Ben Jonson and a Thomas Middleton in its first rank, with Greene, Peele, Kyd, Dekker, Webster, Rowley, Chapman, Ford, Massinger, Beaumont, Fletcher and Tourneur following closely behind.

To return again to the view of a present-day practitioner, Adrian Noble:

> During the thirty-year period in which these plays were written, enormous political shifts were taking place. All that was reflected in the drama. The plays alert the audiences' imagination and edify it, not in a smug way, but because they are truly big experiences, great epic public experiences and the greatest single experience of the age is Shakespeare, where you can have a laugh, followed by a love scene, followed by a battle, followed

by a political intrigue in a council chamber, followed by a rough street scene and all within twenty minutes.

This is the thread which runs through all these plays and the measure of their continuing success is their impact on the public. What we see are big public issues debated in big public plays. They have freedom of form because these playwrights virtually invented their own, even though they stole ideas from all over the place but they were thieves who invented as they went along, saying to themselves 'I'll talk to the audience at this point' or 'I think I'll bring a ghost in here.' In terms of reality it didn't worry them at all because they were creating, play by play, their own worlds. The audiences would have applauded them at the end and then quite possibly gone off and cheered a public hanging.[2]

Epilogue

We are a strange nation. We consider it patriotic and only right to remember and praise military leaders and politicians, many of whom fought wars and introduced policies later found to be disastrously wrong. We can treat as heroes those who made whole nations into colonies or whose decisions led to the deaths of thousands. We hold up as shining examples great inventors, explorers, engineers, as indeed we should, but we take little pride in our theatre. Indeed, the survival of our live theatre and dramatic work in schools is now under real threat.

1993 marked the anniversaries of the deaths of two major European talents, Christopher Marlowe and Guy de Maupassant, both of whom died young. In Britain, Marlowe's quatercentenary passed marked only by small-scale celebrations organised mainly by those working in the theatre and by the BBC who helped sponsor a single, celebratory day. In France, to honour Maupassant, major official celebrations were led by President Mitterrand and the French government.

Notes

CHAPTER 1

1. Frederick S. Boas, *Christopher Marlowe* (Oxford 1940).
2. Ibid.
3. Roland B. Lewis, *The Shakespeare Documents* (Oxford 1940).
4. Mark Eccles, *Shakespeare in Warwickshire* (Wisconsin 1963). Also E. Fripp, *Shakespeare's Stratford* (Oxford 1928).
5. Ibid.

CHAPTER 2

1. A.L. Rowse, *William Shakespeare* (London 1963).
2. Ibid.
3. M. Bradbrook, *The Rise of the Common Player* (Cambridge 1962).
4. *Ben Jonson's Conversations with William Drummond of Hawthornden* (Shakespeare Society 1842).
5. A. Gurr, *The Shakespearean Stage 1574–1642* (Cambridge 1980).
6. Ibid.

CHAPTER 3

1. A.L. Rowse, *William Shakespeare* (London 1963).
2. John Aubrey, *Brief Lives* (Harmondsworth 1972).
3. M. Bradbrook, *John Webster* (London 1980).
4. A.D. Wraight and V.F. Stern, *In Search of Christopher Marlowe* (London 1965).
5. Ibid.
6. S. Schoenbaum, *Shakespeare: A Documentary Life* (2nd ed. Oxford 1977).
7. Ibid.

8. A.L. Rowse, *Shakespeare the Man* (London 1973); Mark Eccles, *Shakespeare in Warwickshire* (Wisconsin 1963); Ivor Brown, *Shakespeare* (London 1949).

CHAPTER 4

1. Stephen Gosson, *Plays Confuted in Five Acts* (pamphlet 1582).
2. A. Gurr, *Playgoing in Shakespeare's London* (Cambridge 1987).
3. Ibid.
4. Ibid.
5. John Stockwood, *A Treatise Against Playhouses* (1587).
6. T.F. Ordish, *Early London Theatres* (London 1971).
7. M. Bradbrook, *The Rise of the Common Player* (Cambridge 1962).
   A. Gurr, *The Shakespearean Stage 1574–1642* (Cambridge 1980).

CHAPTER 5

1. J. Bakeless, *Christopher Marlowe* (New York 1937).
2. T.F. Ordish, *Early London Theatres* (London 1971).
   A. Gurr, *Playgoing in Shakespeare's London* (Cambridge 1987).
3. Duff Cooper, *Sergeant Shakespeare* (London 1949).
4. E.A.J. Honigman, *Shakespeare – The Lost Years* (Manchester 1985).
5. Mark Eccles, *Shakespeare in Warwickshire* (Wisconsin 1963).

CHAPTER 6

1. R.M. McKerrow, ed. *The Works of Thomas Nashe* (London 1904–10).
2. Robert Greene, *Greene's Groatsworth of Wit bought with a Million of Repentance* (London 1922).
3. Ibid.
4. A. Gurr, *Playgoing in Shakespeare's England* (Cambridge 1989).
5. Ibid.
6. G.B. Harrison, *Shakespeare's Fellows* (London 1923).

7. Stephen Gosson, *Plays Confuted in Five Acts* (1582).
8. G.B. Harrison, *Shakespeare's Fellows* (London 1923).
9. All Marlowe biographies include a description of the duel in Hog Lane, including those of J. Bakeless, *Christopher Marlowe* (New York 1937) and A.L. Rowse, *Christopher Marlowe* (London 1964).
10. *A Notable Discovery of Cosenage* and *Second Part of Conney-Catching by Robert Greene* (London 1922).

CHAPTER 7

1. Thomas Seccombe and J.W. Allen in *The Age of Shakespeare Vol II* (London 1904) refer to Marlowe's involvement with *Henry VI* as having long been considered a possibility and there is further discussion of this in numerous biographies, including A.L. Rowse, *William Shakespeare* (London 1963) and Frederick S. Boas, *Christopher Marlowe* (Oxford 1940).
2. It is clear that actors moved between the various companies and that a company might call itself by more than one name. Academics often disagree on dates and make-up of companies although Burbage's group of actors appear to have remained together over a longer period than most. Those wishing to take the matter further might fare best with Andrew Gurr's *The Shakespearean Stage 1574–1642* (Cambridge 1980).
3. R.B. McKerrow, ed. *The Works of Thomas Nashe* (London 1904–10).
4. Robert Greene, *A Notable Discovery of Cosenage* and *Second Part of Conney-Catching* (London 1922).
5. Copies of documents concerning the Arden murder can be found in the Appendix to *Three Elizabethan Domestic Tragedies* (Harmondsworth 1969).
6. R.B. McKerrow, ed. *The Works of Thomas Nashe* (London 1904–10).

CHAPTER 8

1. Daphne du Maurier, *Golden Lads: A Study of Antony Bacon* (London 1975).
2. J.L. Hotson, *The Death of Christopher Marlowe* (London

1926).
3. J. Bakeless, *Christopher Marlowe* (New York 1937).
4. Attributed to the Elizabethan/Jacobean actor, Christopher Beeston. See A.L. Rowse, *William Shakespeare* (London 1963) and E.K.. Chambers, *William Shakespeare: A Study of Facts and Problems* (Oxford 1989).
5. Ivor Brown, *The Women in Shakespeare's Life* (London 1968) and others.
6. A.L. Rowse, *William Shakespeare* (1963) disputed by, among others, S. Schoenbaum in *Shakespeare: A Documentary Life* (2nd ed. Oxford 1977).
7. A.L. Rowse, ed. *The Poems of Shakespeare's Dark Lady* (London 1978).
8. A.L. Rowse, ed. *The Casebook of Simon Foreman* (London 1974).
9. John Aubrey, *Brief Lives* (Harmondsworth 1972).
10. *The Repentance of Robert Greene* (London 1922).
11. G.B. Harrison, *Shakespeare's Fellows* (London 1923).

CHAPTER 9
1. R.A. Foakes and T.R. Rickert, eds. Henslowe's *Diary* (Cambridge 1961) and W.W. Greg, *The Henslowe Papers* (London 1907).
2. Anonymous source quoted by, among others, E.K. Chambers in *The Elizabethan Stage*, vol. III (Oxford 1923).
3. A.D. Wraight and V.F. Stern, *In Search of Christopher Marlowe* (London 1965).
4. For differing views on those responsible for this material, see ibid. and Charles Nicholls, *The Reckoning* (London 1992). Almost all biographies of Marlowe discuss the subject.
5. R.A. Foakes and T.R. Rickerts, eds. Henslowe's *Diary* (Cambridge 1961) and W.W. Greg, *The Henslowe Papers* (London 1907).
6. Charles Nicholls, *The Reckoning* (London 1992), Judith Cook, *The Slicing Edge of Death* (London 1993) (fictionalised but with historical explanations) and others.
7. Reprinted in full in A.D. Wraight and V.F. Stern, *In*

Search of Christopher Marlowe (London 1965).

8. Ibid.
9. In J.L. Hotson, *The Death of Christopher Marlowe* (London 1926) there is a full account of how he discovered the relevant documents, facsimiles and translations of the Inquest Indictment, the letter from the Privy Council asking the university authorities to grant Marlowe his degree and various papers concerning Ingram Frizer, including the charge against him for the cozening of Drew Woodleff.
10. Frederick S. Boas, *Christopher Marlowe* (Oxford 1940).
11. J.L. Hotson, *The Death of Christopher Marlowe* (London 1926).
12. Charles Nicholls, *The Reckoning* (London 1992).
13. Reprinted in full in A.D. Wraight and V.F. Stern, *In Search of Christopher Marlowe* (London 1965).
14. The reader who wants to take the matter further has much material from which to choose. A.L. Rowse dismisses all suggestions of political involvement and goes for the straightforward death in a brawl. Frederick S. Boas goes into great background detail as to the careers of those involved, but remains cautious. Hotson is neutral, merely presenting the documentary evidence. John Bakeless and Wraight and Stern consider the death to be highly suspicious but do not propose a definite theory.
15. Calvin C. Hoffman, *The Murder of the Man who was Shakespeare* (New York 1960).

CHAPTER 10

1. All the correspondence in this chapter is taken from R.A. Foakes and T.R. Rickert, eds. Henslowe's *Diary* (Cambridge 1961) and W.W. Greg, *The Henslowe Papers* (London 1907).

CHAPTER 11

1. For those wanting to study the make-up of the companies in depth there is much material available including: Andrew Gurr, *The Shakespearean Stage 1574–1642*

(Cambridge 1980); M. Bradbrook, *The Rise of the Common Player* (Cambridge 1962); T.F. Ordish, *Early London Theatres* (London 1971).

2. Andrew Gurr, *Playgoing in Shakespeare's London* (Cambridge 1987).
3. Ibid.
4. A.D. Wraight and V.F. Stern, *In Search of Christopher Marlowe* (London 1965).
5. B. Roland Lewis, ed. *The Shakespeare Documents* vols I and II (Oxford 1940).
6. Ibid.
7. *Shakespeare in the Public Record Office* (HMSO 1985).
8. Andrew Gurr, *Playgoing in Shakespeare's London* (Cambridge 1987).
9. B. Roland Lewis, ed. *The Shakespeare Documents* vols I and II (Oxford 1940).

CHAPTER 12

1. From Epigrams, *'On the Famous Voyage'*, in which Jonson takes an imaginary trip down the Fleet River which had become little more than an open sewer. Not for the squeamish.
2. S. Schoenbaum, *Shakespeare: A Documentary Life* (2nd ed. Oxford 1977).
3. Ibid.
4. Ibid.
5. For those who want to read *The Gull's Hornbook* in its entirety, there is a facsimile edition published by the Scolar Press in 1969, otherwise it can be found in most general editions of Dekker's works.

CHAPTER 13

1. *Shakespeare in the Public Record Office* (HMSO 1985).
2. Ibid.
3. B. Roland Lewis, ed. *The Shakespeare Documents* vols I and II (Oxford 1940).
4. Ibid.
5. Ibid.
6. For Jonson's early theatre life: Anne Barton, *Ben Jonson,*

Dramatist (Cambridge 1984) and Marchette Chute, *Ben Jonson of Westminster* (London 1954). Excellent for papers, letters, etc.: the appendix to *Elizabethan and Jacobean Comedies* ed. Brian Gibson (New Mermaids 1984).

7. R.A. Foakes and T.R. Rickert, eds. Henslowe's *Diary* (Cambridge 1969) and W. W. Greg, *The Henslowe Papers* (London 1907).
8. Ibid.
9. Ibid.
10. *Ben Jonson's Conversations with Drummond of Hawthornden* (Shakespeare Society 1842).
11. Jonson's own introduction to his First Folio.

CHAPTER 14

1. A.L. Rowse, *Shakespeare the Man* (London 1973) and others.
2. Act III Scene 3.
3. Charles Nicholls, *The Reckoning* (London 1992).
4. A.L. Rowse, *The England of Elizabeth* (London 1950).
5. Thomas Platter's *Travels in England,* translated by Clare Williams, quoted in Gurr's *Playgoing in Shakespeare's London* (Cambridge 1987).
6. Ibid.

CHAPTER 15

1. The history of Essex, his Court intrigues, relationship with the Queen, the Irish disaster and the abortive rising are the subject of many books for those who want to know more. These include: J.B. Black, *The Reign of Elizabeth* (Oxford 1959); R. Lacey, *Robert, Earl of Essex: An Elizabethan Icarus* (London 1971) and Elizabeth Jenkins, *Elizabeth the Great* (London 1958). The influence of *Richard II* is dealt with by most of them but more specifically in the various Shakespeare biographies, including those of Rowse and Schoenbaum.
2. A.L. Rowse, *William Shakespeare* (London 1963).
3. Elizabeth Jenkins, *Elizabeth the Great* (London 1958).
4. Ibid.

5. Andrew Gurr, *Playgoing in Shakespeare's London* (Cambridge 1987).
6. Elizabeth Jenkins, *Elizabeth the Great* (London 1958).

CHAPTER 16

1. B. Roland Lewis, ed. *The Shakespeare Documents* vols I and II (Oxford 1940).
2. Ibid.
3. John Aubrey, *Brief Lives* (Harmondsworth 1972).
4. Mary Edmond, *Rare Sir William Davenant* (London 1992).
5. A.L. Rowse, ed. *The Casebook of Simon Foreman* (London 1974).
6. *Ben Jonson's Conversations with William Drummond of Hawthornden* (Shakespeare Society 1842).
7. There is a full account of Jonson's problems and imprisonment over *Eastward Ho!* in the appendix to the New Mermaid Anthology, *Elizabethan and Jacobean Comedies* ed. Brian Gibson (1984), along with his correspondence while in gaol.

CHAPTER 17

1. *Tom Tell-Troths Message and His Pen's Complainte* (1600).
2. Henry Peacham, *The Compleat Gentleman: The Art of Living in London* (1622).
3. G.P.V. Akrigg, quoted by Terry Hands in programme notes for the RSC's 1970s production of *Women Beware Women.*
4. A.L. Rowse, *William Shakespeare* (London 1963).
   Ivor Brown, *Shakespeare* (London 1949).
5. Una Ellis-Fermor, *The Jacobean Drama* (London 1936).

CHAPTER 18

1. For those wanting to see the original documentation then it can be tracked down at its various sources. For the rest, copies or facsimiles of documents can be read in:
   B. Roland Lewis, ed. *The Shakespeare Documents* vols I and II (Oxford 1940).

Shakespeare in the Public Record Office (HMSO 1985)
M. Eccles, ed. *Shakespeare in Warwickshire* (Wisconsin 1963).

2. *The Shakespeare Documents* as above.
3. Judith Cook, *Shakespeare's Players* (London 1983).
4. Richard Huggett, *The Curse of Macbeth* (Bath 1981).
5. Conversation with the author.
6. *The Shakespeare Documents* as above.
7. And information following; *Shakespeare in the Public Record Office* (HMSO 1985)
8. Ibid. Details of sale with explanation of Trusteeship.

CHAPTER 19

1. *All the Workes of John Taylor the Water Poet Collected in One Volume* (1630).
2. Ibid.
3. John Aubrey, *Brief Lives* (Harmondsworth 1972).
4. T.S. Eliot *'Whispers of Immortality'* (1920).
5. Quoted in M.C. Bradbrook, *John Webster* (London 1980).
6. G. Bokland, *The Sources of the White Devil* (Uppsala 1957)and *The Duchess of Malfi: Sources, Themes and Characters* (Harvard 1962).
7. Quoted in M.C. Bradbrook, *John Webster* (London 1980).
8. A.L. Rowse, ed. *The Casebook of Simon Foreman* (London 1980).

CHAPTER 20

1. Andrew Gurr, *The Shakespearean Stage 1574–1642* (Cambridge 1980).
2. *Shakespeare in the Public Record Office* (HMSO 1985).
3. B. Roland Lewis, ed. *The Shakespeare Documents* vols I and II (Oxford 1940).
4. *The Collected Works of John Taylor the Water Poet* (London 1630).
5. Ibid.

CHAPTER 21

1. B. Roland Lewis, ed. *The Shakespeare Documents* vols I and II (Oxford 1940).
2. Ibid.
3. *Shakespeare in the Public Records Office* (HMSO 1985).
4. In *The Shakespeare Documents* Roland Lewis lists all the alleged causes of death from a wide variety of sources.
5. A.L. Rowse, *William Shakespeare* (London 1963).

CHAPTER 22

1. *Ben Jonson's Conversations with William Drummond of Hawthornden* (Shakespeare Society 1842).
2. *The Complete Works of Ben Jonson* (London 1883);
   The Collected Works of John Taylor the Water Poet (London 1630).
3. Ibid.
4. And extracts following, *Ben Jonson's Conversations with William Drummond of Hawthornden* (Shakespeare Society 1842).

CHAPTER 23

1. Sir John Chamberlain, quoted in Andrew Gurr's *Playgoing in Shakespeare's London* (Cambridge 1987).
2. Ibid.
3. Robert Anton, *The Philosopher's Satyrs* (1616).
4. Orazio Busino, Chaplain to the Embassy of Venice (1617).
5. Introductions to late nineteenth-century Mermaid Series of collected plays of Elizabethan and Jacobean dramatists; G.B. Harrison, *Shakespeare's Fellows* (London 1923); and many more.

CHAPTER 24

1. John Aubrey, *Brief Lives* (Harmondsworth 1972).
2. Anne Barton, *Ben Jonson, Dramatist* (Cambridge 1984). Marchette Chute, *Ben Jonson of Westminster* (London 1954).
3. Ibid.
4. Ibid.

5. The behaviour of Buckingham's troops, coupled with their bringing disease to the city, had a profound effect. While the West Country was almost entirely for the Royalist cause, Plymouth was not and withstood years of siege almost to starvation point. The resentment lasted hundreds of years.
6. Marchette Chute, *Ben Jonson of Westminster* (London 1954).

CHAPTER 25

1. For Adrian Noble's detailed views on Elizabethan and Jacobean theatre, see the author's *At the Sign of the Swan* (London 1986).
2. Ibid.

Select Bibliography

Christopher Marlowe

Bakeless, J. *Christopher Marlowe* (New York 1937)
Boas, Frederick S. *Christopher Marlowe* (Oxford 1940)
Hotson, J.L. *The Death of Christopher Marlowe* (London 1926)
Nicholl, C. *The Reckoning* (London 1992)
Rowse, A.L. *Christopher Marlowe* (London 1964)
Wraight, A.D. and Stern, V.F. *In Search of Christopher Marlowe* (London 1965)
Christopher Marlowe: Complete Plays and Poems (Everyman Edition, London 1976)

William Shakespeare

Shakespeare in the Public Record Office (HMSO 1985)
The Shakespeare Documents vols I and II ed. B. Roland Lewis (Oxford 1940)
The Shakespeare Apocrypha (Oxford 1912)
Brown, Ivor *Shakespeare* (London 1949)
— *Shakespeare and the Actors* (London 1970)
Chambers, E.K. *William Shakespeare: A Study of Facts and Problems* (Oxford 1989)
Cook, Judith *Women in Shakespeare* (London 1980)
— *Shakespeare's Players* (London 1983)
Eccles, Mark ed. *Shakespeare in Warwickshire* (Wisconsin 1963)
Fripp, E. *Shakespeare's Stratford* (Oxford 1928)
— *Shakespeare's Studies* (Oxford 1930)
Halliday, F.E. *The Life of Shakespeare*
Rowse, A.L. *William Shakespeare* (London 1963)
— *Shakespeare the Man* (London 1973)
Schoenbaum, S. *Shakespeare: A Documentary Life* (2nd ed.

Oxford 1977)
Speaight, R. *Shakespeare, the Man and His Achievement* (London 1977)

Ben Jonson

Barton, *Ben Jonson, Dramatist* (Cambridge 1984)
Chute, M. *Ben Jonson of Westminster* (London 1954)
Herford, C.H. and Simpson, Percy and Evelyn eds. *Ben Jonson* (11 volumes, Oxford 1925–53)
The Complete Works of Ben Jonson (London 1883)
Ben Jonson's Conversations with William Drummond of Hawthornden (Shakespeare Society 1842)

General

Adams, J.Q. ed. *The Dramatic Records of Sir Henry Herbert, Master of the Revels* (New Haven 1917)
Adams, R. *Ben Jonson's Masques and Plays* (New York 1980)
Aubrey, J. *Brief Lives* (Harmondsworth 1972)
Bentley, G.E. *The Profession of Dramatist in Shakespeare's Time* (Princeton 1971)
— *The Jacobean and Caroline Stage* (Oxford 1941)
Black, J.B. *The Reign of Elizabeth* (Oxford 1959)
Bradbrook, M. *The Rise of the Common Player* (Cambridge 1962)
— *John Webster* (London 1980)
Bokland, G. *The Source of the White Devil* (Uppsala 1957)
—*The Duchess of Malfi: Sources, Themes and Characters* (Havard 1962)
Bowers E.T. *Elizabethan Revenge Tragedy 1587–1642* (London 1940)
Chambers, E.K. *The Elizabethan Stage* (Oxford 1923)
Cook, J. *At the Sign of the Swan – An Introduction to Shakespeare's Contemporaries* (London 1986)
Dekker, T. *Selected Prose Works* (Stratford-upon-Avon 1967)
— *A Gull's Hornbook* (Scolar Press 1969)
du Maurier, D. *Golden Lads: A Study of Antony Bacon* (London 1975)
Dunn, T.A. *Philip Massinger* (London 1957)

Edmond, Mary *Rare Sir William Davenant* (London 1992)
Ellis-Fermor, U. *The Jacobean Drama* (London 1936)
Finkelpearl F. *John Marston of the Inner Temple* (London 1969)
Foakes, R.A. and Rickert T.R. eds. Henslowe's *Diary* (Cambridge 1961)
Freeman, A. *Thomas Kyd: Facts and Problems* (London 1967)
Greg, W.W. *The Henslowe Papers* (London 1907)
— *Dramatic Documents from the Elizabethan Playhouses* (Oxford 1931)
Greene, R. *A Notable Discovery of Cosenage* (Bodley Head, London 1923)
— *Greene's Groatsworth of Wit bought with a million of Repentance*
Gurr, A. *The Shakespearean Stage 1574–1642* (Cambridge 1980)
— *Playgoing in Shakespeare's London* (Cambridge 1987)
Handover, P.M. *Arabella Stuart* (London 1957)
Harrison, G.B. *Shakespeare's Fellows* (London 1923)
Haynes, A. *Robert Cecil, 1st Earl of Salisbury* (London 1989)
Holmes, M. *Shakespeare and Burbage* (Chichester 1978)
Hosking, G.L. *The Life and Times of Edward Alleyn*
Jenkins, E. *Elizabeth the Great* (London 1958)
Knights, L.C. *Drama and Society in the Age of Jonson* (London 1937)
Lacey, R. *Robert, Earl of Essex: An Elizabethan Icarus* (London 1971)
Leggatt, C. *Citizen Comedy in the Age of Shakespeare* (London 1973)
Morris, B. *John Webster* (London 1972)
Mulryne, J.R. *Thomas Middleton* (London 1979)
Nicoll, A. ed. *Essays on Shakespeare and Elizabethan Drama* (London 1962)
Ordish, T.F. *Early London Theatres* (London 1971)
Porter, L. (general ed.) *The Revels History of Drama*
vol III 1576–1613 (ed. Leech and Craik) (1975)
vol IV 1613–1660 (ed. Edwards and McLuskie) (1981)
Proutey, C.T. *Life and Works of George Peele* (Yale 1952)
Rowse, A.L. *The England of Elizabeth* (London 1950)

— *The Casebook of Simon Foreman* (ed.) (London 1974)
— *The Poems of Shakespeare's Dark Lady* (ed.) (London 1978)
Salgado, G. *The Elizabethan Underworld* (London 1971)
Seccombe and Allen, *The Age of Shakespeare* (London 1903)
Southern R. *The Staging of Plays before Shakespeare* (London 1973)
Symonds, J.A. *Shakespeare's Predecessors in the English Drama* (London 1981)
Wallis, L.B. *Beaumont and Fletcher* (Oxford 1947)
Wickham, G. *Shakespeare's Dramatic Heritage* (London 1969)
Wilson, F.P. *Marlowe and the Early Shakespeare*
White, M. *Middleton and Tourneur* (Cambridge 1992)

Manuscripts, pamphlets, etc.

The complaint and lamentation of Mistress Arden of Faversham in Kent Roxburgh Collection BM III (1630)
The Spanish Protest Against A Game at Chess ed. E. Wilson and O. Turner, MLR 44 (1949)

Collections

The Collected Works of John Taylor the Water Poet (London 1633)
Elizabethan and Jacobean Comedies ed. Brian Gibson (New Mermaids, London 1984)
Four Early Tudor Comedies ed. W. Tydeman (Penguin Classics 1984)
Three Elizabethan Domestic Tragedies ed. Keith Sturgess (1984)
The Mermaid Series of collected works of Elizabethan and Jacobean dramatists, published in the last decade of the nineteenth century. Volumes include the works of: Beaumont and Fletcher, Chapman, Dekker, Ford, Heywood, Marston, Massinger and Middleton.
Both A. and C. Black in its 'New Revels' series and Manchester University Press have recently started to publish single copies of Elizabethan and Jacobean plays.
Shakespeare texts used have included the Oxford University Press *Complete Works* and the Penguin and Cambridge University Press single editions.

Index

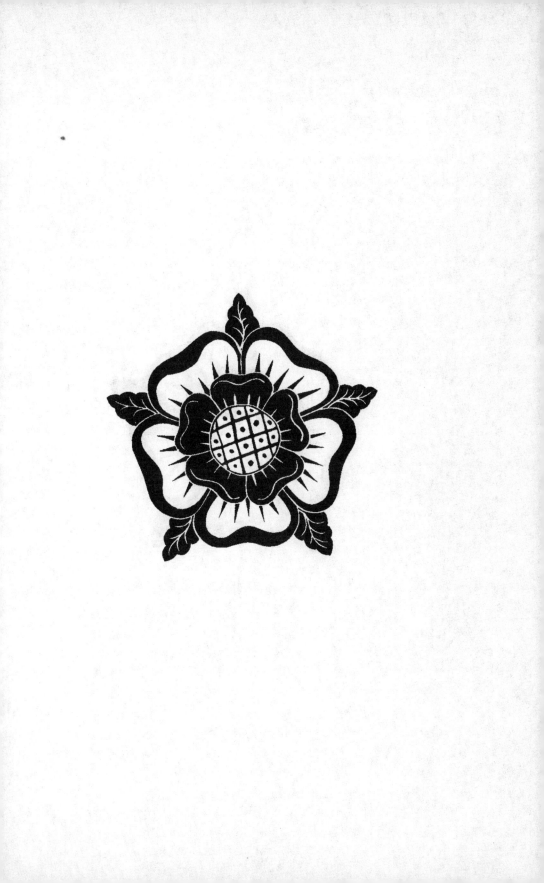